EAST INDIA
Publishing Company

KING ARTHUR and the KINGHTS of the ROUND TABLE
Sir Thomas Malory

Published by the
EAST INDIA PUBLISHING COMPANY
Ottawa, Canada

© 2022 East India Publishing Company

Cover Design by EIPC © 2022
9781774262245

www.eastindiapublishing.com

CONTENTS

INTRODUCTION

King Arthur and the Knights of the Round Table! What magic is in the words! How they carry us straight to the days of chivalry, to the witchcraft of Merlin, to the wonderful deeds of Lancelot and Perceval and Galahad, to the Quest for the Holy Grail, to all that "glorious company, the flower of men," as Tennyson has called the king and his companions! Down through the ages the stories have come to us, one of the few great romances which, like the tales of Homer, are as fresh and vivid to-day as when men first recited them in court and camp and cottage. Other great kings and paladins are lost in the dim shadows of long-past centuries, but Arthur still reigns in Camelot and his knights still ride forth to seek the Grail.

"No little thing shall be
The gentle music of the bygone years,
Long past to us with all their hopes and fears."

So wrote the poet William Morris in The Earthly Paradise. And surely it is no small debt of gratitude we owe the troubadours and chroniclers and poets who through many centuries have sung of Arthur and his champions, each adding to the song the gifts of his own imagination, so building from simple folk-tales one of the most magnificent and moving stories in all literature.

This debt perhaps we owe in greatest measure to three men; to Chrétien de Troies, a Frenchman, who in the twelfth century put many of the old Arthurian legends into verse; to Sir Thomas Malory, who first wrote out most of the stories in English prose, and whose book, the Morte Darthur, was printed by William Caxton, the first English printer, in 1485; and to Alfred, Lord Tennyson, who in his series of poems entitled the Idylls of the King retold the legends in new and beautiful guise in the nineteenth century.

The history of Arthur is so shrouded in the mists of early

England that it is difficult to tell exactly who and what he was. There probably was an actual Arthur, who lived in the island of Britain in the sixth century, but probably he was not a king nor even a prince. It seems most likely that he was a chieftain who led his countrymen to victory against the invading English about the year 500. So proud were his countrymen of his victories that they began to invent imaginary stories of his prowess to add to the fame of their hero, just as among all peoples legends soon spring up about the name of a great leader. As each man told the feats of Arthur he contributed those details that appealed most to his own fancy and each was apt to think of the hero as a man of his own time, dressing and speaking and living as his own kings and princes did, with the result that when we come to the twelfth century we find Geoffrey of Monmouth, in his History of the Kings of Britain, describing Arthur no longer as a half-barbarous Briton, wearing rude armor, his arms and legs bare, but instead as a most Christian king, the flower of mediæval chivalry, decked out in all the gorgeous trappings of a knight of the Crusades.

As the story of Arthur grew it attracted to itself popular legends of all kinds. Its roots were in Britain and the chief threads in its fabric remained British-Celtic. The next most important threads were those that were added by the Celtic chroniclers of Ireland. Then stories that were not Celtic at all were woven into the legend, some from Germanic sources, which the Saxons or the descendants of the Franks may have contributed, and others that came from the Orient, which may have been brought back from the East by men returning from the Crusades. And if it was the Celts who gave us the most of the material for the stories of Arthur it was the French poets who first wrote out the stories and gave them enduring form.

It was the Frenchman, Chrétien de Troies, who lived at the courts of Champagne and of Flanders, who put the old legends into verse for the pleasure of the noble lords and ladies that were his patrons. He composed six Arthurian poems. The first, which was written about 1160 or earlier, related the story of Tristram. The next was called Érec et Énide, and told some of the adventures that were later used by Tennyson in his Geraint and Enid. The third was Cligès, a poem that has little to do with the stories of Arthur and his knights as we have them. Next came the Conte de la Charrette, or Le Chevalier de la Charrette, which set forth the love of Lancelot and Guinevere. Then followed Yvain, or Le Chevalier au Lion, and finally came Perceval, or Le Conte du Graal, which gives the first account of the Holy Grail.

None of these stories are to be found in the work of Geoffrey of Monmouth, who had written earlier in Latin, nor in any of the so-called chronicles. It was Chrétien who took the old folk-tales that men had been telling each other for centuries and put them into sprightly verse for the entertainment of his lords and ladies. He fashioned the stories according to the taste of his own gay courts, and so Arthur and his Queen Guinevere, Lancelot, Perceval and the other knights became far more like French people of the twelfth century than like Britons of the sixth. And in introducing the Holy Grail, that sacred and mystic cup that was supposed to hold drops of the blood of Christ and to have been carried to England by Joseph of Arimathea, Chrétien added to the Arthurian legends an old religious story that had had nothing to do with Arthur originally.

From this point in its history that sturdy ancient English oak, the original story of Arthur and his knights, an account mainly of warlike adventures, sent forth four new branches that have now become part and parcel of the parent legend. These four branches are the story of Merlin, the story of Lancelot, the story of the Holy Grail, and the story of Tristram and Iseult. Some of the writers who came after Chrétien took one of these stories, some another, each enlarging his theme according to his own taste, until each story was the center of a large number of new and romantic offshoots. Practically all of them, however, were bound together by the thread that led from the court of the great King Arthur at Camelot.

The story of Merlin, that man of magic, is the least important of the four branches, though Merlin is still an intensely interesting figure in the story of Arthur that we read to-day. The story of Lancelot was to prove very important; starting as a romance that had very little connection with Arthur, it became with Malory and Tennyson the real center of interest of the plot. The story of the Holy Grail proved almost equally important. In the earliest accounts of this Perceval was the knight chosen above all others to reach the Grail Castle, but Perceval was too rough and worldly a knight to suit the taste of the monks who wrote out the legends and so they created Galahad to take his place as their own ideal of perfection. And into these adventures are woven some of the tales of Sir Gawain, among them the delightful story of Gawain and the Little Maid with the Narrow Sleeves. To the legend of Perceval, Wolfram von Eschenbach, a Bavarian, added the story of the son of Perceval, or Parzival, as he calls him, the story of Lohengrin, the famous Swan-knight. Tristram and Iseult, the fourth of the branches, though less connected with Arthur than either Lancelot or the Holy Grail, became immensely popular with poets and remancers because of its great love story, and is to be found told again and again in widely varying forms all through the Middle Ages.

So we have seen that a British chieftain, winning a great battle in the year 500, became in time celebrated throughout Europe as the greatest king of romance. So far it was mainly the French who had made him famous. Layamon, an English priest, had written a poem in English concerning Arthur shortly after 1200, and told of the founding of the Round Table, but it was to be a considerable time yet before any English writer was to attempt what the French had already done. Chaucer told none of the Arthurian stories, though he placed the scene of his Wife of Bath's Tale at King Arthur's court. An unknown English poet wrote Sir Gawaine and the Green Knight somewhere between 1350 and 1375. It is not until we come to the Morte Darthur of Sir Thomas Malory, finished in 1469 or 1470, that we reach the next great step in the history of the legends since the time of Chrétien de Troies. But in Malory's story Arthur steps forth resplendent, the kingly figure that we have to-day.

Little is known concerning Sir Thomas Malory. He seems to have been a knight and country gentleman of Warwickshire, a member of Parliament in the reign of Henry VI, and later a soldier on the side of Lancaster in the Wars of the Roses. As a result of the victory of the party of York he had to retire from public life when Edward IV came to the throne, and lived quietly at his Warwickshire estate. He was familiar with life at court and with men-at-arms and he knew how popular the stories of King Arthur were becoming in England. So, being a man of education, he set to work to make a collection of the legends, using as his chief sources the French romances.

Malory showed considerable originality in carrying out his plan. He made Arthur the central figure, taking the story of Merlin as an introduction to the birth of Arthur, instead of as a separate legend, and ending his account soon after the death of the king. He omitted a number of the older legends that had little to do with Arthur, many of them good stories, such as that of Sir Gawain and the Green Knight. He made the England of his Arthur something like the England he knew, and his people became real and living instead of fanciful figures out of a far-distant past. His descriptions are vivid and lively and his style so engaging that his work of the fifteenth century is much read to-day. Three characters stand out from all the rest, Arthur, Lancelot, and Guinevere, and these three became in all stories and poems subsequent to Malory's time the main figures of the legends.

Matthew Arnold attributed to Homer three great epic traits, swiftness, simplicity, and nobility. It is these three characteristics that have made the Morte Darthur so deservedly famous.

With the printing of Malory's book by the first English printer, William Caxton, in 1485, we come to the end of the Middle Ages in literature. Manuscripts written out laboriously by monks and clerks were now to give way to the printed page. The age of Elizabeth was less than a century away, one of the golden ages of the poets. Yet few of the Elizabethans touched on the story of Arthur. The main exception was Edmund Spenser, who made Prince Arthur the hero of his great poem The Faerie Queene, but Spenser's Arthur and his knights and ladies have little in common with the figures in the old romances.

The succeeding centuries, great as they were in English writers of genius, paid little attention to Arthur. Milton and Dryden made little use of the legends. Stories of ancient chivalry lost their vogue, novels were becoming popular and the poets chose themes closer to their own times and point of view. Not until the nineteenth century did Arthur come into his own again. Then the Victorian poets turned to him for inspiration. William Morris wrote The Defence of Guenevere, and a host of lesser poets tried their hands on similar themes. Swinburne told the story of Tristram of Lyonesse and the Tale of Balen, and James Russell Lowell composed his beautiful poem The Vision of Sir Launfal. Matthew Arnold wrote Tristram and Iseult. In 1850 Richard Wagner, the great German composer, produced his opera Lohengrin, and followed it with Tristan und Isolde and Parsifal. These tell the old stories in somewhat new form, and follow the early French romances rather than Malory.

But the true descendant of Chrétien de Troies and Malory was Alfred Tennyson. The great work of this poet's life was his Idylls of the King, one of the finest achievements of English literature. He owed his inspiration chiefly to Malory. "The vision of Arthur as I have drawn him," Tennyson said to his son, "had come upon me when, little more than a boy, I first lighted upon Malory." He covered almost the entire field of the legends. The Idylls of the King are The Coming of Arthur, Geraint and Enid, Merlin and Vivien, Lancelot and Elaine, The Holy Grail, Pelleas and Ettarre, Balin and Balan, The Last Tournament, Guinevere, and The Passing of Arthur.

Tennyson gives to the stories far more allegory, far more philosophy than the early poets gave them. His age was interested in philosophy and so, as was the case with each of the earlier poets, Tennyson handled the legends after the fashion of his own times. In his pages we see the characters as actual men and women, subtly drawn, concerned with right and wrong far more than with mere knightly adventures. Arthur and Lancelot and Guinevere hold the center of the stage, and it is the fate of these three that provides the great moving motive of the poems.

To Tennyson we owe the most nearly perfect version of the story that dates back to a dim and legendary England. What verse more beautiful than his to tell of chivalry?

"Then, in the boyhood of the year,
Sir Lancelot and Queen Guinevere
Rode thro' the coverts of the deer,
With blissful treble ringing clear.
She seem'd a part of joyous Spring:
A gown of grass-green silk she wore,
Buckled with golden clasps before;
A light-green tuft of plumes she bore
Closed in a golden ring."

In beauty and dignity and human interest Tennyson gives us the great world of Arthurian legend in its most perfect form.

Malory's Morte Darthur was not Tennyson's only source for the stories of his Idylls. The adventures of Geraint he took from the Mabinogion, a collection of mediæval Welsh tales translated with great charm and accuracy by Lady Charlotte Guest, and published in 1838. Also, though to a very limited extent, he drew some of his incidents from the history of Geoffrey of Monmouth and the other early writers of chronicles.

The great panorama of stories that we group together under the title of King Arthur and the Knights of the Round Table, when they are told in prose, are usually taken from Malory's book, the Morte Darthur, condensed in size, for Malory was frequently verbose, and related in more modern English. In this volume we have used as a basis the version prepared by Sir James Knowles, which is an abridgment of Malory's work as it was printed by Caxton, with a few additions from Geoffrey of Monmouth and other sources. To this we have added the story of Sir Gawain and the Maid with the Narrow Sleeves, which comes originally from the poem of Perceval by Chrétien de Troies.

The stories seem naturally to group themselves into four divisions, The Coming of Arthur and the Founding of the Round Table, The Adventures of the Champions of the Round Table, Sir Galahad and the Quest of the Holy Grail, and The Passing of

Arthur. Into these come all the great characters of the legends and all the surpassing adventures of the king and his knights.

The story of how a half-barbarous British Chieftain became the greatest king of mediæval chivalry is a romance in itself. To him poets and chroniclers of all lands added one valorous knight after another, one amazing adventure on top of another, until the result was the greatest collection of legends that have gathered about any king in history. The story of the origin and growth of these world-famous legends is told in a most delightful book, The Arthur of the English Poets, by Howard Maynadier, and those who wish to get the historical background of King Arthur should turn to its pages.

Those who love brave and knightly deeds, those who love the gorgeous trappings of mediæval romance, come to the story of Arthur and his Round Table, of Lancelot and Perceval and Galahad and Gawain, of Guinevere and Elaine, and of the Quest for the Holy Grail, and there shall be found the glories that you seek. The king and his knights ride out from Camelot. Here shall you join them on their great adventures!

Rupert S. Holland.

THE COMING OF ARTHUR AND THE
FOUNDING OF THE ROUND TABLE

I. MERLIN FORETELLS THE BIRTH OF ARTHUR

King Vortigern the usurper sat upon his throne in London, when, suddenly, upon a certain day, ran in a breathless messenger, and cried aloud—

"Arise, Lord King, for the enemy is come; even Ambrosius and Uther, upon whose throne thou sittest—and full twenty thousand with them—and they have sworn by a great oath, Lord, to slay thee, ere this year be done; and even now they march towards thee as the north wind of winter for bitterness and haste."

At those words Vortigern's face grew white as ashes, and, rising in confusion and disorder, he sent for all the best artificers and craftsmen and mechanics, and commanded them vehemently to go and build him straightway in the furthest west of his lands a great and strong castle, where he might fly for refuge and escape the vengeance of his master's sons—"and, moreover," cried he, "let the work be done within a hundred days from now, or I will surely spare no life amongst you all."

Then all the host of craftsmen, fearing for their lives, found out a proper site whereon to build the tower, and eagerly began to lay in the foundations. But no sooner were the walls raised up above the ground than all their work was overwhelmed and broken down by night invisibly, no man perceiving how, or by whom, or what. And the same thing happening again, and yet again, all the workmen, full of terror, sought out the king, and threw themselves upon their faces before him, beseeching him to interfere and help them or to deliver them from their dreadful work.

Filled with mixed rage and fear, the king called for the astrologers and wizards, and took counsel with them what these things might be, and how to overcome them. The wizards worked their spells and incantations, and in the end declared that nothing but the blood of a youth born without mortal father, smeared on the

11

foundations of the castle, could avail to make it stand. Messengers were therefore sent forthwith through all the land to find, if it were possible, such a child. And, as some of them went down a certain village street, they saw a band of lads fighting and quarreling, and heard them shout at one—"Avaunt, thou imp!—avaunt! Son of no mortal man! go, find thy father, and leave us in peace."

At that the messengers looked steadfastly on the lad, and asked who he was. One said his name was Merlin; another, that his birth and parentage were known by no man; a third, that the foul fiend alone was his father. Hearing the things, the officers seized Merlin, and carried him before the king by force.

But no sooner was he brought to him than he asked in a loud voice, for what cause he was thus dragged there?

"My magicians," answered Vortigern, "told me to seek out a man that had no human father, and to sprinkle my castle with his blood, that it may stand."

"Order those magicians," said Merlin, "to come before me, and I will convict them of a lie."

The king was astonished at his words, but commanded the magicians to come and sit down before Merlin, who cried to them—

"Because ye know not what it is that hinders the foundation of the castle, ye have advised my blood for a cement to it, as if that would avail; but tell me now rather what there is below that ground, for something there is surely underneath that will not suffer the tower to stand?"

The wizards at these words began to fear, and made no answer. Then said Merlin to the king—

"I pray, Lord, that workmen may be ordered to dig deep down into the ground till they shall come to a great pool of water."

This then was done, and the pool discovered far beneath the surface of the ground.

Then, turning again to the magicians, Merlin said, "Tell me now, false sycophants, what there is underneath that pool?"—but they were silent. Then said he to the king, "Command this pool to be drained, and at the bottom shall be found two dragons, great and huge, which now are sleeping, but which at night awake and fight and tear each other. At their great struggle all the ground shakes and trembles, and so casts down thy towers, which, therefore, never yet could find secure foundations."

The king was amazed at these words, but commanded the pool to be forthwith drained; and surely at the bottom of it did they presently discover the two dragons, fast asleep, as Merlin had declared.

But Vortigern sat upon the brink of the pool till night to see what else would happen.

Then those two dragons, one of which was white, the other red, rose up and came near one another, and began a sore fight, and cast forth fire with their breath. But the white dragon had the advantage, and chased the other to the end of the lake. And he, for grief at his flight, turned back upon his foe, and renewed the combat, and forced him to retire in turn. But in the end the red dragon was worsted, and the white dragon disappeared no man knew where.

When their battle was done, the king desired Merlin to tell him what it meant. Whereat he, bursting into tears, cried out this prophecy, which first foretold the coming of King Arthur.

"Woe to the red dragon, which figureth the British nation, for his banishment cometh quickly; his lurking-holes shall be seized by the white dragon—the Saxon whom thou, O king, hast called to the land. The mountains shall be leveled as the valleys, and the rivers of the valleys shall run blood; cities shall be burned, and churches laid in ruins; till at length the oppressed shall turn for a season and prevail against the strangers. For a Boar of Cornwall shall arise and rend them, and trample their necks beneath his feet. The island shall be subject to his power, and he shall take the forests of Gaul. The house of Romulus shall dread him—all the world shall fear him—and his end shall no man know; he shall be immortal in the mouths of the people, and his works shall be food to those that tell them.

"But as for thee, O Vortigern, flee thou the sons of Constantine, for they shall burn thee in thy tower. For thine own ruin wast thou traitor to their father, and didst bring the Saxon heathens to the land. Aurelius and Uther are even now upon thee to revenge their father's murder; and the brood of the white dragon shall waste thy country, and shall lick thy blood. Find out some refuge, if thou wilt! but who may escape the doom of God?"

The king heard all this, trembling greatly; and, convicted of his sins, said nothing in reply. Only he hasted the builders of his tower by day and night, and rested not till he had fled thereto.

In the meantime, Aurelius, the rightful king, was hailed with joy by the Britons, who flocked to his standard, and prayed to be led against the Saxons. But he, till he had first killed Vortigern, would begin no other war. He marched therefore to Cambria, and came before the tower which the usurper had built. Then, crying out to all his knights, "Avenge ye on him who hath ruined Britain and slain my father and your king!" he rushed with many thousands at the castle walls. But, being driven back again and yet again, at length he thought of fire, and ordered blazing brands to be cast into the building from all sides. These, finding soon a proper fuel, ceased not to rage till, spreading to a mighty conflagration, they burned down the tower, and Vortigern within it.

Then did Aurelius turn his strength against Hengist and the Saxons, and, defeating them in many places, weakened their power for a long season, so that the land had peace.

Anon the king, making journeys to and fro, restoring ruined churches and, creating order, came to the monastery near Salisbury, where all those British knights lay buried who had been slain there by the treachery of Hengist. For when in former times Hengist had made a solemn truce with Vortigern, to meet in peace and settle terms, whereby himself and all his Saxons should depart from Britain, the Saxon soldiers carried every one of them beneath his garment a long dagger, and, at a given signal, fell upon the Britons, and slew them, to the number of nearly five hundred.

The sight of the place where the dead lay moved Aurelius to great sorrow, and he cast about in his mind how to make a worthy tomb over so many noble martyrs, who had died there for their country.

14

When he had in vain consulted many craftsmen and builders, he sent, by the advice of the archbishop, for Merlin, and asked him what to do. "If you would honor the burying-place of these men," said Merlin, "with an everlasting monument, send for the Giants' Dance which is in Killaraus, a mountain; in Ireland; for there is a structure of stone there which none of this age could raise without a perfect knowledge of the arts. They are stones of a vast size and wondrous nature, and if they can be placed here as they are there, round this spot of ground, they will stand for ever."

At these words of Merlin, Aurelius burst into laughter, and said, "How is it possible to remove such vast stones from so great a distance, as if Britain, also, had no stones fit for the work?"

"I pray the king," said Merlin, "to forbear vain laughter; what I have said is true, for those stones are mystical and have healing virtues. The giants of old brought them from the furthest coast of Africa, and placed them in Ireland while they lived in that country: and their design was to make baths in them, for use in time of grievous illness. For if they washed the stones and put the sick into the water, it certainly healed them, as also it did them that were wounded in battle; and there is no stone among them but hath the same virtue still."

When the Britons heard this, they resolved to send for the stones, and to make war upon the people of Ireland if they offered to withhold them. So, when they had chosen Uther the king's brother for their chief, they set sail, to the number of 15,000 men, and came to Ireland. There Gillomanius, the king, withstood them fiercely, and not till after a great battle could they approach the Giants' Dance, the sight of which filled them with joy and admiration. But when they sought to move the stones, the strength of all the army was in vain, until Merlin, laughing at their failures, contrived machines of wondrous cunning, which took them down with ease, and placed them in the ships.

When they had brought the whole to Salisbury, Aurelius, with the crown upon his head, kept for four days the feast of Pentecost with royal pomp; and in the midst of all the clergy and the people,

Merlin raised up the stones, and set them round the sepulcher of the knights and barons, as they stood in the mountains of Ireland.

Then was the monument called "Stonehenge," and stands, as all men know, upon the plain of Salisbury to this very day.

Soon thereafter it befell that Aurelius was slain by poison at Winchester, and was himself buried within the Giants' Dance.

At the same time came forth a comet of amazing size and brightness, darting out a beam, at the end whereof was a cloud of fire shaped like a dragon, from whose mouth went out two rays, one stretching over Gaul, the other ending in seven lesser rays over the Irish sea.

At the appearance of this star a great dread fell upon the people, and Uther, marching into Cambria against the son of Vortigern, himself was very troubled to learn what it might mean. Then Merlin, being called before him, cried with a loud voice: "O mighty loss! O stricken Britain! Alas! the great prince is gone from us. Aurelius Ambrosius is dead, whose death will be ours also, unless God help us. Haste, therefore, noble Uther, to destroy the enemy; the victory shall be thine, and thou shalt be king of all Britain. For the star with the fiery dragon signifies thyself; and the ray over Gaul portends that thou shalt have a son, most mighty, whom all those kingdoms shall obey which the ray covers."

Thus, for the second time, did Merlin foretell the coming of King Arthur. And Uther, when he was made king, remembered Merlin's words, and caused two dragons to be made in gold, in likeness of the dragon he had seen in the star. One of these he gave to Winchester Cathedral, and had the other carried into all his wars before him, whence he was ever after called Uther Pendragon, or the dragon's head.

Now, when Uther Pendragon had passed through all the land, and settled it—and even voyaged into all the countries of the Scots, and tamed the fierceness of that rebel people—he came to London, and ministered justice there. And it befell at a certain great banquet and high feast which the king made at Easter-tide, there came, with many other earls and barons, Gorloïs, Duke of Cornwall, and his wife Igerna, who was the most famous beauty in all Britain. And soon thereafter, Gorloïs being slain in battle, Uther determined to make Igerna his own wife. But in order to do this, and enable him to come to her—for she was shut up in the high castle of Tintagil, on the furthest coast of Cornwall—the king sent for Merlin, to take counsel with him and to pray his help. This, therefore, Merlin promised him on one condition—namely, that the king should give him up the first son born of the marriage. For Merlin by his art foreknew that this firstborn should be the long-wished prince, King Arthur.

When Uther, therefore, was at length happily wedded, Merlin came to the castle on a certain day, and said, "Sir, thou must now provide thee for the nourishing of thy child."

And the king, nothing doubting, said, "Be it as thou wilt."

"I know a lord of thine in this land," said Merlin, "who is a man both true and faithful; let him have the nourishing of the child. His name is Sir Ector, and he hath fair possessions both in England and in Wales. When, therefore, the child is born, let him be delivered unto me, unchristened, at yonder postern-gate, and I will bestow him in the care of this good knight."

So when the child was born, the king bid two knights and two ladies to take it, bound in rich cloth of gold, and deliver it to a poor man whom they should discover at the postern-gate. And the child being delivered thus to Merlin, who himself took the guise of a poor man, was carried by him to a holy priest and christened by the name of Arthur, and then was taken to Sir Ector's house, and nourished at Sir Ector's wife's own breasts. And in the same house he remained privily for many years, no man soever knowing where he was, save Merlin and the king.

Anon it befell that the king was seized by a lingering distemper, and the Saxon heathens, taking their occasion, came back from over sea, and swarmed upon the land, wasting it with fire and sword. When Uther heard thereof, he fell into a greater rage than his weakness could bear, and commanded all his nobles to come before him, that he might upbraid them for their cowardice. And when he had sharply and hotly rebuked them, he swore that he himself, nigh unto death although he lay, would lead them forth against the enemy. Then causing a horse-litter to be made, in which he might be carried—for he was too faint and weak to ride—he went up with all his army swiftly against the Saxons.

But they, when they heard that Uther was coming in a litter, disdained to fight him, saying it would be shame for brave men to fight with one half dead. So they retired into their city; and, as it were in scorn of danger, left the gates wide open. But Uther straightway commanding his men to assault the town, they did so without loss of time, and had already reached the gates, when the Saxons, repenting too late of their haughty pride, rushed forth to the defense. The battle raged till night, and was begun again next day; but at last, their leaders, Octa and Eosa, being slain, the Saxons turned their backs and fled, leaving the Britons a full triumph.

The king at this felt so great joy, that, whereas before he could scarce raise himself without help, he now sat upright in his litter by himself, and said, with a laughing and merry face, "They called me the half-dead king, and so indeed I was; but victory to me half dead is better than defeat and the best health. For to die with honor is far better than to live disgraced."

But the Saxons, although thus defeated, were ready still for war. Uther would have pursued them; but his illness had by now so grown, that his knights and barons kept him from the adventure. Whereat the enemy took courage, and left nothing undone to destroy the land; until, descending to the vilest treachery, they resolved to kill the king by poison.

To this end, as he lay sick at Verulum, they sent and poisoned stealthily a spring of clear water, whence he was wont to drink daily; and so, on the very next day, he was taken with the pains of death, as were also a hundred others after him, before the villainy was discovered, and heaps of earth thrown over the well.

The knights and barons, full of sorrow, now took counsel together, and came to Merlin for his help to learn the king's will before he died, for he was by this time speechless. "Sirs, there is no remedy," said Merlin, "and God's will must be done; but be ye all to-morrow before him, for God will make him speak before he die."

18

So on the morrow all the barons, with Merlin, stood round the bedside of the king; and Merlin said aloud to Uther, "Lord, shall thy son Arthur be the king of all this realm after thy days?"

Then Uther Pendragon turned him about, and said, in the hearing of them all, "God's blessing and mine be upon him. I bid him pray for my soul, and also that he claim my crown, or forfeit all my blessing;" and with those words he died.

Then came together all the bishops and the clergy, and great multitudes of people, and bewailed the king; and carrying his body to the convent of Ambrius, they buried it close by his brother's grave, within the "Giants' Dance."

II. THE CROWNING OF ARTHUR AND
THE SWORD EXCALIBUR

Now Arthur the prince had all this time been nourished in Sir Ector's house as his own son, and was fair and tall and comely, being of the age of fifteen years, great in strength, gentle in manner, and accomplished in all exercises proper for the training of a knight.

But as yet he knew not of his father; for Merlin had so dealt, that none save Uther and himself knew aught about him. Wherefore it befell that many of the knights and barons who heard King Uther speak before his death, and call his son Arthur his successor, were in great amazement; and some doubted, and others were displeased.

Anon the chief lords and princes set forth each to his own land, and, raising armed men and multitudes of followers, determined every one to gain the crown for himself; for they said in their hearts, "If there be any such a son at all as he of whom this wizard forced the king to speak, who are we that a beardless boy should have rule over us?"

So the land stood long in great peril, for every lord and baron sought but his own advantage; and the Saxons, growing ever more adventurous, wasted and overran the towns and villages in every part.

Then Merlin went to Brice, the Archbishop of Canterbury, and advised him to require all the earls and barons of the realm and all knights and gentlemen-at-arms to come to him at London, before Christmas, under pain of cursing, that they might learn the will of Heaven who should be king. This, therefore, the archbishop did, and upon Christmas Eve were met together in London all the greatest princes, lords, and barons; and long before day they prayed in St. Paul's Church, and the archbishop besought Heaven for a sign who should be lawful king of all the realm.

And as they prayed, there was seen in the churchyard, set straight before the doorways of the church, a huge square stone having a naked sword stuck in the midst of it. And on the sword was written in letters of gold, "Whoso pulleth out the sword from this stone is born the rightful King of England."

At this all the people wondered greatly; and, when Mass was over, the nobles, knights, and princes ran out eagerly from the church to see the stone and sword; and a law was forthwith made that whoso should pull out the sword should be acknowledged straightway King of Britain.

Then many knights and barons pulled at the sword with all their might, and some of them tried many times, but none could stir or move it.

When all had tried in vain, the archbishop declared the man whom Heaven had chosen was not yet there. "But God," said he, "will doubtless make him known ere many days."

So ten knights were chosen, being men of high renown, to watch and keep the sword; and there was proclamation made through all the land that whosoever would, had leave and liberty to try and pull it from the stone. But though great multitudes of people came, both gentle and simple, for many days, no man could ever move the sword a hair's breadth from its place.

Now, at the New Year's Eve a great tournament was to be held in London, which the archbishop had devised to keep together lords and commons, lest they should grow estranged in the troublous and unsettled times. To the which tournament there came, with many other knights, Sir Ector, Arthur's foster-father, who had great possessions near to London; and with him came his son, Sir Key, but recently made knight, to take his part in the jousting, and young Arthur also to witness all the sports and fighting.

But as they rode towards the jousts, Sir Key found suddenly he had no sword, for he had left it at his father's house; and turning to young Arthur, he prayed him to ride back and fetch it for him. "I will with a good will," said Arthur; and rode fast back after the sword.

But when he came to the house he found it locked and empty,

for all were gone forth to see the tournament. Whereat, being angry and impatient, he said within himself, "I will ride to the churchyard and take with me the sword that sticketh in the stone, for my brother shall not go without a sword this day."

So he rode and came to the churchyard, and alighting from his horse he tied him to the gate, and went to the pavilion, which was pitched near the stone, wherein abode the ten knights who watched and kept it; but he found no knights there, for all were gone to see the jousting.

Then he took the sword by its handle, and lightly and fiercely he pulled it out of the stone, and took his horse and rode until he came to Sir Key and delivered him the sword. But as soon as Sir Key saw it he knew well it was the sword of the stone, and, riding swiftly to his father, he cried out, "Lo! here, sir, is the sword of the stone, wherefore it is I who must be king of all this land."

When Sir Ector saw the sword, he turned back straight with Arthur and Sir Key and came to the churchyard, and there alighting, they went all three into the church, and Sir Key was sworn to tell truly how he came by the sword. Then he confessed it was his brother Arthur who had brought it to him.

Whereat Sir Ector, turning to young Arthur, asked him—"How gottest thou the sword?"

"Sir," said he, "I will tell you. When I went home to fetch my brother's sword, I found nobody to deliver it to me, for all were abroad to the jousts. Yet was I loth to leave my brother swordless, and, bethinking me of this one, I came hither eagerly to fetch it for him, and pulled it out of the stone without any pain."

Then said Sir Ector, much amazed and looking steadfastly on Arthur, "If this indeed be thus, 'tis thou who shalt be king of all this land—and God will have it so—for none but he who should be rightful Lord of Britain might ever draw this sword forth from that stone. But let me now with mine own eyes see thee put back the sword into its place and draw it forth again."

"That is no mastery," said Arthur; and straightway set it in the stone. And then Sir Ector pulled at it himself, and after him Sir

Key, with all his might, but both of them in vain: then Arthur, reaching forth his hand and grasping at the pommel, pulled it out easily, and at once.

Then fell Sir Ector down upon his knees upon the ground before young Arthur, and Sir Key also with him, and straightway did him homage as their sovereign lord.

But Arthur cried aloud, "Alas! mine own dear father and my brother, why kneel ye thus to me?"

"Nay, my Lord Arthur," answered then Sir Ector, "we are of no blood-kinship with thee, and little though I thought how high thy kin might be, yet wast thou never more than foster-child of mine." And then he told him all he knew about his infancy, and how a stranger had delivered him, with a great sum of gold, into his hands to be brought up and nourished as his own born child, and then had disappeared.

But when young Arthur heard of it, he fell upon Sir Ector's neck, and wept, and made great lamentation, "For now," said he, "I have in one day lost my father and my mother and my brother."

"Sir," said Sir Ector presently, "when thou shalt be made king be good and gracious unto me and mine."

"If not," said Arthur, "I were no true man's son at all, for thou art he in all the world to whom I owe the most; and my good lady and mother, thy wife, hath ever kept and fostered me as though I were her own; so if it be God's will that I be king hereafter as thou sayest, desire of me whatever thing thou wilt and I will do it; and God forbid that I should fail thee in it."

"I will but pray," replied Sir Ector, "that thou wilt make my son Sir Key, thy foster-brother, seneschal of all the lands."

"That shall he be," said Arthur; "and never shall another hold that office, save thy son, while he and I do live."

Anon, they left the church and went to the archbishop to tell him that the sword had been achieved. And when he saw the sword in Arthur's hand he set a day and summoned all the princes, knights, and barons to meet again at St. Paul's Church and see the will of Heaven signified. So when they came together, the sword was put back in the stone, and all tried, from the greatest to the least, to move it; but there before them all not one could take it out save Arthur only.

But then befell a great confusion and dispute, for some cried out it was the will of Heaven, and, "Long live King Arthur," but many more were full of wrath and said, "What! would ye give the ancient scepter of this land unto a boy born none know how?" And the contention growing greatly, till nothing could be done to pacify their rage, the meeting was at length broken up by the archbishop and adjourned till Candlemas, when all should meet again.

But when Candlemas was come, Arthur alone again pulled forth the sword, though more than ever came to win it; and the barons, sorely vexed and angry, put it in delay till Easter. But as he had sped before so he did at Easter, and the barons yet once more contrived delays till Pentecost.

But now the archbishop, fully seeing God's will, called together, by Merlin's counsel, a band of knights and gentlemen-at-arms, and set them about Arthur to keep him safely till the Feast of Pentecost. And when at the feast Arthur still again alone prevailed to move the sword, the people all with one accord cried out, "Long live King Arthur! we will have no more delay, nor any other king, for so it is God's will; and we will slay whoso resisteth Him and Arthur;" and wherewithal they kneeled down all at once, and cried for Arthur's grace and pardon that they had so long delayed him from his crown. Then he full sweetly and majestically pardoned them; and taking in his hand the sword, he offered it upon the high altar of the church.

Anon was he solemnly knighted with great pomp by the most famous knight there present, and the crown was placed upon his head; and, having taken oath to all the people, lords and commons, to be true king and deal in justice only unto his life's end, he received homage and service from all the barons who held lands and castles from the crown. Then he made Sir Key, High Steward of England, and Sir Badewaine of Britain, Constable, and Sir Ulfius, Chamberlain: and after this, with all his court and a great retinue of knights and armed men, he journeyed into Wales, and was crowned again in the old city of Caerleon-upon-Usk.

24

Meanwhile those knights and barons who had so long delayed him from the crown, met together and went up to the coronation feast at Caerleon, as if to do him homage; and there they ate and drank such things as were set before them at the royal banquet, sitting with the others in the great hall.

But when after the banquet Arthur began, according to the ancient royal custom, to bestow great boons and fiefs on whom he would, they all with one accord rose up, and scornfully refused his gifts, crying that they would take nothing from a beardless boy come of low or unknown birth, but would instead give him good gifts of hard sword-strokes between neck and shoulders.

Whereat arose a deadly tumult in the hall, and every man there made him ready to fight. But Arthur leaped up as a flame of fire against them, and all his knights and barons drawing their swords, rushed after him upon them and began a full sore battle; and presently the king's party prevailed, and drave the rebels from the hall and from the city, closing the gates behind them; and King Arthur brake his sword upon them in his eagerness and rage.

But amongst them were six kings of great renown and might, who more than all raged against Arthur and determined to destroy him, namely, King Lot, King Nanters, King Urien, King Carados, King Yder, and King Anguisant. These six, therefore, joining their armies together, laid close siege to the city of Caerleon, wherefrom King Arthur had so shamefully driven them.

And after fifteen days Merlin came suddenly into their camp and asked them what this treason meant. Then he declared to them that Arthur was no base adventurer, but King Uther's son, whom they were bound to serve and honor even though Heaven had not vouch-safed the wondrous miracle of the sword. Some of the kings, when they heard Merlin speak thus, marveled and believed him; but others, as King Lot, laughed him and his words to scorn, and mocked him for a conjurer and wizard. But it was agreed with Merlin that Arthur should come forth and speak with the kings.

So he went forth to them to the city gate, and with him the archbishop and Merlin, and Sir Key, Sir Brastias, and a great company of others. And he spared them not in his speech, but spoke to them as king and chieftain, telling them plainly he would make them all bow to him if he lived, unless they choose to do him homage there and then; and so they parted in great wrath, and each side armed in haste.

"What will ye do?" said Merlin to the kings; "ye had best hold your hands, for were ye ten times as many ye should not prevail."

"Shall we be afraid of a dream-reader?" quoth King Lot in scorn.

With that Merlin vanished away and came to King Arthur.

Then Arthur said to Merlin, "I have need now of a sword that shall chastise these rebels terribly."

"Come then with me," said Merlin, "for hard by there is a sword that I can gain for thee."

So they rode out that night till they came to a fair and broad lake, and in the midst of it King Arthur saw an arm thrust up, clothed in white samite, and holding a great sword in the hand.

"Lo! yonder is the sword I spoke of," said Merlin.

Then saw they a damsel floating on the lake in the moonlight. "What damsel is that?" said the king.

"The lady of the lake," said Merlin; "for upon this lake there is a rock, and on the rock a noble palace, where she abideth, and she will come towards thee presently, when thou shalt ask her courteously for the sword."

Therewith the damsel came to King Arthur, and saluted him, and he saluted her, and said, "Lady, what sword is that the arm holdeth above the water? I would that it were mine, for I have no sword."

"Sir King," said the lady of the lake, "that sword is mine, and if thou wilt give me in return a gift whenever I shall ask it of thee, thou shalt have it."

"By my faith," said he, "I will give thee any gift that thou shalt ask."

"Well," said the damsel, "go into yonder barge, and row thyself unto the sword, and take it and the scabbard with thee, and I will ask my gift of thee when I see my time."

So King Arthur and Merlin alighted, and tied their horses to two trees, and went into the barge; and when they came to the sword

26

that the hand held, King Arthur took it by the handle and bore it with him, and the arm and hand went down under the water; and so they came back to land, and rode again to Caerleon.

On the morrow Merlin bade King Arthur to set fiercely on the enemy; and in the meanwhile three hundred good knights went over to King Arthur from the rebels' side. Then at the spring of day, when they had scarce left their tents, he fell on them with might and main, and Sir Badewaine, Sir Key, and Sir Brastias slew on the right and on the left marvelously; and ever in the thickest of the fight King Arthur raged like a young lion, and laid on with his sword, and did wondrous deeds of arms, to the joy and admiration of the knights and barons who beheld him.

Then King Lot, King Carados, and the King of the Hundred Knights—who also was with them—going round to the rear, set on King Arthur fiercely from behind; but King Arthur, turning to his knights, fought ever in the foremost press until his horse was slain beneath him. At that, King Lot rode furiously at him, and smote him down; but rising straightway, and being set again on horseback, he drew his sword Excalibur that he had gained by Merlin from the lady of the lake, which, shining brightly as the light of thirty torches, dazzled the eyes of his enemies. And therewith falling on them afresh with all his knights, he drove them back and slew them in great numbers, and Merlin by his arts scattered among them fire and pitchy smoke, so that they broke and fled. Then all the common people of Caerleon, seeing them give way, rose up with one accord, and rushed at them with clubs and staves, and chased them far and wide, and slew many great knights and lords, and the remainder of them fled and were seen no more. Thus won King Arthur his first battle and put his enemies to shame.

But the six kings, though sorely routed, prepared for a new war, and joining to themselves five others swore together that, whether for weal or woe, they would keep steadfast alliance till they had destroyed King Arthur. Then, with a host of 50,000 men-at-arms on horseback, and 10,000 foot, they were soon ready, and sent forth their fore-riders, and drew from the northern country towards King Arthur, to the castle of Bedgraine.

But he by Merlin's counsel had sent over sea to King Ban of Benwick and King Bors of Gaul, praying them to come and help him in his wars, and promising to help them in return against King Claudas, their foe. To which those kings made answer that they would joyfully fulfil his wish, and shortly after came to London with 300 knights, well arrayed for both peace and war, leaving behind them a great army on the other side of the sea till they had consulted with King Arthur and his ministers how they might best dispose of it.

And Merlin being asked for his advice and help, agreed to go himself and fetch it over sea to England, which in one night he did; and brought with him 10,000 horsemen and led them northward privately to the forest of Bedgraine, and there lodged them in a valley secretly.

Then, by the counsel of Merlin, when they knew which way the eleven kings would ride and sleep, King Arthur with Kings Ban and Bors made themselves ready with their army for the fight, having yet but 30,000 men, counting the 10,000 who had come from Gaul.

"Now shall ye do my advice," said Merlin; "I would that King Ban and King Bors, with all their fellowship of 10,000 men, were led to ambush in this wood ere daylight, and stir not therefrom until the battle hath been long waged. And thou, Lord Arthur, at the spring of day draw forth thine army before the enemy, and dress the battle so that they may at once see all thy host, for they will be the more rash and hardy when they see you have but 20,000 men."

To this the three knights and the barons heartily consented, and it was done as Merlin had devised. So on the morrow when the hosts beheld each other, the host of the north was greatly cheered to find so few led out against them.

Then gave King Arthur the command to Sir Ulfius and Sir Brastias to take 3000 men-at-arms, and to open battle. They therefore setting fiercely on the enemy slew them on the right hand and the left till it was wonderful to see their slaughter.

When the eleven kings beheld so small a band doing such

mighty deeds of arms they were ashamed, and charged them fiercely in return. Then was Sir Ulfius' horse slain under him; but he fought well and marvelously on foot against Duke Eustace and King Clarience, who set upon him grievously, till Sir Brastias, seeing his great peril, pricked towards them swiftly, and so smote the duke through with his spear that horse and man fell down and rolled over. Whereat King Clarience turned upon Sir Brastias, and rushing furiously together they each unhorsed the other and fell both to the ground, and there lay a long time stunned, their horses' knees being cut to the bone. Then came Sir Key the seneschal with six companions, and did wondrous well, till the eleven kings went out against them and overthrew Sir Griflet and Sir Lucas the butler. And when Sir Key saw Sir Griflet unhorsed and on foot, he rode against King Nanters hotly and smote him down, and led his horse to Griflet and horsed him again; with the same spear did Sir Key smite down King Lot and wounded him full sore.

But seeing that, the King of the Hundred Knights rushed at Sir Key and overthrew him in return, and took his horse and gave it to King Lot. And when Sir Griflet saw Sir Key's mischance, he set his spear in rest, and riding at a mighty man-at-arms, he cast him down headlong and caught his horse and led it straightway to Sir Key.

By now the battle was growing perilous and hard, and both sides fought with rage and fury. And Sir Ulfius and Sir Brastias were both afoot and in great danger of their death, and foully stained and trampled under horses' feet. Then King Arthur, putting spurs to his horse, rushed forward like a lion into the midst of all the mêlèe, and singling out King Cradlemont of North Wales, smote him through the left side and overthrew him, and taking his horse by the rein he brought it to Sir Ulfius in haste and said, "Take this horse, mine old friend, for thou hast great need of one, and charge by side of me." And even as he spoke he saw Sir Ector, Sir Key's father, smitten to the earth by the King of the Hundred Knights, and his horse taken to King Cradlemont.

But when King Arthur saw him ride upon Sir Ector's horse

his wrath was very great, and with his sword he smote King Cradlemont upon the helm, and shore off the fourth part thereof and of the shield, and drave the sword onward to the horse's neck and slew the horse, and hurled the king upon the ground.

And now the battle waxed so great and furious that all the noise and sound thereof rang out by water and by wood, so that Kings Ban and Bors, with all their knights and men-at-arms in ambush, hearing the tumult and the cries, trembled and shook for eagerness, and scarce could stay in secret, but made them ready for the fray and dressed their shields and harness.

But when King Arthur saw the fury of the enemy, he raged like a mad lion, and stirred and drove his horse now here, now there, to the right hand and to the left and stayed not in his wrath till he had slain full twenty knights. He wounded also King Lot so sorely in the shoulder that he left the field, and in great pain and dolor cried out to the other kings, "Do ye as I devise, or we shall be destroyed. I, with the King of the Hundred Knights, King Anguisant, King Yder, and the Duke of Cambinet, will take fifteen thousand men and make a circuit, meanwhile that ye do hold the battle with twelve thousand. Then coming suddenly we will fall fiercely on them from behind and put them to the rout, but else shall we never stand against them."

So Lot and four kings departed with their party to one side, and the six other kings dressed their ranks against King Arthur and fought long and stoutly.

But now Kings Ban and Bors, with all their army fresh and eager, broke from their ambush and met face to face the five kings and their host as they came round behind, and then began a frantic struggle with breaking of spears and clashing of swords and slaying of men and horses. Anon King Lot, espying in the midst King Bors, cried out in great dismay, "Our Lady now defend us from our death and fearful wounds; our peril groweth great, for yonder cometh one of the worshipfullest kings and best knights in all the world."

"Who is he?" said the King of the Hundred Knights.

"It is King Bors of Gaul," replied King Lot, "and much I marvel how he may have come with all his host into this land without our knowledge."

"Aha!" cried King Carados, "I will encounter with this king if ye will rescue me when there is need."

"Ride on," said they.

So King Carados and all his host rode softly till they came within a bow-shot of King Bors, and then both hosts, spurring their horses to their greatest swiftness, rushed at each other. And King Bors encountered in the onset with a knight, and struck him through with a spear, so that he fell dead upon the earth; then drawing his sword, he did such mighty feats of arms that all who saw him gazed with wonder. Anon King Ban came also forth upon the field with all his knights, and added yet more fury, sound, and slaughter, till at length both hosts of the eleven kings began to quake, and drawing all together into one body, they prepared to meet the worst, while a great multitude already fled.

Then said King Lot, "Lords, we must take yet other means, or worse loss still awaits us. See ye not what people we have lost in waiting on the footmen, and that it costs ten horsemen to save one of them? Therefore it is my counsel to put away our footmen from us, for it is almost night, and King Arthur will not stay to slaughter them. So they can save their lives in this great wood hard by. Then let us gather into one band all the horsemen that remain, and whoso breaketh rank or leaveth us, let him be straightway slain by him that seeth him, for it is better that we slay a coward than through a coward be all slain. How say ye?" said King Lot; "answer me, all ye kings."

"It is well said," replied they all.

And swearing they would never fail each other, they mended and set right their armor and their shields, and took new spears and set them steadfastly against their thighs, waiting, and so stood still as a clump of trees stands on the plain; and no assaults could shake them, they held so hard together; which when King Arthur saw he marveled greatly, and was very wroth. "Yet," cried he, "I may not blame them, by my faith, for they do as brave men ought to do, and are the best fighting men and knights of most prowess that I ever saw or heard tell of." And so said also Kings Ban and Bors, and praised them greatly for their noble chivalry.

But now came forty noble knights out of King Arthur's host, and prayed that he would suffer them to break the enemy. And when they were allowed, they rode forth with their spears upon their thighs, and spurred their horses to their hottest. Then the eleven kings, with a party of their knights, rushed with set spears as fast and mightily to meet them; and when they were encountered, all the crash and splinter of their spears and armor rang with a mighty din, and so fierce and bloody was their onset that in all that day there had been no such cruel press, and rage, and smiting. At that same moment rode fiercely into the thickest of the struggle King Arthur and Kings Ban and Bors, and slew downright on both hands right and left, until their horses went in blood up to the fetlocks.

And while the slaughter and the noise and shouting were at their greatest, suddenly there came down through the battle Merlin the Wizard, upon a great black horse, and riding to King Arthur, he cried out, "Alas, my Lord! will ye have never done? Of sixty thousand have ye left but fifteen thousand men alive. Is it not time to stay this slaying? for God is ill pleased with ye that ye have never ended, and yonder kings shall not be altogether overthrown this time. But if ye fall upon them any more, the fortune of this day will turn, and go to them. Withdraw, Lord, therefore, to thy lodging, and there now take thy rest, for to-day thou hast won a great victory, and overcome the noblest chivalry of all the world. And now for many years those kings shall not disturb thee. Therefore, I tell thee, fear them no more, for now they are sore beaten, and have nothing left them but their honor; and why shouldest thou slay them to take that?"

Then said King Arthur, "Thou sayest well, and I will take thy counsel." With that he cried out, "Ho!" for the battle to cease, and sent forth heralds through the field to stay more fighting. And gathering all the spoil, he gave it not amongst his own host, but to Kings Ban and Bors and all their knights and men-at-arms, that he might treat them with the greater courtesy as strangers.

Then Merlin took his leave of Arthur and the two other kings, and went to see his master, Blaise, a holy hermit, dwelling in Northumberland, who had nourished him through all his youth. And Blaise was passing glad to see him, for there was a great love ever between them; and Merlin told him how King Arthur had sped in the battle, and how it had ended; and told him the names of every king and knight of worship who was there. So Blaise wrote down the battle, word for word, as Merlin told him; and in the same way ever after, all the battles of King Arthur's days Merlin caused Blaise, his master, to record.

III. ARTHUR DRIVES THE SAXONS FROM HIS REALM

Anon, thereafter, came word to King Arthur that Ryence, King of North Wales, was making war upon King Leodegrance of Camelgard; whereat he was passing wroth, for he loved Leodegrance well, and hated Ryence. So he departed with Kings Ban and Bors and twenty thousand men, and came to Camelgard, and rescued Leodegrance, and slew ten thousand of Ryence's men and put him to flight. Then Leodegrance made a great festival to the three kings, and treated them with every manner of mirth and pleasure which could be devised. And there had King Arthur the first sight of Guinevere, daughter of Leodegrance, whom in the end he married, as shall be told hereafter.

Then did Kings Ban and Bors take leave, and went to their own country, where King Claudas worked great mischief. And King Arthur would have gone with them, but they refused him, saying, "Nay, ye shall not at this time, for ye have yet much to do in these lands of your own; and we with the riches we have won here by your gifts shall hire many good knights, and, by the grace of God, withstand the malice of King Claudas; and if we have need we will send to ye for succor; and likewise ye, if ye have need, send for us, and we will not tarry, by the faith of our bodies."

When the two kings had left, King Arthur rode to Caerleon, and thither came to him his half-sister Belisent, wife to King Lot, sent as a messenger, but in truth to espy his power; and with her came a noble retinue, and also her four sons—Gowain, Gaheris, Agravaine, and Gareth. But when she saw King Arthur and his nobleness, and all the splendor of his knights and service, she forebore to spy upon him as a foe, and told him of her husband's plots against him and his throne. And the king, not knowing that she was his half-sister, made great court to her; and being full of admiration for her beauty, loved her out of measure, and kept her a long season at Caerleon. Wherefore her husband, King Lot, was more than ever King Arthur's enemy, and hated him till death with a passing great hatred.

At that time King Arthur had a marvelous dream, which gave him great disquietness of heart. He dreamed that the whole land was full of many fiery griffins and serpents, which burnt and slew the people everywhere; and then that he himself fought with them, and that they did him mighty injuries, and wounded him nigh to death, but that at last he overcame and slew them all. When he woke, he sat in great heaviness of spirit and pensiveness, thinking what this dream might signify, but by-and-by, when he could by no means satisfy himself what it might mean, to rid himself of all his thoughts of it, he made ready with a great company to ride out hunting.

As soon as he was in the forest, the king saw a great hart before him, and spurred his horse, and rode long eagerly after it, and chased until his horse lost breath and fell down dead from under him. Then, seeing the hart escaped and his horse dead, he sat down by a fountain, and fell into deep thought again. And as he sat there alone, he thought he heard the noise of hounds, as it were some thirty couple in number, and looking up he saw coming towards him the strangest beast that ever he had seen or heard tell of, which ran towards the fountain and drank of the water. Its head was like a serpent's, with a leopard's body and a lion's tail, and it was footed like a stag; and the noise was in its belly, as it were the baying or questing of thirty couple of hounds. While it drank there was no noise within it; but presently, having finished, it departed with a greater sound than ever.

The king was amazed at all this; but being greatly wearied, he fell asleep, and was before long waked up by a knight on foot, who said, "Knight, full of thought and sleepy, tell me if thou sawest a strange beast pass this way?"

"Such a one I saw," said King Arthur to the knight, "but that is now two miles distant at the least. What would you with that beast?"

"Sir," said the knight, "I have followed it for a long time, and have killed my horse, and would to heaven I had another to pursue my quest withal."

At that moment came a yeoman with another horse for the king, which, when the knight saw, he earnestly prayed to be given him. "For I have followed this quest," said he, "twelve months, and either I shall achieve him or bleed of the best blood of my body."

It was King Pellinore who at that time followed the questing beast, but neither he nor King Arthur knew each other.

"Sir Knight," said King Arthur, "leave that quest and suffer me to have it, and I will follow it other twelve months."

"Ah, fool," said the knight, "thy desire is utterly in vain, for it shall never be achieved but by me, or by my next of kin."

Therewith he started to the king's horse, and mounted to the saddle, crying out, "Gramercy, this horse is mine!"

"Well," said the king, "thou mayest take my horse by force, and I will not say nay; but till we prove whether thou or I be best on horseback, I shall not rest content."

"Seek me here," said the knight, "whenever thou wilt, and here by this fountain thou shalt find me;" and so he passed forth on his way.

Then sat King Arthur in a deep fit of study, and bade his yeomen fetch him yet another horse as quickly as they could. And when they left him all alone came Merlin, disguised as a child of fourteen years of age, and saluted the king, and asked him why he was so pensive and heavy.

"I may well be pensive and heavy," he replied, "for here even now I have seen the strangest sight I ever saw."

"That know I well," said Merlin, "as well as thyself, and also all thy thoughts; but thou art foolish to take thought, for it will not amend thee. Also I know what thou art, and know thy father and thy mother."

"That is false," said King Arthur; "how shouldst thou know? thy years are not enough."

"Yea," said Merlin, "but I know better than thou how thou wast born, and better than any man living."

"I will not believe thee," said King Arthur, and was wroth with the child.

So Merlin departed, and came again in the likeness of an old man of fourscore years of age; and the king was glad at his coming, for he seemed wise and venerable. Then said the old man, "Why art thou so sad?"

"For divers reasons," said King Arthur; "for I have seen strange things to-day, and but this moment there was here a child who told me things beyond his years to know."

"Yea," said the old man, "but he told thee truth, and more he would have told thee hadst thou suffered him. But I will tell thee wherefore thou art sad, for thou hast done a thing of late for which God is displeased with thee, and what it is thou knowest in thy heart, though no man else may know."

"What are thou," said King Arthur, starting up all pale, "that tellest me these tidings?"

"I am Merlin," said he, "and I was he in the child's likeness, also."

"Ah," said King Arthur, "thou art a marvelous and right fearful man, and I would ask and tell thee many things this day."

As they talked came one with the king's horses, and so, King Arthur mounting one, and Merlin another, they rode together to Caerleon; and Merlin prophesied to Arthur of his death, and also foretold his own end.

And now King Arthur, having utterly dispersed and overwhelmed those kings who had so long delayed his coronation, turned all his mind to overthrow the Saxon heathens who yet in many places spoiled the land. Calling together, therefore, his knights and men-at-arms, he rode with all his hosts to York, where Colgrin, the Saxon, lay with a great army; and there he fought a mighty battle, long and bloody, and drove him into the city, and besieged him. Then Baldulph, Colgrin's brother, came secretly with six thousand men to assail King Arthur and to raise the siege. But King Arthur was aware of him, and sent six hundred horsemen and three thousand foot to meet and fall on him instead. This therefore they did, encountering them at midnight, and utterly defeated them, till they fled away for life. But Baldulph, full of grief, resolved to share his brother's peril; wherefore he shaved his head and beard, and disguised himself as a jester, and so passed through King Arthur's camp, singing and playing on a harp, till by degrees he drew near to the city walls, where presently he made himself known, and was drawn up by ropes into the town.

Anon, while Arthur closely watched the city, came news that full six hundred ships had landed countless swarms of Saxons, under Cheldric, on the eastern coast. At that he raised the siege, and marched straight to London, and there increased his army, and took counsel with his barons how to drive the Saxons from the land for evermore.

Then with his nephew, Hoel, King of the Armorican Britons, who came with a great force to help him, King Arthur, with a mighty multitude of barons, knights, and fighting men, went swiftly up to Lincoln, which the Saxons lay besieging. And there he fought a passing fierce battle, and made grievous slaughter, killing above six thousand men, till the main body of them turned and fled. But he pursued them hotly into the wood of Celidon, where, sheltering themselves among the trees from his arrows, they made a stand, and for a long season bravely defended themselves. Anon, he ordered all the trees in that part of the forest to be cut down, leaving no shelter or ambush; and with their trunks and branches made a mighty barricade, which shut them in and hindered their escape. After three days, brought nigh to death by famine, they offered to give up their wealth of gold and silver spoils, and to depart forthwith in their empty ships; moreover, to pay tribute to King Arthur when they reached their home, and to leave him hostages till all was paid.

This offer, therefore, he accepted, and suffered them to depart. But when they had been a few hours at sea, they repented of their shameful flight, and turned their ships back again, and landing at Totnes, ravaged all the land as far as the Severn, and, burning and slaying on all sides, bent their steps towards Bath.

When King Arthur heard of their treachery and their return, he burned with anger till his eyes shone like two torches, and then he swore a mighty oath to rest no more until he had utterly destroyed those enemies of God and man, and had rooted them forever out of the land of Britain. Then marching hotly with his armies on to Bath, he cried aloud to them, "Since these detestable and impious heathens disdain to keep their faith with me, I, to keep faith with God, to whom I swear to cherish and defend this realm, will now this day avenge on them the blood of all that they have slain in Britain!"

In like manner after him spoke the archbishop, standing upon a hill, and crying that to-day they should fight both for their country and for Paradise, "For whoso," he said, "shall in this holy war be slain, the angels shall forthwith receive him; for death in this cause shall be penance and absolution for all sins."

At these words every man in the whole army raged with hatred, and pressed eagerly to rush upon those savages.

Anon King Arthur, dressed in armor shining with gold and jewels, and wearing on his head a helmet with a golden dragon, took a shield painted with the likeness of the blessed Mary. Then girding on Excalibur and taking in his right hand his great lance Ron, he placed his men in order and led them out against the enemy, who stood for battle on the slope of Badon Hill, ranged in the form of a wedge, as their custom was. And they, resisting all the onslaughts of King Arthur and his host, made that day a stout defense, and at night lay down upon the hill.

But on the next day Arthur led his army once again to the attack, and with wounds and slaughter such as no man had ever seen before, he drove the heathen step by step before him, backwards and upwards, till he stood with all his noblest knights upon the summit of the hill.

And then men saw him, "red as the rising sun from spur to plume," lift up his sword, and, kneeling, kiss the cross of it; and after, rising to his feet, set might and main with all his fellowship upon the foe, till, as a troop of lions roaring for their prey, they drove them like a scattered herd along the plains, and cut them down till they could cut no more for weariness.

That day King Arthur by himself alone slew with his sword Excalibur four hundred and seventy heathens. Colgrin also, and his brother Baldulph, were slain.

Then the king bade Cador, Duke of Cornwall, follow Cheldric, the chief leader, and the remnant of his hosts, unto the uttermost. He, therefore, when he had first seized their fleet, and filled it with chosen men, to beat them back when they should fly to it at last, chased them and slew them without mercy so long as he could overtake them. And though they crept with trembling hearts for shelter to the coverts of the woods and dens of mountains, yet even so they found no safety, for Cador slew them, even one by one. Last of all he caught and slew Cheldric himself, and slaughtering a great multitude took hostages for the surrender of the rest.

Meanwhile, King Arthur turned from Badon Hill, and freed his nephew Hoel from the Scots and Picts, who besieged him in Alcluld. And when he had defeated them in three sore battles, he drove them before him to a lake, which was one of the most wondrous lakes in all the world, for it was fed by sixty rivers, and had sixty islands, and sixty rocks, and on every island sixty eagles' nests. But King Arthur with a great fleet sailed round the rivers and besieged them in the lake for fifteen days, so that many thousands died of hunger.

Anon the King of Ireland came with an army to relieve them; but Arthur, turning on him fiercely, routed him, and compelled him to retreat in terror to his land. Then he pursued his purpose, which was no less than to destroy the race of Picts and Scots, who, beyond memory, had been a ceaseless torment to the Britons by their barbarous malice.

So bitterly, therefore, did he treat them, giving quarter to none, that at length the bishops of that miserable country with the clergy met together, and, bearing all the holy relics, came barefooted to the king to pray his mercy for their people. As soon as they were led before him they fell down upon their knees, and piteously besought him to spare the few survivors of their countrymen, and grant them any corner of the land where they might live in peace. When he thus heard them, and knew that he had now fully punished them, he consented to their prayer, and withdrew his hosts from any further slaughter.

Then turned he back to his own realm, and came to York for

Christmas, and there with high solemnity observed that holy tide; and being passing grieved to see the ruin of the churches and houses, which the rage of the pagans had destroyed, he rebuilt them, and restored the city to its ancient happy state.

And on a certain day, as the king sat with his barons, there came into the court a squire on horseback, carrying a knight before him wounded to the death, and told the king that hard by in the forest was a knight who had reared up a pavilion by the fountain, "and hath slain my master, a valiant knight, whose name was Nirles; wherefore I beseech thee, Lord, my master may be buried, and that some good knight may avenge his death."

At that stepped forth a squire named Griflet, who was very young, being of the same age with King Arthur, and besought the king, for all the service he had done, to give him knighthood.

"Thou art full young and tender of age," said King Arthur, "to take so high an order upon thee."

"Sir," said Griflet, "I beseech thee make me a knight;" and Merlin also advising the king to grant his request, "Well," said Arthur, "be it then so," and knighted him forthwith. Then said he to him, "Since I have granted thee this favor, thou must in turn grant me a gift."

"Whatsoever thou wilt, my lord," replied Sir Griflet.

"Promise me," said King Arthur, "by the faith of thy body, that when thou hast jousted with this knight at the fountain, thou wilt return to me straightway, unless he slay thee."

"I promise," said Sir Griflet; and taking his horse in haste, he dressed his shield, and took a spear in his hand and rode full gallop till he came to the fountain, by the side of which he saw a rich pavilion, and a great horse standing well saddled and bridled, and on a tree close by there hung a shield of many colors and a long lance.

Then Sir Griflet smote upon the shield with the butt of his spear until he cast it to the ground. At that a knight came out of the pavilion and said, "Fair knight, why smote ye down my shield?"

"Because," said Griflet, "I would joust with thee."

"It were better not," replied the knight; "for thou art young and

41

but latcly made a knight, and thy strength is small compared to mine."

"For all that," said Sir Griflet, "I will joust with ye."

"I am full loth," replied the knight; "but if I must I must."

Then did they wheel their horses far apart, and running them together, the strange knight shivered Sir Griflet's spear to fragments, and smote him through the shield and the left side, and broke his own spear into Sir Griflet's body, so that the truncheon stuck there, and Sir Griflet and his horse fell down. But when the strange knight saw him overthrown, he was sore grieved, and hastily alighted, for he thought that he had slain him. Then he unlaced his helm and gave him air, and tended him carefully till he come out of his swoon, and leaving the truncheon of his spear in his body, he set him upon horse, and commended him to God, and said he had a mighty heart, and if he lived would prove a passing good knight. And so Sir Griflet rode to the court, where, by aid of good physicians, he was healed in time and his life saved.

At that same time there came before the king twelve old men, ambassadors from Lucius Tiberius, Emperor of Rome, and demanded of Arthur tribute unto Cæsar for his realm, or else, said they, the emperor would destroy both him and his land. To whom King Arthur answered that he owed the emperor no tribute, nor would send him any; but said he, "On a fair field I will pay him his proper tribute—with a sharp spear and sword; and by my father's soul that tribute shall he take from me, whether he will or not." So the ambassadors departed passing wroth, and King Arthur was as wroth as they.

But on the morrow of Sir Griflet's hurt, the king commanded to take his horse and armor secretly outside the city walls before sunrise of the next morning, and, rising a long while before dawn, he mounted up and took his shield and spear, and bade his chamberlain tarry till he came again; but he forbore to take Excalibur, for he had given it for safety into charge of his sister, Queen Morgan le Fay. And as the king rode at a soft pace he saw suddenly three villains chasing Merlin and making to attack and slay him. Clapping spurs to his horse, he rushed towards them, and cried out in a terrible voice, "Flee, churls, or take your deaths;" but they, as soon as they perceived a knight, fled away with the haste of hares.

"O Merlin," said the king; "here hadst thou been killed, despite thy many crafts, had I not chanced to pass."

"Not so," said Merlin, "for when I would, I could have saved myself; but thou art nearer to thy death than I, for without special help from heaven thou ridest now towards thy grave."

And as they were thus talking, they came to the fountain and the rich pavilion pitched beside it, and saw a knight sitting all armed on a chair in the opening of the tent. "Sir knight," said King Arthur, "for what cause abidest thou here? to joust with any knight that passeth by? If so, I caution thee to quit that custom."

"That custom," said the knight, "have I followed and will follow, let whosoever will say nay, and if any is aggrieved at it, let him who will amend it."

"I will amend it," said King Arthur.

"And I will defend it," answered the knight.

Then the knight mounted his horse and made himself ready, and charging at each other they met so hard that both their lances splintered into pieces. Then King Arthur drew his sword, but the knight cried out, "Not so; but let us run another tilt together with sharp spears."

"I would with a good will," said King Arthur; "but I have no more spears."

"I have enough of spears," replied the knight, and called a squire, who brought two good new lances.

Then spurring their horses, they rushed together with all their might, and broke each one his own spear short off in his hand. Then the king again put his hand to his sword, but the knight once more cried out, "Nay, yet abide awhile; ye are the best jouster that I ever met with; for the love of knighthood, let us joust yet once again."

So once again they tilted with their fullest force, and this time King Arthur's spear was shivered, but the knight's held whole, and drove so furiously against the king that both his horse and he were hurled to the ground.

At that, King Arthur was enraged and drew his sword and said, "I will attack thee now, Sir knight, on foot, for on horseback I have lost the honor."

"I will be on horseback," said the knight. But when he saw him come on foot, he lighted from his horse, thinking it shame to have so great advantage.

And then began they a strong battle, with many great strokes and grievous blows, and so hewed with their swords that the fragments of their armor flew about the fields, and both so bled that all the ground around was like a marsh of blood. Thus they fought long and mightily, and anon, after brief rest fell to again, and so hurtled together like two wild boars that they both rolled to the ground. At last their swords clashed furiously together, and the knight's sword shivered the king's in two.

Then said the knight, "Now art thou in my power, to save thee or to slay. Yield therefore as defeated, and a recreant knight, or thou shalt surely die."

"As for death," replied King Arthur, "welcome be it when it cometh; but as for yielding me to thee as a recreant because of this poor accident upon my sword, I had far liefer die than be so shamed."

So saying, he sprang on the knight, and took him by the middle and threw him down, and tore off his helm. But the knight, being a huge man, wrestled and struggled in a frenzy with the king until he brought him under, and tore off his helm in turn, and would have smitten off his head.

At that came Merlin and said, "Knight, hold thy hand, for if thou slayest yonder knight, thou puttest all this realm to greater loss and damage than ever realm was in; for he is a man of greater worship than thou dreamest of."

"Who then is he?" cried the knight.

Then would he have slain him for dread of his wrath, but Merlin cast a spell upon the knight, so that he fell suddenly to the earth in a deep sleep. Then raising up the king, he took the knight's horse for himself and rode away.

"Alas," said King Arthur, "what hast thou done, Merlin? hast thou slain this good knight by thy crafts? There never lived a better knight; I had rather lose my kingdom for a year than have him dead."

"Be not afraid," said Merlin; "he is more whole and sound than thou art, and is but in a sleep, wherefrom in three hours' time he will awake. I told thee what a knight he was, and how near thou was to death. There liveth not a better knight than he in all the world, and hereafter he shall do thee good service. His name is King Pellinore, and he shall have two sons, who shall be passing valiant men, and, save one another, shall have no equal in prowess and in purity of life. The one shall be named Percival, and the other Lamoracke of Wales."

So they rode on to Caerleon, and all the knights grieved greatly when they heard of this adventure, that the king would jeopardize his person thus alone. Yet could they not hide their joy at serving under such a noble chief, who adventured his own life as much as did the poorest knight among them all.

IV. THE KING'S MANY AND GREAT ADVENTURES

The land of Britain being now in peace, and many great and valiant knights therein ready to take part in whatsoever battles or adventures might arise, King Arthur resolved to follow all his enemies to their own coasts. Anon he fitted out a great fleet, and sailing first to Ireland, in one battle he miserably routed the people of the country. The King of Ireland also he took prisoner, and forced all earls and barons to pay him homage.

Having conquered Ireland, he went next to Iceland and subdued it also, and the winter being then arrived, returned to Britain.

In the next year he set forth to Norway, whence many times the heathen had descended on the British coasts; for he was determined to give so terrible a lesson to those savages as should be told through all their tribes both far and near, and make his name fearful to them.

As soon as he was come, Riculf, the king, with all the power of that country, met and gave him battle; but, after mighty slaughter, the Britons had at length the advantage, and slew Riculf and a countless multitude besides.

Having thus defeated them, they set the cities on fire, dispersed the country people, and pursued the victory till they had reduced all Norway, as also Dacia, under the dominion of King Arthur.

Now, therefore, having thus chastised those pagans who so long had harassed Britain, and put his yoke upon them, he voyaged on to Gaul, being steadfastly set upon defeating the Roman governor of that province, and so beginning to make good the threats which he had sent the emperor by his ambassadors.

So soon as he was landed on the shores of Gaul, there came to him a countryman who told him of a fearful giant in the land of Brittany, who had slain, murdered, and devoured many people, and had lived for seven years upon young children only, "insomuch," said the man, "that all the children of the country are destroyed; and but the other day he seized upon our duchess, as she rode out with her men, and took her away to his lodging in a cave of a mountain, and though five hundred people followed her, yet could they give her no help or rescue, but left her shrieking and crying lamentably in the giant's hands; and, Lord, she is thy cousin Hoel's wife, who is of thy near kindred; wherefore, as thou art a rightful king, have pity on this lady; and as thou art a valiant conqueror, avenge us and deliver us."

"Alas!" said King Arthur, "this is a great mischief that ye tell of. I had rather than the best realm I have, that I had rescued that lady ere the giant laid his hand on her; but tell me now, good fellow, canst thou bring me where this giant haunteth?"

"Yea, Lord!" replied the man; "lo, yonder, where thou seest two great fires, there shalt thou find him, and more treasure also than is in all Gaul besides."

Then the king returned to his tent, and, calling Sir Key and Sir Bedwin, desired them to get horses ready for himself and them, for that after evensong he would ride a pilgrimage with them alone to St. Michael's Mount. So in the evening they departed, and rode as fast as they could till they came near the mount, and there alighted; and the king commanded the two knights to await him at the hill foot, while he went up alone.

Then he ascended the mountain till he came to a great fire. And there he found a sorrowful widow wringing her hands and weeping miserably, sitting by a new-made grave. And saluting her, King Arthur prayed her wherefore she made such heavy lamentations.

"Sir knight," she said, "speak softly, for yonder is a devil, who, if he hear thy voice, will come and straightway slay thee. Alas! what dost thou here? Fifty such men as thou were powerless to resist him. Here lieth dead my lady, Duchess of Brittany, wife to Sir Hoel, who was the fairest lady in the world, foully and shamefully slaughtered by that fiend! Beware that thou go not too nigh, for he hath overcome and vanquished fifteen kings, and hath made himself a coat of precious stones, embroidered with their beards; but if thou art so hardy, and wilt speak with him, at yonder great fire he is at supper."

"Well," said King Arthur, "I will accomplish mine errand, for all thy fearful words;" and so went forth to the crest of the hill, and saw where the giant sat at supper, gnawing on a limb of a man, and baking his huge frame by the fire, while three damsels turned three spits, whereon were spitted, like larks, twelve young children lately born.

When King Arthur saw all that, his heart bled for sorrow, and he trembled for rage and indignation; then lifting up his voice he cried aloud—"God, that wieldeth all the world, give thee short life and shameful death, and may the devil have thy soul! Why hast thou slain those children and that fair lady! Wherefore arise, and prepare thee to perish, thou glutton and fiend, for this day thou shalt die by my hands."

Then the giant, mad with fury at these words, started up, and seizing a great club, smote the king, and struck his crown from off his head. But King Arthur smote him with his sword so mightily in return, that all his blood gushed forth in streams.

At that the giant, howling in great anguish, threw away his club of iron, and caught the king in both his arms and strove to crush his ribs together. But King Arthur struggled and writhed, and twisted him about so that the giant could not hold him tightly; and as they fiercely wrestled, they both fell, and rolling over one another, tumbled—wrestling, and struggling, and fighting frantically—from rock to rock, till they came to the sea.

And as they tore and strove and tumbled, the king ever and anon smote at the giant with his dagger, till his arms stiffened in death around King Arthur's body, and groaning horribly, he died. So presently the two knights came and found the king locked fast in the giant's arms, and very faint and weary, and loosed him from their hold.

Then the king bade Sir Key to "smite off the giant's head, and set it on the truncheon of a spear, and bear it to Sir Hoel, and tell him that his enemy is slain; and afterwards let it be fastened to the castle gate, that all the people may behold it. And go ye two up on the mountain and fetch me my shield and sword, and also the great club of iron ye will see there; and as for the treasure, ye shall find there wealth beyond counting, but take as much as ye will, for I have his kirtle and the club, I desire no more."

Then the knights fetched the club and kirtle, as the king had ordered, and took the treasure to themselves, as much as they could carry, and returned to the army. But when this deed was noised abroad, all the people came in multitudes to thank the king, who told them "to give thanks to God, and to divide the giant's spoils amongst them equally." And King Arthur desired Sir Hoel to build a church upon the mount, and dedicate it to the Archangel Michael.

On the morrow, all the host moved onwards into the country of Champagne, and Flollo, the Roman tribune, retired before them into Paris. But while he was preparing to collect more forces from the neighboring countries, King Arthur came upon him unawares; and besieged him in the town.

And when a month had passed, Flollo—full of grief at the starvation of his people, who died in hundreds day by day—sent to King Arthur, and desired that they two might fight together; for he was a man of mighty stature and courage, and thought himself sure of the victory. This challenge, King Arthur, full weary of the siege, accepted with great joy, and sent back word to Flollo that he would meet him whensoever he appointed.

And a truce being made on both sides, they met together the next day on the island without the city, where all the people also were gathered to see the issue. And as the king and Flollo rode up to the lists, each was so nobly armed and horsed, and sat so mightily upon his saddle, that no man could tell which way the battle would end.

When they had saluted one another, and presented themselves against each other with their lances aloft, they put spurs to their horses and began a fierce encounter. But King Arthur, carrying his spear more warily, struck it on the upper part of Flollo's breast, and flung him from his saddle to the earth. Then drawing his sword, he cried to him to rise, and rushed upon him; but Flollo, starting up, met him with his spear couched, and pierced the breast of King Arthur's horse, and overthrew both horse and man.

The Britons, when they saw their king upon the ground, could scarcely keep themselves from breaking up the truce and falling on the Gauls. But as they were about to burst the barriers, and rush upon the lists, King Arthur hastily arose, and, guarding himself with his shield, ran with speed on Flollo. And now they renewed the assault with great rage, being sorely bent upon each other's death.

At length, Flollo, seizing his advantage, gave King Arthur a huge stroke upon the helm, which nigh overthrew him, and drew forth his blood in streams.

But when King Arthur saw his armor and shield all red with blood, he was inflamed with fury, and lifting up Excalibur on high, with all his might, he struck straight through the helmet into Flollo's head, and smote it into halves; and Flollo falling backwards, and tearing up the ground with his spurs, expired.

As soon as this news spread, the citizens all ran together, and, opening the gates, surrendered the city to the conqueror.

And when he had overrun the whole province with his arms, and reduced it everywhere to subjection, he returned again to Britain, and held his court at Caerleon, with greater state than ever.

Anon he invited thereto all the kings, dukes, earls, and barons, who owed him homage, that he might treat them royally, and reconcile them to each other, and to his rule.

And never was there a city more fit and pleasant for such festivals. For on one side it was washed by a noble river, so that the kings and princes from the countries beyond sea might conveniently sail up to it; and on the other side, the beauty of the groves and meadows, and the stateliness and magnificence of the royal palaces, with lofty gilded roofs, made it even rival the grandeur of Rome. It was famous also for two great and noble churches, whereof one was built in honor of the martyr Julius, and adorned with a choir of virgins who had devoted themselves wholly to the service of God; and the other, founded in memory of St. Aaron, his companion, maintained a convent of canons, and was the third metropolitan church of Britain. Besides, there was a college of two hundred philosophers, learned in astronomy, and all the other sciences and arts.

In this place, therefore, full of such delights, King Arthur held his court, with many jousts and tournaments, and royal huntings, and rested for a season after all his wars.

And on a certain day there came into the court a messenger from Ryence, King of North Wales, bearing this message from his master: That King Ryence had discomfited eleven kings, and had compelled each one of them to cut off his beard; that he had trimmed a mantle with these beards, and lacked but one more beard to finish it; and that he therefore now sent for King Arthur's beard, which he required of him forthwith, or else he would enter his lands and burn and slay, and never leave them till he had taken by force not his beard only, but his head also.

When King Arthur heard these words he flushed all scarlet, and rising in great anger said, "Well it is for thee that thou speakest another man's words with thy lips, and not thine own. Thou hast said thy message, which is the most insolent and villainous that ever man heard sent to any king: now hear my reply. My beard is yet too young to trim that mantle of thy master's with; yet, young although I be, I owe no homage either to him or any man—nor will ever owe. But, young although I be, I will have thy master's homage upon both his knees before this year be past, or else he shall lose his head, by the faith of my body, for this message is the shamefullest I ever heard speak of. I see well thy king hath never yet met with a worshipful man; but tell him that King Arthur will have his head or his worship right soon."

Then the messenger departed, and Arthur, looking round upon his knights, demanded of them if any there knew this King Ryence. "Yea," answered Sir Noran, "I know him well, and there be few better or stronger knights upon a field than he; and he is passing proud and haughty in his heart; wherefore I doubt not, Lord, he will make war on thee with mighty power."

"Well," said King Arthur, "I shall be ready for him, and that shall he find."

While the king thus spoke, there came into the hall a damsel having on a mantle richly furred, which she let fall, and showed herself to be girded with a noble sword. The king being surprised at this, said, "Damsel, wherefore art thou girt with that sword, for it beseemeth thee not?" "Sir," said she, "I will tell thee. This sword wherewith I am thus girt gives me great sorrow and encumbrance, for I may not be delivered from it till I find a knight faithful and pure and true, strong of body and of valiant deeds, without guile or treachery, who shall be able to draw it from its scabbard, which no man else can do. And I have but just now come from the court of King Ryence, for there they told me many great and good knights were to be ever found; but he and all his knights have tried to draw it forth in vain—for none of them can move it."

"This is a great marvel," said King Arthur; "I will myself try to draw forth this sword, not thinking in my heart that I am the best knight, but rather to begin and give example that all may try after me." Saying this, he took the sword and pulled at it with all his might, but could not shake or move it.

"Thou needest not strive so hard, Lord," said the damsel, "for whoever may be able to pull it forth shall do so very easily."

"Thou sayest well," replied the king, remembering how he had himself drawn forth the sword from the stone before St. Paul's. "Now try ye, all my barons; but beware ye be not stained with shame, or any treachery, or guile." And turning away his face from them, King Arthur mused full heavily on sins within his breast he knew of, and which his failure brought to mind right sadly.

Then all the barons present tried each after other, but could none of them succeed; whereat the damsel greatly wept, and said, "Alas, alas! I thought in this court to have found the best knight, without shame or treachery or treason."

Now by chance there was at that time a poor knight with King Arthur, who had been prisoner at his court for half a year or more, charged with slaying unawares a knight who was a cousin of the king's. He was named Balin le Savage, and had been by the good offices of the barons delivered from prison, for he was of good and valiant address and gentle blood. He being secretly present at the court saw this advantage, and felt his heart rise high within him, and longed to try the sword as did the others; but being poor and poorly clad, he was ashamed to come forward in the press of knights and nobles. But in his heart he felt assured that he could do better—if Heaven willed—than any knight among them all.

So as the damsel left the king, he called to her and said, "Damsel, I pray thee of thy courtesy, suffer me to try the sword as well as all these lords; for though I be but poorly clad, I feel assurance in my heart."

The damsel looked at him, saw in him a likely and an honest man, but because of his poor garments could not think him to be any knight of worship, and said, "Sir, there is no need to put me to any more pain or labor; why shouldst thou succeed where so many worthy ones have failed?"

"Ah, fair lady," answered Balin, "worthiness and brave deeds are not shown by fair raiment but manhood and truth lie hid within the heart. There be many worshipful knights unknown to all the people."

"By my faith, thou sayest truth," replied the damsel; "try therefore, if thou wilt, what thou canst do."

So Balin took the sword by the girdle and hilt, and drew it lightly out, and looking on its workmanship and brightness, it pleased him greatly.

But the king and all the barons marveled at Sir Balin's fortune, and many knights were envious of him, for, "Truly," said the damsel, "this is a passing good knight, and the best man I have ever found, and the most worshipfully free from treason, treachery, or villainy, and many wonders shall he achieve.

"Now, gentle and courteous knight," continued she, turning to Balin, "give me the sword again."

"Nay," said Sir Balin, "save it be taken from me by force, I shall preserve this sword for evermore."

"Thou art not wise," replied the damsel, "to keep it from me; for if thou wilt do so, thou shall slay with it the best friend thou hast, and the sword shall be thine own destruction also."

"I will take whatever adventure God may send," said Balin; "but the sword will I keep, by the faith of my body."

"Thou will repent it shortly," said the damsel; "I would take the sword for thy sake rather than for mine, for I am passing grieved and heavy for thy sake, who wilt not believe the peril I foretell thee." With that she departed, making great lamentation.

Then Balin sent for his horse and armor, and took his leave of King Arthur, who urged him to stay at his court. "For," said he, "I believe that thou art displeased that I showed thee unkindness; blame me not overmuch, for I was misinformed against thee, and knew not truly what a knight of worship thou art. Abide in this court with my good knights, and I will so advance thee that thou shalt be well pleased."

"God thank thee, Lord," said Balin, "for no man can reward thy bounty and thy nobleness; but at this time I must needs depart, praying thee ever to hold me in thy favor."

"Truly," said King Arthur, "I am grieved for thy departure; but tarry not long, and thou shalt be right welcome to me and all my knights when thou returnest, and I will repair my neglect and all that I have done amiss against thee."

"God thank thee, Lord," again said Balin, and made ready to depart.

But meanwhile came into the court a lady upon horseback, full richly dressed, and saluted King Arthur, and asked him for the gift that he had promised her when she gave him his sword Excalibur, "for," said she, "I am the lady of the lake."

"Ask what thou wilt," said the king, "and thou shalt have it, if I have power to give."

"I ask," said she, "the head of that knight who hath just achieved the sword, or else the damsel's head who brought it, or else both; for the knight slew my brother, and the lady caused my father's death."

"Truly," said King Arthur, "I cannot grant thee this desire; it were against my nature and against my name; but ask whatever else thou wilt, and I will do it."

"I will demand no other thing," said she.

And as she spake came Balin, on his way to leave the court, and saw her where she stood, and knew her straightway for his mother's murderess, whom he had sought in vain three years. And when they told him that she had asked King Arthur for his head, he went up straight to her and said, "May evil have thee! Thou desirest my head, therefore shalt thou lose thine"; and with his sword he lightly smote her head off, in the presence of the king and all the court.

"Alas, for shame!" cried out King Arthur, rising up in wrath; "why hast thou done this, shaming both me and my court? I am beholden greatly to this lady, and under my safe conduct came she here; thy deed is passing shameful; never shall I forgive thy villainy."

"Lord," cried Sir Balin, "hear me; this lady was the falsest living, and by her witchcraft hath destroyed many, and caused my mother also to be burnt to death by her false arts and treachery."

"What cause soever thou mightest have had," said the king, "thou shouldst have forborne her in my presence. Deceive not thyself, thou shalt repent this sin, for such a shame was never brought upon my court; depart now from my face with all the haste thou mayest."

Then Balin took up the head of the lady and carried it to his lodgings, and rode forth with his squire from out the town. Then said he, "Now must we part; take ye this head and bear it to my friends in Northumberland, and tell them how I speed, and that our worst foe is dead; also tell them that I am free from prison, and of the adventure of my sword."

"Alas!" said the squire, "ye are greatly to blame to have so displeased King Arthur."

"As for that," said Sir Balin, "I go now to find King Ryence, and destroy him or lose my life; for should I take him prisoner, and lead him to the court, perchance King Arthur would forgive me, and become my good and gracious lord."

"Where shall I meet thee again?" said the squire.

"In King Arthur's court," said Balin.

V. SIR BALIN FIGHTS WITH HIS BROTHER, SIR BALAN

Now there was a knight at the court more envious than the others of Sir Balin, for he counted himself one of the best knights in Britain. His name was Lancear; and going to the king, he begged leave to follow after Sir Balin and avenge the insult he had put upon the court. "Do thy best," replied the king, "for I am passing wroth with Balin."

In the meantime came Merlin, and was told of this adventure of the sword and lady of the lake.

"Now hear me," said he, "when I tell ye that this lady who hath brought the sword is the falsest damsel living."

"Say not so," they answered, "for she hath a brother a good knight, who slew another knight this damsel loved; so she, to be revenged upon her brother, went to the Lady Lile, of Avilion, and besought her help. Then Lady Lile gave her the sword, and told her that no man should draw it forth but one, a valiant knight and strong, who should avenge her on her brother. This, therefore, was the reason why the damsel came here."

"I know it all as well as ye do," answered Merlin; "and would to God she had never come hither, for never came she into any company but to do harm; and that good knight who hath achieved the sword shall be himself slain by it, which shall be great harm and loss, for a better knight there liveth not; and he shall do unto my lord the king great honor and service."

Then Sir Lancear, having armed himself at all points, mounted, and rode after Sir Balin, as fast as he could go, and overtaking him, he cried aloud, "Abide, Sir knight! wait yet awhile, or I shall make thee do so."

Hearing him cry, Sir Balin fiercely turned his horse, and said, "Fair knight, what wilt thou with me? wilt thou joust?"

"Yea," said Sir Lancear, "it is for that I have pursued thee."

"Peradventure," answered Balin, "thou hadst best have stayed at home, for many a man who thinketh himself already victor, endeth by his own downfall. Of what court art thou?"

"Of King Arthur's court," cried Lancear, "and I am come to revenge the insult thou hast put on it this day."

"Well," said Sir Balin, "I see that I must fight thee, and I repent to be obliged to grieve King Arthur or his knights; and thy quarrel seemeth full foolish to me, for the damsel that is dead worked endless evils through the land, or else I had been loth as any knight that liveth to have slain a lady."

"Make thee ready," shouted Lancear, "for one of us shall rest forever in this field."

But at their first encounter Sir Lancear's spear flew into splinters from Sir Balin's shield, and Sir Balin's lance pierced with such might through Sir Lancear's shield, that it rove the hauberk also, and passed through the knight's body and the horse's crupper. And Sir Balin turning fiercely round again, drew out his sword, and knew not that he had already slain him; and then he saw him lie a corpse upon the ground.

At that same moment came a damsel riding towards him as fast as her horse could gallop, who, when she saw Sir Lancear dead, wept and sorrowed out of measure, crying, "O, Sir Balin, two bodies hast thou slain, and one heart; and two hearts in one body; and two souls also hast thou lost."

Therewith she took the sword from her dead lover's side—for she was Sir Lancear's lady-love—and setting the pommel of it on the ground, ran herself through the body with the blade.

When Sir Balin saw her dead he was sorely hurt and grieved in spirit, and repented the death of Lancear, which had also caused so fair a lady's death. And being unable to look on their bodies for sorrow, he turned aside into a forest, where presently as he rode, he saw the arms of his brother, Sir Balan. And when they were met they put off their helms, and embraced each other, kissing, and weeping for joy and pity. Then Sir Balin told Sir Balan all his late adventures, and that he was on his way to King Ryence, who at that time was besieging Castle Terrabil. "I will be with thee," answered Sir Balan, "and we will help each other, as brethren ought to do."

Anon by chance, as they were talking, came King Mark, of Cornwall, by that way, and when he saw the two dead bodies of Sir Lancear and his lady lying there, and heard the story of their death, he vowed to build a tomb to them before he left that place. So pitching his pavilion there, he sought through all the country round to find a monument, and found at last a rich and fair one in a church, which he took and raised above the dead knight and his damsel, writing on it—"Here lieth Lancear, son of the King of Ireland, who, at his own request, was slain by Balin; and here beside him also lieth his lady Colombe, who slew herself with her lover's sword for grief and sorrow."

Then as Sir Balin and Sir Balan rode away, Merlin met with them, and said to Balin, "Thou hast done thyself great harm not to have saved that lady's life who slew herself; and because of it, thou shalt strike the most Dolorous Stroke that ever man struck, save he that smote our Lord. For thou shalt smite the truest and most worshipful of living knights, who shall not be recovered from his wounds for many years, and through that stroke three kingdoms shall be overwhelmed in poverty and misery."

"If I believed," said Balin, "what thou sayest, I would slay myself to make thee a liar."

At that Merlin vanished suddenly away; but afterwards he met them in disguise towards night, and told them he could lead them to King Ryence, whom they sought. "For this night he is to ride with sixty lances only through a wood hard by."

So Sir Balin and Sir Balan hid themselves within the wood, and at midnight came out from their ambush among the leaves by the highway, and waited for the king, whom presently they heard approaching with his company. Then did they suddenly leap forth and smote at him and overthrew him and laid him on the ground, and turning on his company wounded and slew forty of them, and put the rest to flight. And returning to King Ryence they would have slain him there, but he craved mercy, and yielded to their grace, crying, "Knights full of prowess, slay me not; for by my life ye may win something—but my death can avail ye nought."

"Ye say truth," said the two knights, and put him in a horse-litter, and went swiftly through all the night, till at cock-crow they came to King Arthur's palace. There they delivered him to the warders and porters, to be brought before the king, with this message—"That he was sent to King Arthur by the knight of the two swords" (for so was Balin known by name, since his adventure with the damsel) "and by his brother." And so they rode away again ere sunrise.

Within a month or two thereafter, King Arthur being somewhat sick, went forth outside the town, and had his pavilion pitched in a meadow, and there abode, and laid him down on a pallet to sleep, but could get no rest. And as he lay he heard the sound of a great horse, and looking out of the tent door, saw a knight ride by, making great lamentation.

"Abide, fair sir," said King Arthur, "and tell me wherefore thou makest this sorrow."

"Ye may little amend it," said the knight, and so passed on.

Presently after Sir Balin, rode, by chance, past that meadow, and when he saw the king he alighted and came to him on foot, and kneeled and saluted him.

"By my head," said King Arthur, "ye be welcome, Sir Balin;" and then he thanked him heartily for revenging him upon King Ryence, and for sending him so speedily a prisoner to his castle, and told him how King Nero, Ryence's brother, had attacked him afterwards to deliver Ryence from prison; and how he had defeated him and slain him, and also King Lot, of Orkney, who was joined with Nero, and whom King Pellinore had killed in the battle. Then when they had thus talked, King Arthur told Sir Balin of the sullen knight that had just passed his tent, and desired him to pursue him and to bring him back.

So Sir Balin rode and overtook the knight in a forest with a damsel, and said, "Sir knight, thou must come back with me unto my lord, King Arthur, to tell him the cause of thy sorrow, which thou hast refused even now to do."

"That will I not," replied the knight, "for it would harm me much, and do him no advantage."

"Sir," said Sir Balin, "I pray thee make ready, for thou must needs go with me—or else I must fight with thee and take thee by force."

"Wilt thou be warrant for safe conduct, if I go with thee?" inquired the knight.

"Yea, surely," answered Balin, "I will die else."

So the knight made ready to go with Sir Balin, and left the damsel in the wood.

But as they went, there came one invisible, and smote the knight through the body with a spear. "Alas," cried Sir Herleus (for so was he named), "I am slain under thy guard and conduct, by that traitor knight called Garlon, who through magic and witchcraft rideth invisibly. Take, therefore, my horse, which is better than thine, and ride to the damsel whom we left, and follow the quest I had in hand, as she will lead thee—and revenge my death when thou best mayest."

"That will I do," said Sir Balin, "by my knighthood, and so I swear to thee."

Then went Sir Balin to the damsel, and rode forth with her; she carrying ever with her the truncheon of the spear wherewith Sir Herleus had been slain. And as they went, a good knight, Perin de Mountbelgard, joined their company, and vowed to take adventure with them wheresoever they might go. But presently as they passed a hermitage fast by a churchyard, came the knight Garlon, again invisible, and smote Sir Perin through the body with a spear, and slew him as he had slain Sir Herleus. Whereat, Sir Balin greatly raged, and swore to have Sir Garlon's life, whenever next he might encounter and behold him in his bodily shape. Anon, he and the hermit buried the good knight Sir Perin, and rode on with the damsel till they came to a great castle, whereinto they were about to enter. But when Sir Balin had passed through the gateway, the portcullis fell behind him suddenly, leaving the damsel on the outer side, with men around her, drawing their swords as if to slay her.

When he saw that, Sir Balin climbed with eager haste by wall and tower, and leaped into the castle moat, and rushed towards the damsel and her enemies, with his sword drawn, to fight and slay them. But they cried out, "Put up thy sword, Sir knight, we will not fight thee in this quarrel, for we do nothing but an ancient custom of this castle."

Then they told him that the lady of the castle was passing sick, and had lain ill for many years, and might never more be cured, unless she had a silver dish full of the blood of a pure maid and a king's daughter. Wherefore the custom of the castle was, that never should a damsel pass that way but she must give a dish full of her blood. Then Sir Balin suffered them to bleed the damsel with her own consent, but her blood helped not the lady of the castle. So on the morrow they departed, after right good cheer and rest.

Then they rode three or four days without adventure, and came at last to the abode of a rich man, who sumptuously lodged and fed them. And while they sat at supper Sir Balin heard a voice of some one groaning grievously. "What noise is this?" said he.

"Forsooth," said the host, "I will tell you. I was lately at a tournament, and there I fought a knight who is brother to King Pelles, and overthrew him twice, for which he swore to be revenged on me through my best friend, and so he wounded my son, who cannot be recovered till I have that knight's blood, but he rideth through witchcraft always invisibly, and I know not his name."

"Ah," said Sir Balin, "but I know him; his name is Garlon, and he hath slain two knights, companions of mine own, in the same fashion, and I would rather than all the riches in this realm that I might meet him face to face."

"Well," said his host, "let me now tell thee that King Pelles hath proclaimed in all the country a great festival, to be held at Listeniss, in twenty days from now, whereto no knight may come without a lady. At that great feast we might perchance find out this Garlon, for many will be there; and if it please thee we will set forth together."

So on the morrow they rode all three towards Listeniss, and

traveled fifteen days, and reached it on the day the feast began. Then they alighted and stabled their horses, and went up to the castle, and Sir Balin's host was denied entrance, having no lady with him. But Sir Balin was right heartily received, and taken to a chamber, where they unarmed him, and dressed him in rich robes, of any color that he chose, and told him he must lay aside his sword. This, however, he refused, and said, "It is the custom of my country for a knight to keep his sword ever with him; and if I may not keep it here, I will forthwith depart." Then they gave him leave to wear his sword. So he went to the great hall, and was set among knights of rank and worship, and his lady before him.

Soon he found means to ask one who sat near him, "Is there not here a knight whose name is Garlon?"

"Yonder he goeth," said his neighbor, "he with that black face; he is the most marvelous knight alive, for he rideth invisibly, and destroyeth whom he will."

"Ah, well," said Balin, drawing a long breath, "is that indeed the man? I have aforetime heard of him."

Then he mused long within himself, and thought, "If I shall slay him here and now, I shall not escape myself; but if I leave him, peradventure I shall never meet with him again at such advantage; and if he live, how much more harm and mischief will he do!"

But while he deeply thought, and cast his eyes from time to time upon Sir Garlon, that false knight saw that he watched him, and thinking that he could at such a time escape revenge, he came and smote Sir Balin on the face with the back of his hand, and said, "Knight, why dost thou so watch me? be ashamed, and eat thy meat, and do that which thou camest for."

"Thou sayest well," cried Sir Balin, rising fiercely; "now will I straightway do that which I came to do, as thou shalt find." With that he whirled his sword aloft and struck him downright on the head, and clove his skull asunder to the shoulder.

"Give me the truncheon," cried out Sir Balin to his lady, "wherewith he slew thy knight." And when she gave it him— for she had always carried it about with her, wherever she had gone—he smote him through the body with it, and said, "With

62

that truncheon didst thou treacherously murder a good knight, and now it sticketh in thy felon body."

Then he called to the father of the wounded son, who had come with him to Listeniss, and said, "Now take as much blood as thou wilt, to heal thy son withal."

But now arose a terrible confusion, and all the knights leaped from the table to slay Balin, King Pelles himself the foremost, who cried out, "Knight, thou hast slain my brother at my board; die, therefore, die, for thou shalt never leave this castle."

"Slay me, thyself, then," shouted Balin.

"Yea," said the king, "that will I! for no other man shall touch thee, for the love I bear my brother."

Then King Pelles caught in his hand a grim weapon and smote eagerly at Balin, but Balin put his sword between his head and the king's stroke, and saved himself but lost his sword, which fell down smashed and shivered into pieces by the blow. So being weaponless he ran to the next room to find a sword, and so from room to room, with King Pelles after him, he in vain ever eagerly casting his eyes round every place to find some weapon.

At last he ran into a chamber wondrous richly decked, where was a bed all dressed with cloth of gold, the richest that could be thought of, and one who lay quite still within the bed; and by the bedside stood a table of pure gold, borne on four silver pillars, and on the table stood a marvelous spear, strangely wrought.

When Sir Balin saw the spear he seized it in his hand, and turned upon King Pelles, and smote at him so fiercely and so sore that he dropped swooning to the ground.

But at that Dolorous and awful Stroke the castle rocked and rove throughout, and all the walls fell crashed and breaking to the earth, and Balin himself fell also in their midst, struck as it were to stone, and powerless to move a hand or foot. And so three days he lay amidst the ruins, until Merlin came and raised him up and brought him a good horse, and bade him ride out of that land as swiftly as he could.

"May I not take the damsel with me I brought hither?" said Sir Balin.

"Lo! where she lieth dead," said Merlin. "Ah, little knowest thou, Sir Balin, what thou hast done; for in this castle and that chamber which thou didst defile, was the blood of our Lord Christ! and also that most holy cup—the Sangreal—wherefrom the wine was drunk at the last supper of our Lord. Joseph of Arimathea brought it to this land, when first he came here to convert and save it. And on that bed of gold it was himself who lay, and the strange spear beside him was the spear wherewith the soldier Longus smote our Lord, which evermore had dripped with blood. King Pelles is the nearest kin to Joseph in direct descent, wherefore he held these holy things in trust; but now have they all gone at thy dolorous stroke, no man knoweth whither; and great is the damage to this land, which until now hath been the happiest of all lands, for by that stroke thou hast slain thousands, and by the loss and parting of the Sangreal, the safety of this realm is put in peril, and its great happiness is gone for evermore."

Then Balin departed from Merlin, struck to his soul with grief and sorrow, and said, "In this world shall we meet never more."

So he rode forth through the fair cities and the country, and found the people lying dead on every side. And all the living cried out on him as he passed, "O Balin, all this misery hast thou done! For the dolorous stroke thou gavest King Pelles, three countries are destroyed, and doubt not but revenge will fall on thee at last!"

When he had passed the boundary of those countries, he was somewhat comforted, and rode eight days without adventure. Anon he came to a cross, whereon was written in letters of gold, "It is not for a knight alone to ride towards this castle." Looking up, he saw a hoary ancient man come towards him, who said, "Sir Balin le Savage, thou passest thy bounds this way; therefore turn back again, it will be best for thee;" and with these words he vanished.

Then did he hear a horn blow as it were the death-note of some hunted beast. "That blast," said Balin, "is blown for me, for I am the prey; though yet I be not dead." But as he spoke he saw a hundred ladies with a great troop of knights come forth to meet him with bright faces and great welcome, who led him to the castle and made a great feast, with dancing and minstrelsy and all manner of joy.

Then the chief lady of the castle said, "Knight with the two swords, thou must encounter and fight with a knight hard by, who dwelleth on an island, for no man may pass this way without encountering him."

"It is a grievous custom," answered Sir Balin.

"There is but one knight to defeat," replied the lady.

"Well," said Sir Balin, "be it as thou wilt. I am ready and quite willing, and though my horse and my body be full weary, yet is my heart not weary, save of life. And truly I were glad if I might meet my death."

"Sir," said one standing by, "methinketh your shield is not good; I will lend you a bigger."

"I thank thee, sir," said Balin, and took the unknown shield and left his own, and so rode forth, and put himself and horse into a boat and came to the island.

As soon as he had landed, he saw come riding towards him, a knight dressed all in red, upon a horse trapped in the same color. When the red knight saw Sir Balin, and the two swords he wore, he thought it must have been his brother (for the red knight was Sir Balan), but when he saw the strange arms on his shield, he forgot the thought, and came against him fiercely. At the first course they overthrew each other, and both lay swooning on the ground; but Sir Balin was the most hurt and bruised, for he was weary and spent with traveling. So Sir Balan rose up first to his feet and drew his sword, and Sir Balin painfully rose against him and raised his shield. Then Sir Balan smote him through the shield and brake his helmet; and Sir Balin, in return, smote at him with his fated sword, and had wellnigh slain his brother. And so they fought till their breaths failed.

Then Sir Balin, looking up, saw all the castle towers stand full of ladies. So they went again to battle, and wounded each other full sore, and paused, and breathed again, and then again began the fight; and this for many times they did, till all the ground was red with blood. And by now, each had full grievously wounded the other with seven great wounds, the least of which might have destroyed the mightiest giant in the world. But still they rose against each other, although their hauberks now were all unnailed, and they smiting at each other's naked bodies with their sharp swords. At the last, Sir Balan, the younger brother, withdrew a little space and laid him down.

Then said Sir Balin le Savage, "What knight art thou? for never before have I found a knight to match me thus."

"My name," said he, all faintly, "is Balan, brother to the good knight Sir Balin."

"Ah, God!" cried Balin, "that ever I should see this day!" and therewith fell down backwards in a swoon.

Then Sir Balan crept with pain upon his feet and hands, and put his brother's helmet off his head, but could not know him by his face, it was so hewed and bloody. But presently, when Sir Balin came to, he said, "Oh! Balan, mine own brother, thou hast slain me, and I thee! All the wide world saw never greater grief!"

"Alas!" said Sir Balan, "that I ever saw this day; and through mishap alone I knew thee not, for when I saw thy two swords, if it had not been for thy strange shield, I should have known thee for my brother."

"Alas!" said Balin, "all this sorrow lieth at the door of one unhappy knight within the castle, who made me change my shield. If I might live, I would destroy that castle and its evil customs."

"It were well done," said Balan, "for since I first came hither I have never been able to depart, for here they made me fight with one who kept this island, whom I slew, and by enchantment I might never quit it more; nor couldst thou, brother, hadst thou slain me, and escaped with thine own life."

Anon came the lady of the castle, and when she heard their talk, and saw their evil case, she wrung her hands and wept bitterly. So Sir Balan prayed the lady of her gentleness that, for his true service, she would bury them both together in that place. This she granted, weeping full sore, and said it should be done right solemnly and richly, and in the noblest manner possible. Then did they send for a priest, and received the holy sacrament at his hands. And Balin said, "Write over us upon our tomb, that here two brethren slew each other; then shall never good knight or pilgrim pass this way but he will pray for both our souls." And anon Sir Balan died, but Sir Balin died not till the midnight after; and then they both were buried.

On the morrow of their death came Merlin, and took Sir Balin's sword and fixed on it a new pommel, and set it in a mighty stone, which then, by magic, he made float upon the water. And so, for many years, it floated to and fro around the island, till it swam down the river to Camelot, where young Sir Galahad achieved it, as shall be told hereafter.

VI. THE MARRIAGE OF ARTHUR AND GUINEVERE AND THE FOUNDING OF THE ROUND TABLE

It befell upon a certain day, that King Arthur said to Merlin, "My lords and knights do daily pray me now to take a wife; but I will have none without thy counsel, for thou hast ever helped me since I came first to this crown."

"It is well," said Merlin, "that thou shouldst take a wife, for no man of bounteous and noble nature should live without one; but is there any lady whom thou lovest better than another?"

"Yea," said King Arthur, "I love Guinevere, the daughter of King Leodegrance, of Camelgard, who also holdeth in his house the Round Table that he had from my father Uther; and as I think, that damsel is the gentlest and the fairest lady living."

"Sir," answered Merlin, "as for her beauty, she is one of the fairest that do live; but if ye had not loved her as ye do, I would fain have had ye choose some other who was both fair and good. But where a man's heart is set, he will be loth to leave." This Merlin said, knowing the misery that should hereafter happen from this marriage.

Then King Arthur sent word to King Leodegrance that he mightily desired to wed his daughter, and how that he had loved her since he saw her first, when with Kings Ban and Bors he rescued Leodegrance from King Ryence of North Wales.

When King Leodegrance heard the message, he cried out, "These be the best tidings I have heard in all my life—so great and worshipful a prince to seek my daughter for his wife! I would fain give him half my lands with her straightway, but that he needeth none—and better will it please him that I send him the Round Table of King Uther, his father, with a hundred good knights towards the furnishing of it with guests, for he will soon find means to gather more, and make the table full."

Then King Leodegrance delivered his daughter Guinevere to the messengers of King Arthur, and also the Round Table with the hundred knights.

So they rode royally and freshly, sometimes by water and sometimes by land, towards Camelot. And as they rode along in the spring weather, they made full many sports and pastimes. And, in all those sports and games, a young knight lately come to Arthur's, court, Sir Lancelot by name, was passing strong, and won praise from all, being full of grace and hardihood; and Guinevere also ever looked on him with joy. And always in the eventide, when the tents were set beside some stream or forest, many minstrels came and sang before the knights and ladies as they sat in the tent-doors, and many knights would tell adventures; and still Sir Lancelot was foremost, and told the knightliest tales, and sang the goodliest songs, of all the company.

And when they came to Camelot, King Arthur made great joy, and all the city with him; and riding forth with a great retinue he met Guinevere and her company, and led her through the streets all filled with people, and in the midst of all their shoutings and the ringing of church bells, to a palace hard by his own.

Then, in all haste, the king commanded to prepare the marriage and the coronation with the stateliest and most honorable pomp that could be made. And when the day was come, the archbishops led the king to the cathedral, whereto he walked, clad in his royal robes, and having four kings, bearing four golden swords, before him; a choir of passing sweet music going also with him.

In another part, was the queen dressed in her richest ornaments, and led by archbishops and bishops to the Chapel of the Virgins, the four queens also of the four kings last mentioned walked before her, bearing four white doves, according to ancient custom; and after her there followed many damsels, singing and making every sign of joy.

And when the two processions were come to the churches, so wondrous was the music and the singing, that all the knights and barons who were there pressed on each other, as in the crowd of battle, to hear and see the most they might.

When the king was crowned, he called together all the knights that came with the Round Table from Camelgard, and twenty-eight others, great and valiant men, chosen by Merlin out of all the realm, towards making up the full number of the table. Then the Archbishop of Canterbury blessed the seats of all the knights, and when they rose again therefrom to pay their homage to King Arthur, there was found upon the back of each knight's seat his name, written in letters of gold. But upon one seat was found written, "This is the Siege Perilous, wherein if any man shall sit save him whom Heaven hath chosen, he shall be devoured by fire."

Anon came young Gawain, the king's nephew, praying to be made a knight, whom the king knighted then and there. Soon after came a poor man, leading with him a tall fair lad of eighteen years of age, riding on a lean mare. And falling at the king's feet, the poor man said, "Lord, it was told me, that at this time of thy marriage thou wouldst give to any man the gift he asked for, so it were not unreasonable."

"That is the truth," replied King Arthur, "and I will make it good."

"Thou sayest graciously and nobly," said the poor man. "Lord, I ask nothing else but that thou wilt make my son here a knight."

"It is a great thing that thou askest," said the king. "What is thy name?"

"Aries, the cowherd," answered he.

"Cometh this prayer from thee or from thy son?" inquired King Arthur.

"Nay, lord, not from myself," said he, "but from him only, for I have thirteen other sons, and all of them will fall to any labor that I put them to. But this one will do no such work for anything that I or my wife may do, but is for ever shooting or fighting, and running to see knights and joustings, and torments me both night and day that he be made a knight."

"What is thy name?" said the king to the young man.

"My name is Tor," said he.

Then the king, looking at him steadfastly, was well pleased with his face and figure, and with his look of nobleness and strength.

"Fetch all thy other sons before me," said the king to Aries. But when he brought them, none of them resembled Tor in size or shape or feature.

Then the king knighted Tor, saying, "Be thou to thy life's end a good knight and a true, as I pray God thou mayest be; and if thou provest worthy, and of prowess, one day thou shalt be counted in the Round Table." Then turning to Merlin, Arthur said, "Prophesy now, O Merlin, shall Sir Tor become a worthy knight, or not?"

"Yea, lord," said Merlin, "so he ought to be, for he is the son of that King Pellinore whom thou hast met, and proved to be one of the best knights living. He is no cowherd's son."

Presently after came in King Pellinore, and when he saw Sir Tor he knew him for his son, and was more pleased than words can tell to find him knighted by the king. And Pellinore did homage to King Arthur, and was gladly and graciously accepted of the king; and then was led by Merlin to a high seat at the Table Round, near to the Perilous Seat.

But Sir Gawain was full of anger at the honor done King Pellinore, and said to his brother Gaheris, "He slew our father, King Lot, therefore will I slay him."

"Do it not yet," said he; "wait till I also be a knight, then will I help ye in it: it is best ye suffer him to go at this time, and not trouble this high feast with blood-shed."

"As ye will, be it," said Sir Gawain.

Then rose the king and spake to all the Table Round, and charged them to be ever true and noble knights, to do neither outrage nor murder, nor any unjust violence, and always to flee treason; also by no means ever to be cruel, but give mercy unto him that asked for mercy, upon pain of forfeiting the liberty of his court forevermore. Moreover, at all times, on pain of death, to give all succor unto ladies and young damsels; and lastly, never to take part in any wrongful quarrel, for reward or payment. And to all this he swore them knight by knight.

Then he ordained that, every year at Pentecost, they should all come before him, wheresoever he might appoint a place, and give account of all their doings and adventures of the past twelve-month. And so, with prayer and blessing, and high words of cheer, he instituted the most noble order of the Round Table, whereto the best and bravest knights in all the world sought afterwards to find admission.

Then was the high feast made ready, and the king and queen sat side by side, before the whole assembly; and great and royal was the banquet and the pomp.

And as they sat, each man in his place, Merlin went round and said, "Sit still awhile, for ye shall see a strange and marvelous adventure."

So as they sat, there suddenly came running through the hall, a white hart, with a white hound next after him, and thirty couple of black running hounds, making full cry; and the hart made circuit of the Table Round, and past the other tables; and suddenly the white hound flew upon him and bit him fiercely, and tore out a piece from his haunch. Whereat the hart sprang suddenly with a great leap, and overthrew a knight sitting at the table, who rose forthwith, and, taking up the hound, mounted, and rode fast away.

But no sooner had he left, than there came in a lady, mounted on a white palfrey, who cried out to the king, "Lord, suffer me not to have this injury!—the hound is mine which that knight taketh." And as she spake, a knight rode in all armed, on a great horse, and suddenly took up the lady and rode away with her by force, although she greatly cried and moaned.

Then the king desired Sir Gawain, Sir Tor, and King Pellinore to mount and follow this adventure to the uttermost; and told Sir Gawain to bring back the hart, Sir Tor the hound and knight, and King Pellinore the knight and the lady.

So Sir Gawain rode forth at a swift pace, and with him Gaheris, his brother, for a squire. And as they went, they saw two knights fighting on horseback, and when they reached them they divided them and asked the reason of their quarrel. "We fight for a foolish matter," one replied, "for we be brethren; but there came by a white hart this way, chased by many hounds, and thinking it was an adventure for the high feast of King Arthur, I would have followed it to have gained worship; whereat my younger brother here declared he was the better knight and would go after it instead, and so we fight to prove which of us be the better knight."

"This is a foolish thing," said Sir Gawain. "Fight with all strangers, if ye will, but not brother with brother. Take my advice, set on against me, and if ye yield to me, as I shall do my best to make ye, ye shall go to King Arthur and yield ye to his grace."

"Sir knight," replied the brothers, "we are weary, and will do thy wish without encountering thee; but by whom shall we tell the king that we were sent?"

"By the knight that followeth the quest of the white hart," said Sir Gawain. "And now tell me your names, and let us part."

"Sorlous and Brian of the Forest," they replied; and so they went their way to the king's court.

Then Sir Gawain, still following his quest by the distant baying of the hounds, came to a great river, and saw the hart swimming over and near to the further bank. And as he was about to plunge in and swim after, he saw a knight upon the other side, who cried, "Come not over here, Sir knight, after that hart, save thou wilt joust with me."

"I will not fail for that," said Sir Gawain; and swam his horse across the stream.

Anon they got their spears, and ran against each other fiercely; and Sir Gawain smote the stranger off his horse, and turning, bade him yield.

"Nay," replied he, "not so; for though ye have the better of me on horseback, I pray thee, valiant knight, alight, and let us match together with our swords on foot."

"What is thy name?" quoth Gawain.

"Allardin of the Isles," replied the stranger.

Then they fell on each other; but soon Sir Gawain struck him through the helm, so deeply and so hard, that all his brains were scattered, and Sir Allardin fell dead. "Ah," said Gaheris, "that was a mighty stroke for a young knight!"

Then did they turn again to follow the white hart, and let slip three couple of greyhounds after him; and at the last they chased him to a castle, and there they overtook and slew him, in the chief courtyard.

At that there rushed a knight forth from a chamber, with a drawn sword in his hand, and slew two of the hounds before their eyes, and chased the others from the castle, crying, "Oh, my white hart! alas, that thou art dead! for thee my sovereign lady gave to me, and evil have I kept thee; but if I live, thy death shall be dear bought." Anon he went within and armed, and came out fiercely, and met Sir Gawain face to face.

"Why have ye slain my hounds?" said Sir Gawain; "they did but after their nature: and ye had better have taken vengeance on me than on the poor dumb beasts."

"I will avenge me on thee, also," said the other, "ere thou depart this place."

Then did they fight with each other savagely and madly, till the blood ran down to their feet. But at last Sir Gawain had the better, and felled the knight of the castle to the ground. Then he cried out for mercy, and yielded to Sir Gawain, and besought him as he was a knight and gentleman to save his life. "Thou shalt die," said Sir Gawain, "for slaying my hounds."

"I will make thee all amends within my power," replied the knight.

But Sir Gawain would have no mercy, and unlaced his helm to strike his head off; and so blind was he with rage, that he saw not where a lady ran out from her chamber and fell down upon his enemy. And making a fierce blow at him, he smote off by mischance the lady's head.

"Alas!" cried Gaheris, "foully and shamefully have ye done—the shame shall never leave ye! Why give ye not your mercy unto them that ask it? a knight without mercy is without worship also."

Then Sir Gawain was sore amazed at that fair lady's death, and knew not what to do, and said to the fallen knight, "Arise, for I will give thee mercy."

"Nay, nay," said he, "I care not for thy mercy now, for thou hast slain my lady and my love—that of all earthly things I loved the best."

"I repent me sorely of it," said Sir Gawain, "for I meant to have struck thee: but now shalt thou go to King Arthur and tell him this adventure, and how thou hast been overcome by the knight that followeth the quest of the white hart."

"I care not whether I live or die, or where I go," replied the knight.

So Sir Gawain sent him to the court to Camelot, making him bear one dead greyhound before and one behind him on his horse. "Tell me thy name before we part," said he.

"My name is Athmore of the Marsh," he answered.

Then went Sir Gawain into the castle, and prepared to sleep there and began to unarm; but Gaheris upbraided him, saying, "Will ye disarm in this strange country? bethink ye, ye must needs have many enemies about."

No sooner had he spoken than there came out suddenly four knights, well armed, and assailed them hard, saying to Sir Gawain, "Thou new-made knight, how hast thou shamed thy knighthood! a knight without mercy is dishonored! Slayer of fair ladies, shame to thee evermore! Doubt not thou shalt thyself have need of mercy ere we leave thee."

Then were the brothers in great jeopardy, and feared for their lives, for they were but two to four, and weary with traveling; and one of the four knights shot Sir Gawain with a bolt, and hit him through the arm, so that he could fight no more. But when there was nothing left for them but death, there came four ladies forth and prayed the four knights' mercy for the strangers. So they gave Sir Gawain and Gaheris their lives, and made them yield themselves prisoners.

On the morrow, came one of the ladies to Sir Gawain, and talked with him, saying, "Sir knight, what cheer?"

"Not good," said he.

"It is your own default, sir," said the lady, "for ye have done a passing foul deed in slaying that fair damsel yesterday—and ever shall it be great shame to you. But ye be not of King Arthur's kin."

"Yea, truly am I," said he; "my name is Gawain, son of King Lot of Orkney, whom King Pellinore slew—and my mother, Belisent, is half-sister to the king."

When the lady heard that, she went and presently got leave for him to quit the castle; and they gave him the head of the white hart to take with him, because it was in his quest; but made him also carry the dead lady with him—her head hung round his neck and her body lay before him on his horse's neck.

So in that fashion he rode back to Camelot; and when the king and queen saw him, and heard tell of his adventures, they were heavily displeased, and, by order of the queen, he was put upon his trial before a court of ladies—who judged him to be evermore, for all his life, the knight of ladies' quarrels, and to fight always on their side, and never against any, except he fought for one lady and his adversary for another; also they charged him never to refuse mercy to him that asked it, and swore him to it on the Holy Gospels. Thus ended the adventure of the white hart.

Meanwhile, Sir Tor had made him ready, and followed the knight who rode away with the hound. And as he went, there suddenly met him in the road a dwarf, who struck his horse so viciously upon the head with a great staff, that he leaped backwards a spear's length.

"Wherefore so smitest thou my horse, foul dwarf?" shouted Sir Tor.

"Because thou shalt not pass this way," replied the dwarf, "unless thou fight for it with yonder knights in those pavilions," pointing to two tents, where two great spears stood out, and two shields hung upon two trees hard by.

"I may not tarry, for I am on a quest I needs must follow," said Sir Tor.

"Thou shalt not pass," replied the dwarf, and therewith blew his horn. Then rode out quickly at Sir Tor one armed on horseback, but Sir Tor was quick as he, and riding at him bore him from his horse, and made him yield. Directly after came another still more fiercely, but with a few great strokes and buffets Sir Tor unhorsed him also, and sent them both to Camelot to King Arthur. Then came the dwarf and begged Sir Tor to take him in his service, "for," said he, "I will serve no more recreant knights."

"Take then a horse, and come with me," said Tor.

"Ride ye after the knight with the white hound?" said the dwarf; "I can soon bring ye where he is."

So they rode through the forest till they came to two more tents. And Sir Tor alighting, went into the first, and saw three damsels lie there, sleeping. Then went he to the other, and found another lady also sleeping, and at her feet the white hound he sought for, which instantly began to bay and bark so loudly, that the lady woke. But Sir Tor had seized the hound and given it to the dwarf's charge.

"What will ye do, Sir knight?" cried out the lady; "will ye take away my hound from me by force?"

"Yea, lady," said Sir Tor; "for so I must, having the king's command; and I have followed it from King Arthur's court, at Camelot, to this place."

"Well," said the lady, "ye will not go far before ye be ill handled, and will repent ye of the quest."

"I shall cheerfully abide whatsoever adventure cometh, by the grace of God," said Sir Tor; and so mounted his horse and began to ride back on his way. But night coming on, he turned aside to a hermitage that was in the forest, and there abode till the next day, making but sorrowful cheer of such poor food as the hermit had to give him, and hearing a Mass devoutly before he left on the morrow.

And in the early morning, as he rode forth with the dwarf towards Camelot, he heard a knight call loudly after him, "Turn, turn! Abide, Sir knight, and yield me up the hound thou tookest from my lady." At which he turned, and saw a great and strong knight, armed full splendidly, riding down upon him fiercely through a glade of the forest.

Now Sir Tor was very ill provided, for he had but an old courser, which was as weak as himself, because of the hermit's scanty fare. He waited, nevertheless, for the strange knight to come, and at the first onset with their spears, each unhorsed the other, and then fell to with their swords like two mad lions. Then did they smite through one another's shields and helmets till the fragments flew on all sides, and their blood ran out in streams; but yet they carved and rove through the thick armor of the hauberks, and gave each other great and ghastly wounds. But in the end, Sir Tor, finding the strange knight faint, doubled his strokes until he beat him to the earth. Then did he bid him yield to his mercy.

"That will I not," replied Abellius, "while my life lasteth and my soul is in my body, unless thou give me first the hound."

"I cannot," said Sir Tor, "and will not, for it was my quest to bring again that hound and thee unto King Arthur, or otherwise to slay thee."

With that there came a damsel riding on a palfrey, as fast as she could drive, and cried out to Sir Tor with a loud voice, "I pray thee, for King Arthur's love, give me a gift."

"Ask," said Sir Tor, "and I will give thee."

"Gramercy," said the lady, "I ask the head of this false knight Abellius, the most outrageous murderer that liveth."

"I repent me of the gift I promised," said Sir Tor. "Let him make thee amends for all his trespasses against thee."

"He cannot make amends," replied the damsel, "for he hath slain my brother, a far better knight than he, and scorned to give him mercy, though I kneeled for half an hour before him in the mire, to beg it, and though it was but by a chance they fought, and for no former injury or quarrel. I require my gift of thee as a true knight, or else will I shame thee in King Arthur's court; for this Abellius is the falsest knight alive, and a murderer of many."

When Abellius heard this, he trembled greatly, and was sore afraid, and yielded to Sir Tor, and prayed his mercy.

"I cannot now, Sir knight," said he, "lest I be false to my promise. Ye would not take my mercy when I offered it; and now it is too late."

Therewith he unlaced his helmet, and took it off; but Abellius, in dismal fear, struggled to his feet, and fled, until Sir Tor overtook him, and smote off his head entirely with one blow.

"Now, sir," said the damsel, "it is near night, I pray ye come and lodge at my castle hard by."

"I will, with a good will," said he, for both his horse and he had fared but poorly since they left Camelot.

So he went to the lady's castle and fared sumptuously, and saw her husband, an old knight, who greatly thanked him for his service, and urged him oftentimes to come again.

On the morrow he departed, and reached Camelot by noon, where the king and queen rejoiced to see him, and the king made him Earl; and Merlin prophesied that these adventures were but little to the things he should achieve hereafter.

Now while Sir Gawain and Sir Tor had fulfilled their quests, King Pellinore pursued the lady whom the knight had seized away from the wedding-feast. And as he rode through the woods, he saw in a valley a fair young damsel sitting by a well-side, and a wounded knight lying in her arms, and King Pellinore saluted her as he passed by.

As soon as she perceived him she cried out, "Help, help me, knight, for our Lord's sake!" But Pellinore was far too eager in his quest to stay or turn, although she cried a hundred times to him for help; at which she prayed to heaven he might have such sore need before he died as she had now. And presently thereafter her knight died in her arms; and she, for grief and love, slew herself with his sword.

But King Pellinore rode on till he met a poor man, and asked him had he seen a knight pass by that way, leading by force a lady with him.

"Yea, surely," said the man, "and greatly did she moan and cry; but even now another knight is fighting with him to deliver the lady; ride on and thou shalt find them fighting still."

At that King Pellinore rode swiftly on, and came to where he saw the two knights fighting, hard by where two pavilions stood. And when he looked in one of them, he saw the lady that was his quest, and with her the two squires of the two knights who fought.

"Fair lady," said he, "ye must come with me unto King Arthur's court."

"Sir knight," said the two squires, "yonder be two knights fighting for this lady; go part them, and get their consent to take her, ere thou touch her."

"Ye say well," said King Pellinore, and rode between the combatants, and asked them why they fought.

"Sir knight," said the one, "yon lady is my cousin, mine aunt's daughter, whom I met borne away against her will, by this knight here, with whom I therefore fight to free her."

"Sir knight," replied the other, whose name was Hantzlake of Wentland, "this lady got I, by my arms and prowess, at King Arthur's court to-day."

"That is false," said King Pellinore; "ye stole the lady suddenly, and fled away with her, before any knight could arm to stay thee. But it is my service to take her back again. Neither of ye shall therefore have her; but if ye will fight for her, fight with me now and here."

"Well," said the knights, "make ready, and we will assail thee with all our might."

Then Sir Hantzlake ran King Pellinore's horse through with his sword, so that they might be all alike on foot. But King Pellinore at that was passing wroth, and ran upon Sir Hantzlake, with a cry, "Keep well thy head!" and gave him such a stroke upon the helm as clove him to the chin, so that he fell dead to the ground. When he saw that, the other knight refused to fight, and kneeling down said, "Take my cousin the lady with thee, as thy quest is; but as thou art a true knight, suffer her to come to neither shame nor harm."

So the next day King Pellinore departed for Camelot, and took the lady with him; and as they rode in a valley full of rough stones, the damsel's horse stumbled and threw her, so that her arms were sorely bruised and hurt. And as they rested in the forest for the pain to lessen, night came on, and there they were compelled to make their lodging. A little before midnight they heard the trotting of a horse. "Be ye still," said King Pellinore, "for now we may hear of some adventure," and therewith he armed her. Then he heard two knights meet and salute each other, in the dark; one riding from Camelot, the other from the north.

"What tidings at Camelot?" said one.

"By my head," said the other, "I have but just left there, and have espied King Arthur's court, and such a fellowship is there as never may be broke or overcome; for wellnigh all the chivalry of the world is there, and all full loyal to the king, and now I ride back homewards to the north to tell our chiefs, that they waste not their strength in wars against him."

"As for all that," replied the other knight, "I am but now from the north, and bear with me a remedy, the deadliest poison that ever was heard tell of, and to Camelot will I with it; for there we have a friend close to the king, and greatly cherished of him, who hath received gifts from us to poison him, as he hath promised soon to do."

"Beware," said the first knight, "of Merlin, for he knoweth all things, by the devil's craft."

"I will not fear for that," replied the other, and so rode on his way.

Anon King Pellinore and the lady passed on again; and when they came to the well at which the lady with the wounded knight had sat, they found both knight and damsel utterly devoured by lions and wild beasts, all save the lady's head.

When King Pellinore saw that, he wept bitterly, saying, "Alas! I might have saved her life had I but tarried a few moments in my quest."

"Wherefore make so much sorrow now?" said the lady.

"I know not," answered he, "but my heart grieveth greatly for this poor lady's death, so fair she was and young."

Then he required a hermit to bury the remains of the bodies, and bare the lady's head with him to Camelot, to the court.

When he was arrived, he was sworn to tell the truth of his quest before the King and Queen, and when he had entered the Queen somewhat upbraided him, saying, "Ye were much to blame that ye saved not that lady's life."

"Madam," said he, "I shall repent it all my life."

"Ay, king," quoth Merlin, who suddenly came in, "and so ye ought to do, for that lady was your daughter, not seen since infancy by thee. And she was on her way to court, with a right good young knight, who would have been her husband, but was slain by treachery of a felon knight, Lorraine le Savage, as they came; and because thou wouldst not abide and help her, thy best friend shall fail thee in thine hour of greatest need, for such is the penance ordained thee for that deed."

Then did King Pellinore tell Merlin secretly of the treason he had heard in the forest, and Merlin by his craft so ordered that the knight who bare the poison was himself soon after slain by it, and so King Arthur's life was saved.

VII. THE ADVENTURE OF ARTHUR
AND SIR ACCOLON OF GAUL

Being now happily married, King Arthur for a season took his pleasure, with great tournaments, and jousts, and huntings. So once upon a time the king and many of his knights rode hunting in a forest, and Arthur, King Urience, and Sir Accolon of Gaul, followed after a great hart, and being all three well mounted, they chased so fast that they outsped their company, and left them many miles behind; but riding still as rapidly as they could go, at length their horses fell dead under them. Then being all three on foot, and seeing the stag not far before them, very weary and nigh spent—"What shall we do," said King Arthur, "for we are hard bested?" "Let us go on afoot," said King Urience, "till we can find some lodging." At that they saw the stag lying upon the bank of a great lake, with a hound springing at his throat, and many other hounds trooping towards him. So, running forward, Arthur blew the death-note on his horn, and slew the hart. Then lifting up his eyes he saw before him on the lake a barge, all draped down to the water's edge, with silken folds and curtains, which swiftly came towards him, and touched upon the sands; but when he went up close and looked in, he saw no earthly creature. Then he cried out to his companions, "Sirs, come ye hither, and let us see what there is in this ship." So they all three went in, and found it everywhere throughout furnished, and hung with rich draperies of silk and gold.

By this time eventide had come, when suddenly a hundred torches were set up on all sides of the barge, and gave a dazzling light, and at the same time came forth twelve fair damsels, and saluted King Arthur by his name, kneeling on their knees, and telling him that he was welcome, and should have their noblest cheer, for which the king thanked them courteously. Then did they lead him and his fellows to a splendid chamber, where was a table spread with all the richest furniture, and costliest wines and viands; and there they served them with all kinds of wines and meats, till Arthur wondered at the splendor of the feast, declaring he had never in his life supped better, or more royally. After supper they led him to another chamber, than which he had never beheld a richer, where he was left to rest. King Urience, also, and Sir Accolon were each conducted into rooms of like magnificence. And so they all three fell asleep, and being very weary slept deeply all that night.

But when the morning broke, King Urience found himself in his own house in Camelot, he knew not how; and Arthur awaking found himself in a dark dungeon, and heard around him nothing but the groans of woeful knights, prisoners like himself. Then said King Arthur, "Who are ye, thus groaning and complaining?" And some one answered him, "Alas, we be all prisoners, even twenty good knights, and some of us have lain here seven years—some more—nor seen the light of day for all that time." "For what cause?" said King Arthur. "Know ye not then yourself?" they answered—"we will soon tell you. The lord of this strong castle is Sir Damas, and is the falsest and most traitorous knight that liveth; and he hath a younger brother, a good and noble knight, whose name is Outzlake. This traitor Damas, although passing rich, will give his brother nothing of his wealth, and save what Outzlake keepeth to himself by force, he hath no share of the inheritance. He owneth, nevertheless, one fair rich manor, whereupon he liveth, loved of all men far and near. But Damas is as altogether hated as his brother is beloved, for he is merciless and cowardly: and now for many years there hath been war between these brothers, and Sir Outzlake evermore defieth Damas to come forth and fight with him, body to body, for the inheritance; and if he be too cowardly, to find some champion knight that will fight for him. And Damas hath agreed to find some champion, but never yet hath found a knight to take his evil cause in hand, or wager battle for him. So with a strong band of men-at-arms he lieth ever in ambush, and taketh captive every passing knight who may unwarily go near and bringeth him into this castle, and desireth him either to fight Sir Outzlake, or to lie for evermore indurance. And thus hath he dealt with all of us, for we all scorned to take up such a cause for such a false foul knight—but rather one by one came here, where many a good knight hath died of hunger and disease. But if one of us would fight, Sir Damas would deliver all the rest."

"God of his mercy send you deliverance," said King Arthur, and sat turning in his mind how all these things should end, and how he might himself gain freedom for so many noble hearts.

Anon there came a damsel to the king, saying, "Sir, if thou wilt fight for my lord thou shalt be delivered out of prison, but else nevermore shalt thou escape with thy life." "Nay," said King Arthur, "that is but a hard choice, yet had I rather fight than die in prison, and if I may deliver not myself alone, but all these others, I will do the battle." "Yea," said the damsel, "it shall be even so." "Then," said King Arthur, "I am ready now, if but I had a horse and armor." "Fear not," said she, "that shalt thou have presently, and shalt lack nothing proper for the fight." "Have I not seen thee," said the king, "at King Arthur's court? for it seemeth that thy face is known to me." "Nay," said the damsel, "I was never there; I am Sir Damas' daughter, and have never been but a day's journey from this castle." But she spoke falsely, for she was one of the damsels of Morgan le Fay, the great enchantress, who was King Arthur's half-sister.

When Sir Damas knew that there had been at length a knight found who would fight for him, he sent for Arthur, and finding him a man so tall and strong, and straight of limb, he was passingly well pleased, and made a covenant with him, that he should fight unto the uttermost for his cause, and that all the other knights should be delivered. And when they were sworn to each other on the Holy Gospels, all those imprisoned knights were straightway led forth and delivered, but abode there one and all to see the battle.

In the meanwhile there had happened to Sir Accolon of Gaul a strange adventure; for when he awoke from his deep sleep upon the silken barge, he found himself upon the edge of a deep well, and in instant peril of falling thereinto. Whereat, leaping up in great affright, he crossed himself and cried aloud, "May God preserve my lord King Arthur and King Urience, for those damsels in the ship have betrayed us, and were doubtless devils and no women; and if I may escape this misadventure, I will certainly destroy them wheresoever I may find them." With that there came to him a dwarf with a great mouth, and a flat nose, and saluted him, saying that he came from Queen Morgan le Fay. "And she greeteth you well," said he, "and biddeth you be strong of heart, for to-morrow you shall do battle with a strange knight, and therefore she hath sent you here Excalibur, King Arthur's sword, and the scabbard likewise. And she desireth you as you do love her to fight this battle to the uttermost, and without any mercy, as you have promised her you would fight when she should require it of you; and she will make a rich queen forever of any damsel that shall bring her that knight's head with whom you are to fight."

"Well," said Sir Accolon, "tell you my lady Queen Morgan, that I shall hold to that I promised her, now that I have this sword— and," said he, "I suppose it was to bring about this battle that she made all these enchantments by her craft." "You have guessed rightly," said the dwarf, and therewithal he left him.

Then came a knight and lady, and six squires, to Sir Accolon, and took him to a manor house hard by, and gave him noble cheer; and the house belonged to Sir Outzlake, the brother of Sir Damas, for so had Morgan le Fay contrived with her enchantments. Now Sir Outzlake himself was at that time sorely wounded and disabled, having been pierced through both his thighs by a spear-thrust. When, therefore, Sir Damas sent down messengers to his brother, bidding him make ready by to-morrow morning, and be in the field to fight with a good knight, for that he had found a champion ready to do battle at all points, Sir Outzlake was sorely annoyed and distressed, for he knew he had small chance of victory, while yet he was disabled by his wounds; notwithstanding, he determined to take the battle in hand, although he was so weak that he must needs be lifted to his saddle. But when Sir Accolon of Gaul heard this, he sent a message to Sir Outzlake offering to take the battle in his stead, which cheered Sir Outzlake mightily, who thanked Sir Accolon with all his heart, and joyfully accepted him.

So, on the morrow, King Arthur was armed and well horsed, and asked Sir Damas, "When shall we go to the field?" "Sir," said Sir Damas, "you shall first hear mass." And when mass was done, there came a squire on a great horse, and asked Sir Damas if his knight were ready, "for our knight is already in the field." Then King Arthur mounted on horseback, and there around were all the knights, and barons, and people of the country; and twelve of them were chosen to wait upon the two knights who were about to fight. And as King Arthur sat on horseback, there came a damsel from Morgan le Fay, and brought to him a sword, made like Excalibur, and a scabbard also, and said to him, "Morgan le Fay sendeth you here your sword for her great love's sake." And the king thanked her, and believed it to be as she said; but she traitorously deceived him, for both sword and scabbard were counterfeit, brittle, and false, and the true sword Excalibur was in the hands of Sir Accolon. Then, at the sound of a trumpet, the champions set themselves on opposite side of the field, and giving rein and spur to their horses urged them to so great a speed that each smiting the other in the middle of the shield, rolled his opponent to the ground, both horse and man. Then starting up immediately, both drew their swords and rushed swiftly together. And so they fell to eagerly, and gave each other many great and mighty strokes.

And as they were thus fighting, the damsel Vivien, lady of the lake, who loved King Arthur, came upon the ground, for she knew by her enchantments how Morgan le Fay had craftily devised to have King Arthur slain by his own sword that day, and therefore came to save his life. And Arthur and Sir Accolon were now grown hot against each other, and spared not strength nor fury in their fierce assaults; but the king's sword gave way continually before Sir Accolon's, so that at every stroke he was sore wounded, and his blood ran from him so fast that it was a marvel he could stand. When King Arthur saw the ground so sore be-blooded, he bethought him in dismay that there was magic treason worked upon him, and that his own true sword was changed, for it seemed to him that the sword in Sir Accolon's hand was Excalibur, for fearfully it drew his blood at every blow, while what he held himself kept no sharp edge, nor fell with any force upon his foe.

"Now, knight, look to thyself, and keep thee well from me," cried out Sir Accolon. But King Arthur answered not, and gave him such a buffet on the helm as made him stagger and nigh fall upon the ground. Then Sir Accolon withdrew a little, and came on with Excalibur on high, and smote King Arthur in return with such a mighty stroke as almost felled him; and both being now in hottest wrath, they gave each other grievous and savage blows. But Arthur all the time was losing so much blood that scarcely could he keep upon his feet, yet so full was he of knighthood, that knightly he endured the pain, and still sustained himself, though now he was so feeble that he thought himself about to die. Sir Accolon, as yet, had lost no drop of blood, and being very bold and confident in Excalibur, even grew more vigorous and hasty in his assaults. But all men who beheld them said they never saw a knight fight half so well as did King Arthur, and all the people were so grieved for him that they besought Sir Damas and Sir Outzlake to make up their quarrel and so stay the fight; but they would not.

So still the battle raged, till Arthur drew a little back for breath and a few moments' rest; but Accolon came on after him, following fiercely and crying loud, "It is no time for me to suffer thee to rest," and therewith set upon him. Then Arthur, full of scorn and rage, lifted up his sword and struck Sir Accolon upon the helm so mightily that he drove him to his knees; but with the force of that great stroke his brittle, treacherous sword broke short off at the hilt, and fell down in the grass among the blood, leaving the pommel only in his hand. At that, King Arthur thought within himself that all was over, and secretly prepared his mind for death, yet kept himself so knightly sheltered by his shield that he lost no ground, and made as though he yet had hope and cheer. Then said Sir Accolon, "Sir knight, thou now art overcome and canst endure no longer, seeing thou art weaponless, and hast lost already so much blood. Yet am I fully loth to slay thee; yield, then, therefore, to me as recreant." "Nay," said King Arthur, "that may I not, for I have promised to do battle to the uttermost by the faith of my body while my life lasteth; and I had rather die with honor than live with shame; and if it were possible for me to die an hundred times, I had rather die as often than yield me to thee, for though I lack weapons, I shall lack no worship, and it shall be to thy shame to slay me weaponless." "Aha," shouted then Sir Accolon, "as for the shame, I will not spare; look to thyself, sir knight, for thou art even now but a dead man." Therewith he drove at him with pitiless force, and struck him nearly down; but Arthur evermore waxing in valor as he waned in blood, pressed on Sir Accolon with his shield, and hit at him so fiercely with the pommel in his hand, as hurled him three strides backward.

This, therefore, so confused Sir Accolon, that rushing up, all dizzy, to deliver once again a furious blow, even as he struck, Excalibur, by Vivien's magic, fell from out his hands upon the earth. Beholding which, King Arthur lightly sprang to it, and grasped it, and forthwith felt it was his own good sword, and said to it, "Thou hast been from me all too long, and done me too much damage." Then spying the scabbard hanging by Sir Accolon's side, he sprang and pulled it from him, and cast it away as far as he could throw it; for so long as he had worn it, Arthur knew his life would have been kept secure. "Oh, knight!" then said the king, "thou hast this day wrought me much damage by this sword, but now art thou come to thy death, for I shall not warrant thee but that thou shalt suffer, ere we part, somewhat of that thou hast made me suffer." And therewithal King Arthur flew at him with all his might, and pulled him to the earth, and then struck off his helm, and gave him on the head a fearful buffet, till the blood leaped forth. "Now will I slay thee!" cried King Arthur; for his heart was hardened, and his body all on fire with fever, till for a moment he forgot his knightly mercy. "Slay me thou mayest," said Sir Accolon, "for thou art the best knight I ever found, and I see well that God is with thee; and I, as thou hast, have promised to fight this battle to the uttermost, and never to be recreant while I live; therefore shall I never yield me with my mouth, and God must do with my body what he will." And as Sir Accolon spoke, King Arthur thought he knew his voice; and parting all his blood-stained hair from out his eyes, and leaning down towards him, saw, indeed, it was his friend and own true knight. Then said he—keeping his own visor down—"I pray thee tell me of what country art thou, and what court?" "Sir knight," he answered, "I am of King Arthur's court, and my name is Sir Accolon of Gaul." Then said the king, "Oh, sir knight! I pray thee tell me who gave thee this sword? and from whom thou hadst it?"

Then said Sir Accolon, "Woe worth this sword, for by it I have gotten my death. This sword hath been in my keeping now for almost twelve months, and yesterday Queen Morgan le Fay, wife of King Urience, sent it to me by a dwarf, that therewith I might in some way slay her brother, King Arthur; for thou must understand that King Arthur is the man she hateth most in all the world, being full of envy and jealousy because he is of greater worship and renown than any other of her blood. She loveth me also as much as she doth hate him; and if she might contrive to slay King Arthur by her craft and magic, then would she straightway kill her husband also, and make me the king of all this land, and herself my queen, to reign with me; but now," said he, "all that is over, for this day I am come to my death."

"It would have been sore treason of thee to destroy thy lord," said Arthur. "Thou sayest truly," answered he; "but now that I have told thee, and openly confessed to thee all that foul treason whereof I now do bitterly repent, tell me, I pray thee, whence art thou, and of what court?" "O, Sir Accolon!" said King Arthur, "learn that I am myself King Arthur." When Sir Accolon heard this he cried aloud, "Alas, my gracious lord! have mercy on me, for I knew thee not." "Thou shalt have mercy," said he, "for thou knewest not my person at this time; and though by thine own confession thou art a traitor, yet do I blame thee less, because thou hast been blinded by the false crafts of my sister Morgan le Fay, whom I have trusted more than all others of my kin, and whom I now shall know well how to punish." Then did Sir Accolon cry loudly, "O, lords, and all good people! this noble knight that I have fought with is the noblest and most worshipful in all the world; for it is King Arthur, our liege lord and sovereign king; and full sorely I repent that I have ever lifted lance against him, though in ignorance I did it."

Then all the people fell down on their knees and prayed the pardon of the king for suffering him to come to such a strait. But he replied, "Pardon ye cannot have, for, truly, ye have nothing sinned; but here ye see what ill adventure may ofttimes befall knights-errant, for to my own hurt, and his danger also, I have fought with one of my own knights."

Then the king commanded Sir Damas to surrender to his brother the whole manor, Sir Outzlake only yielding him a palfrey every year; "for," said he scornfully, "it would become thee better to ride on than a courser;" and ordered Damas, upon pain of death, never again to touch or to distress knights-errant riding on their adventures; and also to make full compensation and satisfaction to the twenty knights whom he had held in prison. "And if any of them," said the king, "come to my court complaining that he hath not had full satisfaction of thee for his injuries, by my head, thou shalt die therefor."

Afterwards, King Arthur asked Sir Outzlake to come with him to his court, where he should become a knight of his, and, if his deeds were noble, be advanced to all he might desire.

So then he took his leave of all the people and mounted upon horseback, and Sir Accolon went with him to an abbey hard by, where both their wounds were dressed. But Sir Accolon died within four days after. And when he was dead, the king sent his body to Queen Morgan, to Camelot, saying that he sent her a present in return for the sword Excalibur which she had sent him by the damsel.

So, on the morrow, there came a damsel from Queen Morgan to the king, and brought with her the richest mantle that ever was seen, for it was set as full of precious stones as they could stand against each other, and they were the richest stones that ever the king saw. And the damsel said, "Your sister sendeth you this mantle, and prayeth you to take her gift, and in whatsoever thing she hath offended you, she will amend it at your pleasure." To this the king replied not, although the mantle pleased him much. With that came in the lady of the lake, and said, "Sir, put not on this mantle till thou hast seen more; and in nowise let it be put upon thee, or any of thy knights, till ye have made the bringer of it first put it on her." "It shall be done as thou dost counsel," said the king. Then said he to the damsel that came from his sister, "Damsel, I would see this mantle ye have brought me upon yourself." "Sir," said she, "it will not beseem me to wear a knight's garment." "By my head," said King Arthur, "thou shalt wear it ere it go on any other person's back!" And so they put it on her by force, and forthwith the garment burst into a flame and burned the damsel into cinders. When the king saw that, he hated that false witch Morgan le Fay with all his heart, and evermore was deadly quarrel between her and Arthur to their lives' end.

VIII. ARTHUR IS CROWNED EMPEROR AT ROME

And now again the second time there came ambassadors from Lucius Tiberius, Emperor of Rome, demanding, under pain of war, tribute and homage from King Arthur, and the restoration of all Gaul, which he had conquered from the tribune Flollo.

When they had delivered their message, the king bade them withdraw while he consulted with his knights and barons what reply to send. Then some of the younger knights would have slain the ambassadors, saying that their speech was a rebuke to all who heard the king insulted by it. But when King Arthur heard that, he ordered none to touch them upon pain of death; and sending officers, he had them taken to a noble lodging, and there entertained with the best cheer. "And," said he, "let no dainty be spared, for the Romans are great lords; and though their message please me not, yet must I remember mine honor."

Then the lords and knights of the Round Table were called on to declare their counsel—what should be done upon this matter; and Sir Cador of Cornwall speaking first, said, "Sir, this message is the best news I have heard for a long time, for we have been now idle and at rest for many days, and I trust that thou wilt make sharp war upon the Romans, wherein, I doubt not, we shall all gain honor."

"I believe well," said Arthur, "that thou art pleased, Sir Cador; but that is scarce an answer to the Emperor of Rome, and his demand doth grieve me sorely, for truly I will never pay him tribute; wherefore, lords, I pray ye counsel me. Now, I have understood that Belinus and Brennius, knights of Britain, held the Roman Empire in their hands for many days, and also Constantine, the son of Helen, which is open evidence, not only that we owe Rome no tribute, but that I, being descended from them, may, of right, myself claim the empire."

Then said King Anguish of Scotland, "Sir, thou oughtest of

right to be above all other kings, for in all Christendom is there not thine equal; and I counsel thee never to obey the Romans. For when they reigned here they grievously distressed us, and put the land to great and heavy burdens; and here, for my part, I swear to avenge me on them when I may, and will furnish thee with twenty thousand men-at-arms, whom I will pay and keep, and who shall wait on thee with me, when it shall please thee."

Then the King of Little Britain rose and promised King Arthur thirty thousand men; and likewise many other kings, and dukes, and barons, promised aid—as the lord of West Wales thirty thousand men, Sir Ewaine and his cousin thirty thousand men, and so forth; Sir Lancelot also, and every other knight of the Round Table, promised each man a great host.

So the king, passing joyful at their courage and good will, thanked them all heartily, and sent for the ambassadors again, to hear his answer. "I will," said he, "that ye now go back straightway unto the Emperor your master, and tell him that I give no heed to his words, for I have conquered all my kingdoms by the will of God and by my own right arm, and I am strong enough to keep them, without paying tribute to any earthly creature. But, on the other hand, I claim both tribute and submission from himself, and also claim the sovereignty of all his empire, whereto I am entitled by the right of my own ancestors—sometime kings of this land. And say to him that I will shortly come to Rome, and by God's grace will take possession of my empire and subdue all rebels. Wherefore, lastly, I command him and all the lords of Rome that they forthwith pay me their homage, under pain of my chastisement and wrath."

Then he commanded his treasurers to give the ambassadors great gifts, and defray all their charges, and appointed Sir Cador to convey them worshipfully out of the land.

So when they returned to Rome and came before Lucius, he was sore angry at their words, and said, "I thought this Arthur would have instantly obeyed my orders and have served me as humbly as any other king; but because of his fortune in Gaul, he hath grown insolent."

"Ah, lord," said one of the ambassadors, "refrain from such vain words, for truly I and all with me were fearful at his royal majesty and angry countenance. I fear me thou hast made a rod for thee more sharp than thou hast counted on. He meaneth to be master of this empire; and is another kind of man than thou supposest, and holdeth the most noble court of all the world. We saw him on the new year's day, served at his table by nine kings, and the noblest company of other princes, lords, and knights that ever was in all the world; and in his person he is the most manly-seeming man that liveth, and looketh like to conquer all the earth."

Then Lucius sent messengers to all the subject countries of Rome, and brought together a mighty army, and assembled sixteen kings, and many dukes, princes, lords, and admirals, and a wondrous great multitude of people. Fifty giants also, born of fiends, were set around him for a body-guard. With all that host he straightway went from Rome, and passed beyond the mountains into Gaul, and burned the towns and ravaged all the country of that province, in rage for its submission to King Arthur. Then he moved on towards Little Britain.

Meanwhile, King Arthur having held a parliament at York, left the realm in charge of Sir Badewine and Sir Constantine, and crossed the sea from Sandwich to meet Lucius. And so soon as he was landed, he sent Sir Gawain, Sir Bors, Sir Lionel, and Sir Bedivere to the Emperor, commanding him "to move swiftly and in haste out of his land, and, if not, to make himself ready for battle, and not continue ravaging the country and slaying harmless people." Anon, those noble knights attired themselves and set forth on horseback to where they saw, in a meadow, many silken tents of divers colors, and the Emperor's pavilion in the midst, with a golden eagle set above it.

Then Sir Gawain and Sir Bors rode forward, leaving the other two behind in ambush, and gave King Arthur's message. To which the Emperor replied, "Return, and tell your lord that I am come to conquer him and all his land."

At this, Sir Gawain burned with anger, and cried out, "I had rather than all France that I might fight with thee alone!"

"And I also," said Sir Bors.

Then a knight named Ganius, a near cousin of the Emperor, laughed out aloud, and said, "Lo! how these Britons boast and are full of pride, bragging as though they bare up all the world!"

At these words, Sir Gawain could refrain no longer, but drew forth his sword and with one blow shore off Ganius' head; then with Sir Bors, he turned his horse and rode over waters and through woods, back to the ambush, where Sir Lionel and Sir Bedivere were waiting. The Romans followed fast behind them till the knights turned and stood, and then Sir Bors smote the foremost of them through the body with a spear, and slew him on the spot. Then came on Calibere, a huge Pavian, but Sir Bors overthrew him also. And then the company of Sir Lionel and Sir Bedivere brake forth from their ambush and fell on the Romans, and slew and hewed them down, and forced them to return and flee, chasing them to their tents.

But as they neared the camp, a great host more rushed forth, and turned the battle backwards, and in the turmoil, Sir Bors and Sir Berel fell into the Romans' hands. When Sir Gawain saw that, he drew his good sword Galotine, and swore to see King Arthur's face no more if those two knights were not delivered; and then, with good Sir Idrus, made so sore an onslaught that the Romans fled and left Sir Bors and Sir Berel to their friends. So the Britons returned in triumph to King Arthur, having slain more than ten thousand Romans, and lost no man of worship from amongst themselves.

When the Emperor Lucius heard of that discomfiture he arose, with all his army, to crush King Arthur, and met him in the vale of Soissons. Then speaking to all his host, he said, "Sirs, I admonish you that this day ye fight and acquit yourselves as men; and remembering how Rome is chief of all the earth, and mistress of the universal world, suffer not these barbarous and savage Britons to abide our onset." At that, the trumpets blew so loud, that the ground trembled and shook.

Then did the rival hosts draw near each other with great shoutings; and when they closed, no tongue can tell the fury of their smiting, and the sore struggling, wounds, and slaughter. Then King Arthur, with his mightiest knights, rode down into the thickest of the fight, and drew Excalibur, and slew as lightning slays for swiftness and for force. And in the midmost crowd he met a giant, Galapas by name, and struck off both his legs at the knee-joints; then saying, "Now art thou a better size to deal with!" smote his head off at a second blow: and the body killed six men in falling down.

Anon, King Arthur spied where Lucius fought and worked great deeds of prowess with his own hands. Forthwith he rode at him, and each attacked the other passing fiercely; till at the last, Lucius struck King Arthur with a fearful wound across the face, and Arthur, in return, lifting up Excalibur on high, drove it with all his force upon the Emperor's head, shivering his helmet, crashing his head in halves, and splitting his body to the breast. And when the Romans saw their Emperor dead, they fled in hosts of thousands; and King Arthur and his knights, and all his army followed them, and slew one hundred thousand men.

Then returning to the field, King Arthur rode to the place where Lucius lay dead, and round him the kings of Egypt and Ethiopia, and seventeen other kings, with sixty Roman senators, all noble men. All these he ordered to be carefully embalmed with aromatic gums, and laid in leaden coffins, covered with their shields and arms and banners. Then calling for three senators who were taken prisoners, he said to them, "As the ransom of your lives, I will that ye take these dead bodies and carry them to Rome, and there present them for me, with these letters saying I will myself be shortly there. And I suppose the Romans will beware how they again ask tribute of me; for tell them, these dead bodies that I send them are for the tribute they have dared to ask of me; and if they wish for more, when I come I will pay them the rest."

So, with that charge, the three senators departed with the dead bodies, and went to Rome; the body of the Emperor being carried in a chariot blazoned with the arms of the empire, all alone, and the bodies of the kings two and two in chariots following.

After the battle, King Arthur entered Lorraine, Brabant, and

Flanders, and thence, subduing all the countries as he went, passed into Germany, and so beyond the mountains into Lombardy and Tuscany. At length he came before a city which refused to obey him, wherefore he sat down before it to besiege it. And after a long time thus spent, King Arthur called Sir Florence, and told him they began to lack food for his hosts—"And not far from hence," said he, "are great forests full of cattle belonging to my enemies. Go then, and bring by force all that thou canst find; and take with thee Sir Gawain, my nephew, and Sir Clegis, Sir Claremond, the Captain of Cardiff, and a strong band."

Anon, those knights made ready, and rode over holts and hills, and through forests and woods, till they came to a great meadow full of fair flowers and grass, and there they rested themselves and their horses that night. And at the dawn of the next day, Sir Gawain took his horse and rode away from his fellows to seek some adventure. Soon he saw an armed knight walking his horse by a wood's side, with his shield laced to his shoulder, and no attendant with him save a page, bearing a mighty spear; and on his shield were blazoned three gold griffins. When Sir Gawain spied him, he put his spear in rest, and riding straight to him, asked who he was. "A Tuscan," said he; "and thou mayest prove me when thou wilt, for thou shalt be my prisoner ere we part."

Then said Sir Gawain, "Thou vauntest thee greatly, and speakest proud words; yet I counsel thee, for all thy boastings, look to thyself the best thou canst."

At that they took their spears and ran at each other with all the might they had, and smote each other through their shields into their shoulders; and then drawing swords smote with great strokes, till the fire sprang out of their helms. Then was Sir Gawain enraged, and with his good sword Galotine struck his enemy through shield and hauberk, and splintered into piece all the precious stones of it, and made so huge a wound that men might see both lungs and liver. At that the Tuscan, groaning loudly, rushed on to Sir Gawain, and gave him a deep slanting stroke, and made a mighty wound and cut a great vein asunder, so that he bled fast. Then he cried out, "Bind thy wound quickly up, Sir knight, for thou be-bloodest all thy horse and thy fair armor, and all the surgeons of the world shall never staunch thy blood; for so shall it be to whomsoever is hurt with this good sword."

Then answered Sir Gawain, "It grieveth me but little, and thy boastful words give me no fear, for thou shalt suffer greater grief and sorrow ere we part; but tell me quickly who can staunch this blood."

"That can I do," said the strange knight, "and will, if thou wilt aid and succor me to become christened, and to believe in God, which now I do require of thee upon thy manhood."

"I am content," said Sir Gawain; "and may God help me to grant all thy wishes. But tell me first, what soughtest thou thus here alone, and of what land art thou?"

"Sir," said the knight, "my name is Prianius, and my father is a great prince, who hath rebelled against Rome. He is descended from Alexander and Hector, and of our lineage also were Joshua and Maccabæus. I am of right the king of Alexandria, and Africa, and all the outer isles, yet I would believe in the Lord thou worshipest, and for thy labor I will give thee treasure enough. I was so proud in heart that I thought none my equal, but now have I encountered with thee, who hast given me my fill of fighting; wherefore, I pray thee, Sir knight, tell me of thyself."

"I am no knight," said Sir Gawain; "I have been brought up many years in the wardrobe of the noble prince King Arthur, to mind his armor and array."

"Ah," said Prianius, "if his varlets be so keen and fierce, his knights must be passing good! Now, for the love of heaven, whether thou be knight or knave, tell me thy name."

"By heaven!" said Gawain, "now will I tell thee the truth. My name is Sir Gawain, and I am a knight of the Round Table."

"Now am I better pleased," said Prianius, "than if thou hadst given me all the province of Paris the rich. I had rather have been torn by wild horses than that any varlet should have won such victory over me as thou hast done. But now, Sir knight, I warn thee that close by is the Duke of Lorraine, with sixty thousand good men of war; and we had both best flee at once, for he will find us else, and we be sorely wounded and never likely to recover. And let my page be careful that he blow no horn, for hard by are a hundred knights, my servants; and if they seize thee, no ransom of gold or silver would acquit thee."

Then Sir Gawain rode over a river to save himself, and Sir Prianius after him, and so they both fled till they came to his companions who were in the meadow, where they spent the night. When Sir Whishard saw Sir Gawain so hurt, he ran to him weeping, and asked him who it was had wounded him; and Sir Gawain told him how he had fought with that man—pointing to Prianius—who had salves to heal them both. "But I can tell ye other tidings," said he—"that soon we must encounter many enemies, for a great army is close to us in our front."

Then Prianius and Sir Gawain alighted and let their horses graze while they unarmed, and when they took this armor and their clothing off, the hot blood ran down freshly from their wounds till it was piteous to see. But Prianius took from his page a vial filled from the four rivers that flow out of Paradise, and anointed both their wounds with a certain balm, and washed them with that water, and within an hour afterwards they were both as sound and whole as ever they had been. Then, at the sound of a trumpet, all the knights were assembled to council; and after much talking, Prianius said, "Cease your words, for I warn you in yonder wood ye shall find knights out of number, who will put out cattle for a decoy to lead you on; and ye are not seven hundred!"

"Nevertheless," said Sir Gawain, "let us at once encounter them, and see what they can do; and may the best have the victory."

Then they saw suddenly an earl named Sir Ethelwold, and the Duke of Duchmen come leaping out of ambush of the woods in front, with many a thousand after them, and all rode straight down to the battle. And Sir Gawain, full of ardor and courage, comforted his knights, saying, "They all are ours." Then the seven hundred knights, in one close company, set spurs to their horses and began to gallop, and fiercely met their enemies. And then were men and horses slain and overthrown on every side, and in and out amidst them all, the knights of the Round Table pressed and thrust, and smote down to the earth all who withstood them, till at length the whole of them turned back and fled.

"By heaven!" said Sir Gawain, "this gladdeneth well my heart, for now behold them as they flee! they are full seventy thousand less in number than they were an hour ago!"

Thus was the battle quickly ended, and a great host of high lords and knights of Lombardy and Saracens left dead upon the field. Then Sir Gawain and his company collected a great plenty of cattle, and of gold and silver, and all kind of treasure, and returned to King Arthur, where he still kept the siege.

"Now God be thanked," cried he; "but who is he that standeth yonder by himself, and seemeth not a prisoner?"

"Sir," said Sir Gawain, "he is a good man with his weapons, and hath matched me; but cometh hither to be made a Christian. Had it not been for his warnings, we none of us should have been here this day. I pray thee, therefore, let him be baptized, for there can be few nobler men, or better knights."

So Prianius was christened, and made a duke and knight of the Round Table.

Presently afterwards, they made a last attack upon the city, and entered by the walls on every side; and as the men were rushing to the pillage, came the Duchess forth, with many ladies and damsels, and kneeled before King Arthur; and besought him to receive their submission. To whom the king made answer, with a noble countenance, "Madam, be well assured that none shall harm ye, or your ladies; neither shall any that belong to thee be hurt; but the Duke must abide my judgment." Then he commanded to stay the assault and took the keys from the Duke's eldest son, who brought them kneeling. Anon the Duke was sent a prisoner to Dover for his life, and rents and taxes were assigned for dowry of the Duchess and her children.

Then went he on with all his hosts, winning all towns and castles, and wasting them that refused obedience, till he came to Viterbo. From thence he sent to Rome, to ask the senators whether they would receive him for their lord and governor. In answer, came out to him all the Senate who remained alive, and the Cardinals, with a majestic retinue and procession; and laying great treasures at his feet, they prayed him to come in at once to Rome, and there be peaceably crowned as Emperor. "At this next Christmas," said King Arthur, "will I be crowned, and hold my Round Table in your city."

Anon he entered Rome, in mighty pomp and state; and after him came all his hosts, and his knights, and princes, and great lords, arrayed in gold and jewels, such as never were beheld before. And then was he crowned Emperor by the Pope's hands, with all the highest solemnity that could be made.

Then after his coronation, he abode in Rome for a season, settling his lands and giving kingdoms to his knights and servants, to each one after his deserving, and in such wise fashion that no man among them all complained. Also he made many dukes and earls, and loaded all his men-at-arms with riches and great treasures.

When all this was done, the lords and knights, and all the men of great estate, came together before him, and said, "Noble Emperor! by the blessing of Eternal God, thy mortal warfare is all finished, and thy conquests all achieved; for now in all the world is none so great and mighty as to dare make war with thee. Wherefore we beseech and heartily pray thee of thy noble grace, to turn thee homeward, and give us also leave to see our wives and homes again, for now we have been from them a long season, and all thy journey is completed with great honor and worship."

"Ye say well," replied he, "and to tempt God is no wisdom; therefore make ready in all haste, and turn we home to England."

So King Arthur returned with his knights and lords and armies, in great triumph and joy, through all the countries he had conquered, and commanded that no man, upon pain of death, should rob or do any violence by the way. And crossing the sea, he came at length to Sandwich, where Queen Guinevere received him, and made great joy at his arrival. And through all the realm of Britain was there such rejoicing as no tongue can tell.

IX. SIR GAWAIN AND THE MAID
WITH THE NARROW SLEEVES

Now it happened that as Sir Gawain was riding one day through the country he encountered a troop of knights, followed by a squire, who led a Spanish charger, and about whose neck was hung a shield. Gawain rode up to the squire and said, "Tell me, what is yonder troop that hath ridden by?"

The squire answered, "Sir, Meliance of Lis, a brave and hardy knight."

"Is it to him you belong?" Sir Gawain asked.

"Nay, sir," said the squire, "my master is Teudaves, a knight as worthy as this one."

"Teudaves I know," said Gawain. "Whither fareth he? Tell me the truth."

"He proceedeth to a tourney, sir, which this Meliance of Lis hath undertaken against Thiébault of Tintagel. If you will take my advice you will throw yourself into the castle, and take part against the outsiders."

"Was it not," cried Gawain, "in the house of this Thiébault that Meliance of Lis was nurtured?"

"Aye, sir, so God save me!" said the squire. "His father loved Thiébault and trusted him so much that on his death-bed he committed to his care his little son, whom Thiébault cherished and protected, until the time came when the youth petitioned his daughter to give him her love; but she replied that she would never do that until he should be made a knight. The youth, being ardent, forthwith had himself knighted, and then returned to the maiden. 'Nay,' answered the girl to his renewed suit, 'it shall never be, until in my presence you shall have achieved such feats of arms that I will know my love hath cost you somewhat; for those things which come suddenly are not so sweet as those we earn. If you

103

wish my love, take a tournament of my father. I desire to be certain that my love would be well placed in case I were to grant it.' What she suggested he performed, for love hath such lordship over lovers that those who are under his power would never dare refuse whatever it pleased him to enjoin. And you, sir, sluggish will you be if you do not enter the castle, for they will need you greatly, if you might help them."

To which Sir Gawain answered, "Brother, go thy way, it would be wise of you, and let my affairs be." So the squire departed, and Gawain rode towards Tintagel, for there was no other way by which he could pass.

Now Thiébault had summoned all his kith and kin, who had come, high and low, old and young; but he could not get the permission of his council to joust with his master, for the councillors feared lest he should utterly ruin their castle. Therefore the gates had been walled up with stones and mortar, leaving as the only approach one small postern, which had a gate made of copper, as much as a cart could haul. Sir Gawain rode to the gate, behind the troop that bore his harness, for there was no other road within seven leagues. He found the postern shut and so he turned into a close below the tower, that was fenced with a palisade. He dismounted under an oak and hung up his shields. Thither came the folk from the castle, most of them sorry that the tourney had been abandoned; in the fortress was an aged nobleman, great in land and lineage, whose word no one disputed. A long way off the troop had been pointed out to him, and before they rode into the close he went to Thiébault, and said, "Sir, so God save me, I have seen two companions of King Arthur, worthy men, who ride this way; I advise you to tourney with good hope, for we have brave knights, and servants, and archers, who will slay their horses, and I am certain they will joust before this gate; if their pride shall bring them the gain will be ours, and theirs will be the loss and the shame."

As a result of this counsel Thiébault allowed those who wished to take their arms and sally forth. The knights were right glad, and their squires ran after their horses, while the dames and the damsels climbed high places to see the tourney. Below, in the meadow, they saw the arms of Sir Gawain, and at first thought that there were two knights, because two shields hung from the tree. They cried out that they were fortunate to see two such knights arm. So some thought; but others exclaimed, "Fair Lord God, this knight hath arms and steeds sufficient for two; if he hath no companion, what will he do with two shields? Never was seen a knight who carried two shields at one and the same time. It is very strange if one man means to bear two shields."

While the ladies talked and the knights went forth from the castle the elder daughter of Thiébault mounted to the tower, she on account of whom the tournament had been undertaken, and with her her younger sister, whose sleeves were so quaint that she was called the Maid with the Narrow Sleeves, for she wore them tight. Dames and damsels climbed the tower with them, and the tourney was joined in front of the castle. None bore himself so well as Meliance of Lis, by the testimony of his fair friend, who said to those about her, "Ladies, never did I see a knight who delighted me as doth Meliance of Lis. Is it not a pleasure to see such a knight? That man must have a good seat and be skillful in the use of lance and shield who beareth himself so excellently."

Thereupon her sister, who sat by her side, said that she saw a fairer knight. The elder maiden was angry and rose to strike her sister. But the ladies interfered, and held her back, so that she missed her blow, which greatly incensed her.

In the tournament many lances were shivered, shields pierced, and knights unhorsed; and it went hard with the knight who met Meliance of Lis, for there was none he did not throw on the hard ground. If his lance broke, he dealt great blows with his sword; and he bore himself better than any other knight on either side, to the great joy of his fair friend, who could not resist exclaiming, "Ladies, it is wonderful! Behold the best bachelor knight of whom minstrel hath ever sung or whom eyes have ever seen, the fairest and bravest of all those in the tourney!"

Then the little girl cried, "I see a handsomer one, and 'tis like, a better!"

The elder sister grew hot. "Ha, girl, you were malapert when you were so unlucky as to blame one whom I praised! Take that, to teach you better another time!" So saying, she slapped her sister, so hard that she left on the little girl's cheek the print of her five fingers. But the ladies who sat near scolded her and took her away.

After that they fell to talking of Sir Gawain. One of the damsels said, "The knight beneath yonder tree, why doth he delay to take arms?" A second damsel, who was ruder, exclaimed, "He hath sworn to keep the peace." And a third added, "He is a merchant. Don't tell me that he desireth to joust; he bringeth horses to market." "He is a money-changer," said a fourth. "The goods he hath he meaneth to sell to poor bachelors. Trust me, he hath money or raiment in those chests."

"You have wicked tongues!" cried the little girl. "And you lie! Do you think a merchant would bear such huge lances? You tire me to death, talking such nonsense! By the faith that I owe the Holy Spirit, he seemeth to me a knight rather than a merchant or a money-changer. He is a knight, and he looketh like one!"

The ladies all cried with one voice, "Fair sweet friend, if he looketh so, it doth not follow that he is so. He putteth it on because he wisheth to cheat the tariff. But in spite of all his cleverness he is a fool, for he will be taken up and hung for a cheat."

Now Gawain heard all that the ladies said about him, and he was ashamed and annoyed. But he thought, and thought rightly, that he lay under an accusation of treason, and that it was his duty to keep his pledge or forever disgrace himself and his line. It was for this reason that he took no part in the tourney, lest, if he fought, he should be wounded or taken prisoner.

Meliance of Lis called for great lances, to strike harder blows. Until night fell the tourney continued before the gate; the man who took any booty carried it to some place where he thought it would be safe. Then the ladies saw a squire, tall and strong, who held a piece of a lance and bore on his neck a steel cap. One of the ladies, who was foolish, called to him, saying, "Sir squire, so God help me, it is foolish of you to make prize of that tester, those arms and croup-piece. If you do a squire's duty you deserve a squire's wage. Below, in yonder meadow, is a man who hath riches he cannot defend. Unwise is he who misseth his gain while he hath the power to take it. He seemeth the most debonair of knights, and yet he would not stir if one plucked his beard. If you are wise, take the armor and the treasure, none will hinder you."

The squire went into the meadow and struck one of Gawain's horses, crying, "Vassal, are you sick that all day long you gape here and have done nothing, neither pierced shield nor shivered lance?"

Sir Gawain answered, "Pray, what is it to you why I tarry? You shall know, but not now. Get you gone about your business."

The squire withdrew, for Gawain was not the type of man to whom he would dare say anything unpleasant.

The tourney ended, after many knights had been killed and many horses captured. The outsiders had had the best, and the people of the castle gained by the intermission. At parting they all agreed that on the morrow with songs they would meet again and continue the encounter. So for that night they separated and those who had sallied forth returned to the castle, followed by Sir Gawain. At the gate he met the nobleman who had advised his lord to engage in the tourney. This man accosted him pleasantly, and said, "Fair sir, in this castle your hostel is ready. If it pleaseth you, remain here, for if you should go on it would be long before you arrived at a lodging; therefore I urge you to stay."

"I will tarry, your mercy!" said Gawain. "I have heard worse words."

The man led the guest to his house, talking of this and that, and asked him why on that day he had not borne arms. Sir Gawain explained how he had been accused of treason and was bound to be on his guard against prison and wounds until he could free himself from the reproach that was cast upon him, for it would be to the dishonor of himself and his friends if he should fail to appear at the time appointed.

The nobleman praised him, and said that if this was the reason he had done right. With that he led Gawain to his house, where they dismounted. The people of the castle blamed him, wondering how his lord would take it; while the elder daughter of Thiébault did her best to make trouble for Gawain, on account of her sister, with whom she was angry. "Sir," she said to her father, "on this day you have suffered no loss, but made a gain, greater than you think; you have only to go and take it. The man who hath brought it will not dare to defend it, for he is wily. Lances and shields he bringeth, with palfreys and chargers, and maketh himself resemble a knight to cheat the customs, so that he may pass free when he cometh to sell his wares. Render him his deserts. He is with Garin, the son of Bertan, who hath taken him to lodge at his house. I just saw him pass."

Thiébault took his horse, for he himself wished to go there. The little girl, who saw him leave, went out secretly by a back gate and straight down the hill to the house of Garin, who had two fair daughters. When these saw their little lady they should have been glad, and glad they were, each took her by a hand and led her into the house, kissing her eyes and lips.

In the meantime Garin and his son Herman had left the house and were going up to the castle to speak to their lord. Midway there they met Thiébault and saluted him. He asked whither Garin was going and said he had intended to pay him a visit. "By my faith," said the nobleman, "that will not displease me, and at my house you shall see the fairest of knights."

"It is even he whom I seek," said Thiébault, "to arrest him. He is a merchant who selleth horses and pretendeth to be a knight."

"Alas," said Garin, "'tis a churlish speech I hear you make! I am your man and you are my master, but on the spot I renounce your homage, and in the name of all my line now defy you, rather than suffer you to disgrace my house."

"Indeed," answered Thiébault, "I have no wish to do any such thing. Neither you nor your house shall ever receive aught but honor from me; not but what I have been counseled so to proceed."

"Your great mercy!" exclaimed the nobleman. "It will be my honor if you will visit my guest."

So side by side they went on until they reached the house. When Sir Gawain saw them, he rose out of courtesy, and said,

"Welcome!" The two saluted him and took their seats beside him. Then the nobleman, who was the lord of that country, asked why he had taken no part in the tourney, and Gawain narrated how a knight had accused him of treason and how he was on his way to defend himself in a royal court. "Doubtless," answered the lord, "that is sufficient excuse. But where is the battle to be held?"

"Sir, before the king of Cavalon, whither I am journeying."

"And I," said the nobleman, "will guide you. Since you must needs pass through a poor country, I will provide you with food and packbeasts to carry it."

Gawain answered that he had no need to accept anything, for if it could be bought he would have food and lodging wherever he went.

With these words Thiébault took leave. As he departed, from the opposite direction he saw come his little daughter, who embraced Gawain's leg, and said, "Fair sir, listen! I have come to complain of my sister, who hath beaten me. So please you, do me justice!"

Gawain made no answer, for he did not know what she meant. He put his hand on her head, while the girl pulled him, saying, "To you, fair sir, I complain of my sister. I do not love her, since to-day she hath done me great shame for your sake."

"Fair one, what have I to do with that? How can I do you justice against your sister?"

Thiébault, who had taken leave, heard his child's entreaty, and said, "Girl, who bade you come here and complain to this knight?"

Gawain asked, "Fair sweet sir, is this maid your daughter?"

"Aye; but never mind what she says. A girl is a silly creature."

"Certes," said Gawain, "I should be churlish if I did not do what she desires. Tell me, my sweet child and fair, in what manner I can justify you against your sister."

"If it pleaseth you, for love of me, bear arms in the tourney."

"Tell me, dear friend," said Gawain, "have you ever before made petition to any knight?"

"No, sir."

"Never mind her," exclaimed her father. "Pay no heed to her folly."

Sir Gawain answered, "Sir, so aid me the Lord God, for so little a girl, she hath spoken very well, and I will not refuse her. To-morrow, if she wisheth, I will be her knight."

"Your mercy, fair sweet sir!" cried the child, who was overjoyed, and bowed down to his feet.

Without more words they parted. Thiébault carried his daughter back on the neck of his palfrey. As they rode up the hill be asked her what the quarrel had been about, and she told him the story from beginning to end, saying, "Sir, I was vexed with my sister, who declared that Meliance of Lis was the best of all the knights; and I, who had seen this knight in the meadow, could not help saying that I had seen a fairer, whereupon my sister called me a silly girl and beat me. Fie on me, if I take it from her! I would cut off both my braids close to my head, which would be a great loss, if to-morrow in the tourney this knight would conquer Meliance of Lis, and put an end to the fuss of madam, my sister! She talked so much that she tired all the ladies; but a little rain will hush a great wind."

"Fair child," said her father, "I command and allow you, in courtesy, to send him some love-token, a sleeve or a wimple."

The child, who was simple, answered, "With pleasure since you bid me. But my sleeves are so small, I should not like to send them. Most likely he would not care for them."

"Daughter, say no more," said Thiébault. "I will think about it. I am very glad." So saying, he took her in his arms, and had great joy of embracing and kissing her, until he came in front of his palace. But when his elder daughter saw him approach, with the child before him, she was vexed, and exclaimed, "Sir, whence cometh my sister, the Maid with the Narrow Sleeves? She is full of her tricks; she hath been quick about it; where did you find her?"

"And you," he answered, "what is it to you? Hush, for she is better than you are. You pulled her hair and beat her, which grieveth me. You acted rudely; you were discourteous."

When she heard her father's rebuke, the maid was greatly abashed.

Thiébault had brought from his chests a piece of red samite, and he bade his people cut out and make a sleeve, wide and long. Then he called his daughter and said, "Child, to-morrow rise betimes and visit the knight before he leaveth his hostel. For love's sake you will give him this new sleeve, which he will wear in the tourney when he goeth thither."

The girl answered that so soon as ever she saw the clear dawn she would dress herself and go. With that her father went his way, while she, in great glee, charged her companions that they should not let her oversleep but should wake her when day broke, if they would have her love them. They did as she wished, and when it dawned caused her to wake and dress. All alone she went to the house where Sir Gawain lodged, but, early though it was, the knights had risen and gone to the monastery to hear mass sung. She waited until they had offered long orisons and listened to the service, as much as was right. When they returned the child rose to greet Sir Gawain, and cried, "Sir, on this day may God save and honor you! For love of me, wear the sleeve which I carry in my hand."

"With pleasure," he answered; "friend, your mercy!"

After that the knights were not slow to take arms, and came pouring out of the town, while the damsels again went up to the walls and the dames of the castle saw the troops of brave and hardy knights approach.

They rode with loose rein, and in front was Meliance of Lis, who went so fast that he left the rest in the rear, two rods and more. When his maiden saw her friend she could not keep quiet, but cried, "Ladies, yonder comes the man who hath the lordship of chivalry!"

As swiftly as his horse would carry him Sir Gawain charged Meliance of Lis, who did not evade the blow, but met it boldly, and shivered his lance. On his part Sir Gawain smote so hard that he grieved Meliance, whom he flung on the field; the steed he grasped by the rein and gave to a varlet, bidding him take it to the lady on whose account he had entered the tourney, and say that his master had sent her the first spoil he had made that day. The youth took the charger, saddled as it was, and led it towards the girl, who was sitting at the window of the tower, whence she had watched the joust, and when she saw the encounter she cried to her sister, "Sister, there lies Meliance of Lis, whom you praised so highly! A wise man ought to give praise where it is due. You see, I was right yesterday when I said I saw a better knight."

Thus she teased her sister, who grew angry, and cried, "Child, hold your tongue! If you say another word, I will slap you so that you will not have a foot to stand on!" "Oh, sister," answered the little girl, "remember God! You ought not to beat me because I told you the truth. I saw him tumble as well as you; I think he will not be able to get up. Be as cross as you please, I must say that there is not a lady here who did not see him fall flat on the ground."

Her sister would have struck her, had she been able, but the ladies around would not allow it.

With that came the squire, who held the rein in his right hand. He saw the girl sitting at the window and presented the steed. She thanked him a hundred times, and bade the steed be taken in charge. The squire returned to tell his master, who seemed the lord of the tournament, for there was no knight so gallant that he did not cast from the saddle, if he reached him with the lance. On that day he captured four steeds. The first he sent to the little girl, the second to the wife of the nobleman who had been so kind, and the third and fourth to his own daughters.

The tourney was over and the knights entered the city. On both sides the honor belonged to Sir Gawain. It was not yet noon when he returned from the encounter; the city was full of knights, who ran after him, asking who he was and of what land. At the gate of his hostel he was met by the damsel, who did naught but grasp his stirrup, salute him, and cry, "A thousand mercies, fair sweet sir!" He answered frankly, "Friend, before I am recreant to your service, may I be aged and bald! I shall never be so remote, but a message will bring me. If I know your need, I shall come at the first summons, whatever business be mine!"

While they talked her father came and wished Sir Gawain to

stay with him for that night; but first he begged, that if his guest pleased, he would tell his name. Sir Gawain answered, "Sir, I am called Gawain. My name was never concealed, nor have I ever told it before it hath been asked."

When Thiébault knew that the knight was Sir Gawain his heart was full of joy, and he exclaimed, "Sir, be pleased to lodge with me, and accept my service. Hitherto I have done you little worship, and never did I set eyes on a knight whom so much I longed to honor."

In spite of urging, Sir Gawain refused to stay. The little girl, who was good and clever, clasped his foot and kissed it, commending him to God. Sir Gawain asked why she had done that, and the girl replied that she had kissed his foot in order that he should remember her wherever he went. He answered, "Doubt it not, fair sweet friend! I shall never forget you, after I have parted hence."

With that Sir Gawain took leave of his host and the others, who one and all commended him to God. That night he slept in an abbey, and had all that was necessary.

THE CHAMPIONS OF THE ROUND TABLE

X. THE ADVENTURES OF SIR LANCELOT

Then, at the following Pentecost, was held a feast of the Round Table at Caerleon, with high splendor; and all the knights thereof resorted to the court, and held many games and jousts. And therein Sir Lancelot increased in fame and worship above all men, for he overthrew all comers, and never was unhorsed or worsted, save by treason and enchantment.

When Queen Guinevere had seen his wondrous feats, she held him in great favor, and smiled more on him than on any other knight. And ever since he first had gone to bring her to King Arthur, had Lancelot thought on her as fairest of all ladies, and done his best to win her grace. So the queen often sent for him, and bade him tell of his birth and strange adventures: how he was only son of great King Ban of Brittany, and how, one night, his father, with his mother Helen and himself, fled from his burning castle; how his father, groaning deeply, fell to the ground and died of grief and wounds, and how his mother, running to her husband, left himself alone; how, as he thus lay wailing, came the lady of the lake, and took him in her arms and went with him into the midst of the waters, where, with his cousins Lionel and Bors, he had been cherished all his childhood until he came to King Arthur's court; and how this was the reason why men called him Lancelot du Lake.

Anon it was ordained by King Arthur, that in every year at Pentecost there should be held a festival of all the knights of the Round Table at Caerleon, or such other place as he should choose. And at those festivals should be told publicly the most famous adventures of any knight during the past year.

So, when Sir Lancelot saw Queen Guinevere rejoiced to hear his wanderings and adventures, he resolved to set forth yet again, and win more worship still, that he might more increase her favor. Then he bade his cousin Sir Lionel make ready, "for," said he, "we two will seek adventure." So they mounted their horses—armed at all points—and rode into a vast forest; and when they had passed through it, they came to a great plain, and the weather being very hot about noontide, Sir Lancelot greatly longed to sleep. Then Sir Lionel espied a great apple-tree standing by a hedge, and said, "Brother, yonder is a fair shadow where we may rest ourselves and horses."

"I am full glad of it," said Sir Lancelot, "for all these seven years I have not been so sleepy."

So they alighted there, and tied their horses up to sundry trees; and Sir Lionel waked and watched while Sir Lancelot fell asleep, and slept passing fast.

In the meanwhile came three knights, riding as fast flying as ever they could ride, and after them followed a single knight; but when Sir Lionel looked at him, he thought he had never seen so great and strong a man, or so well furnished and appareled. Anon he saw him overtake the last of those who fled, and smite him to the ground; then came he to the second, and smote him such a stroke that horse and man went to the earth; then rode he to the third, likewise, and struck him off his horse more than a spear's length. With that he lighted from his horse, and bound all three knights fast with the reins of their own bridles.

When Sir Lionel saw this he thought the time was come to prove himself against him, so quietly and cautiously, lest he should wake Sir Lancelot, he took his horse and mounted and rode after him. Presently overtaking him, he cried aloud to him to turn, which instantly he did, and smote Sir Lionel so hard that horse and man went down forthwith. Then took he up Sir Lionel, and threw him bound over his own horse's back; and so he served the three other knights, and rode them away to his own castle. There they were disarmed, stripped naked, and beaten with thorns, and afterwards thrust into a deep prison, where many more knights, also, made great moans and lamentations, saying, "Alas, alas! there is no man can help us but Sir Lancelot, for no other knight can match this tyrant Turquine, our conqueror."

But all this while, Sir Lancelot lay sleeping soundly under the apple-tree. And, as it chanced, there passed that way four queens, of high estate, riding upon four white mules, under four canopies of green silk borne on spears, to keep them from the sun. As they rode thus, they heard a great horse grimly neigh, and, turning them about, soon saw a sleeping knight that lay all armed under an apple-tree; and when they saw his face, they knew it was Sir Lancelot of the Lake.

Then they began to strive which of them should have the care of him. But Queen Morgan le Fay, King Arthur's half sister, the great sorceress, was one of them, and said, "We need not strive for him, I have enchanted him, so that for six hours more he shall not wake. Let us take him to my castle, and, when he wakes, himself shall choose which one of us he would rather serve." So Sir Lancelot was laid upon his shield and borne on horseback between two knights, to the castle, and there laid in a cold chamber, till the spell should pass.

Anon, they sent him a fair damsel, bearing his supper, who asked him, "What cheer?"

"I cannot tell, fair damsel," said he, "for I know not how I came into this castle, if it were not by enchantment."

"Sir," said she, "be of good heart, and to-morrow at dawn of day, ye shall know more."

And so she left him alone, and there he lay all night. In the morning early came the four queens to him, passing richly dressed; and said, "Sir knight, thou must understand that thou art our prisoner, and that we know thee well for King Ban's son, Sir Lancelot du Lake. And though we know full well there is one lady only in this world may have thy love, and she Queen Guinevere— King Arthur's wife—yet now are we resolved to have thee to serve one of us; choose, therefore, of us four which thou wilt serve. I am Queen Morgan le Fay, Queen of the land of Gore, and here also is the Queen of Northgales, and the Queen of Eastland, and the Queen of the Out Isles. Choose, then, at once, for else shalt thou abide here, in this prison, till thy death."

"It is a hard case," said Sir Lancelot, "that either I must die, or choose one of you for my mistress! Yet had I rather die in this prison than serve any living creature against my will. So take this for my answer. I will serve none of ye, for ye be false enchantresses. And as for my lady, Queen Guinevere, whom lightly ye have spoken of, were I at liberty I would prove it upon you or upon yours she is the truest lady living to her lord the king."

"Well," said the queen, "is this your answer, that ye refuse us all?"

"Yea, on my life," said Lancelot, "refused ye be of me."

So they departed from him in great wrath, and left him sorrowfully grieving in his dungeon.

At noon the damsel came to him and brought his dinner, and asked him as before, "What cheer?"

"Truly, fair damsel," said Sir Lancelot, "in all my life never so ill."

"Sir," replied she, "I grieve to see ye so, but if ye do as I advise, I can help ye out of this distress, and will do so if you promise me a boon."

"Fair damsel," said Sir Lancelot, "right willingly will I grant it thee, for sorely do I dread these four witch-queens, who have destroyed and slain many a good knight with their enchantments."

Then said the damsel, "Sir, wilt thou promise me to help my father on next Tuesday, for he hath a tournament with the King of Northgales, and last Tuesday lost the field through three knights of King Arthur's court, who came against him. And if next Tuesday thou wilt aid him, to-morrow, before daylight, by God's grace, I will deliver thee."

"Fair maiden," said Sir Lancelot, "tell me thy father's name and I will answer thee."

"My father is King Bagdemagus," said she.

"I know him well," replied Sir Lancelot, "for a noble king and a good knight; and by the faith of my body I will do him all the service I am able on that day."

"Gramercy to thee, Sir knight," said the damsel. "To-morrow, when thou art delivered from this place, ride ten miles hence unto an abbey of white monks, and there abide until I bring my father to thee."

"So be it," said Sir Lancelot, "as I am a true knight."

So she departed, and on the morrow, early, came again, and let him out of twelve gates, differently locked, and brought him to his armor; and when he was all armed, she brought him his horse also, and lightly he saddled him, and took a great spear in his hand, and mounted and rode forth, saying, as he went, "Fair damsel, I shall not fail thee, by the grace of God."

And all that day he rode in a great forest, and could find no highway, and spent the night in the wood; but the next morning found his road, and came to the abbey of white monks. And there he saw King Bagdemagus and his daughter waiting for him. So when they were together in a chamber, Sir Lancelot told the king how he had been betrayed by an enchantment, and how his brother Lionel was gone he knew not where, and how the damsel had delivered him from the castle of Queen Morgan le Fay. "Wherefore while I live," said he, "I shall do service to herself and all her kindred."

"Then am I sure of thy aid," said the king, "on Tuesday now next coming?"

"Yea, sir, I shall not fail thee," said Sir Lancelot; "but what knights were they who last week defeated thee, and took part with the King of Northgales?"

"Sir Mador de la Port, Sir Modred, and Sir Gahalatine," replied the king.

"Sir," said Sir Lancelot, "as I understand, the tournament shall take place but three miles from this abbey; send then to me here, three knights of thine, the best thou hast, and let them all have plain white shields, such as I also will; then will we four come suddenly into the midst between both parties, and fall upon thy enemies, and grieve them all we can, and none will know us who we are."

So, on the Tuesday, Sir Lancelot and the three knights lodged themselves in a small grove hard by the lists. Then came into the field the King of Northgales, with one hundred and sixty helms, and the three knights of King Arthur's court, who stood apart by themselves. And when King Bagdemagus had arrived, with eighty helms, both companies set all their spears in rest and came together with a mighty clash, wherein were slain twelve knights of King Bagdemagus, and six of the King of Northgales; and the party of King Bagdemagus was driven back.

With that, came Sir Lancelot, and thrust into the thickest of the press, and smote down with one spear five knights, and brake the backs of four, and cast down the King of Northgales, and brake his thigh by the fall. When the three knights of Arthur's court saw this, they rode at Sir Lancelot, and each after other attacked him; but he overthrew them all, and smote them nigh to death. Then, taking a new spear, he bore down to the ground sixteen more knights, and hurt them all so sorely, that they could carry arms no more that day. And when his spear at length was broken, he took yet another, and smote down twelve knights more, the most of whom he wounded mortally, till in the end the party of the King of Northgales would joust no more, and the victory was cried to King Bagdemagus.

Then Sir Lancelot rode forth with King Bagdemagus to his castle, and there he feasted with great cheer and welcome, and received many royal gifts. And on the morrow he took leave and went to find his brother Lionel.

Anon, by chance, he came to the same forest where the four queens had found him sleeping, and there he met a damsel riding on a white palfrey. When they had saluted each other, Sir Lancelot said, "Fair damsel, knowest thou where any adventures may be had in this country?"

"Sir knight," said she, "there are adventures great enough close by if thou darest prove them."

"Why should I not," said he, "since for that cause I came here?"

"Sir," said the damsel, "hard by this place there dwelleth a knight that cannot be defeated by any man, so great and perilously strong he is. His name is Sir Turquine, and in the prisons of his castle lie three score knights and four, mostly from King Arthur's court, whom he hath taken with his own hands. But promise me, ere thou undertakest their deliverance, to go and help me afterwards, and free me and many other ladies that are distressed by a false knight."

"Bring me but to this felon Turquine," quoth Sir Lancelot, "and I will afterwards fulfill all your wishes."

So the damsel went before, and brought him to a ford, and a tree whereon a great brass basin hung; and Sir Lancelot beat with his spear-end upon the basin, long and hard, until he beat the bottom of it out, but he saw nothing. Then he rode to and fro before the castle gates for wellnigh half an hour, and anon saw a great knight riding from the distance, driving a horse before him, across which hung an armed man bound. And when they came near, Sir Lancelot knew the prisoner for a knight of the Round Table. By that time, the great knight who drove the prisoner saw Sir Lancelot, and each of them began to settle his spear, and to make ready.

"Fair sir," then said Sir Lancelot, "put off that wounded knight, I pray thee, from his horse, and let him rest while thou and I shall prove our strength upon each other; for, as I am told, thou doest, and hast done, great shame and injury to knights of the Round Table. Wherefore, I warn thee now, defend thyself."

"If thou mayest be of the Round Table," answered Turquine, "I defy thee, and all thy fellows."

"That is saying overmuch," said Sir Lancelot.

Then, setting their lances in rest, they spurred their horses towards each other, as fast as they could go, and smote so fearfully upon each other's shields, that both their horses' backs brake under them. As soon as they could clear their saddles, they took their shields before them, and drew their swords, and came together eagerly, and fought with great and grievous strokes; and soon they both had many grim and fearful wounds, and bled in streams. Thus they fought two hours and more, thrusting and smiting at each other, wherever they could hit.

Anon, they both were breathless, and stood leaning on their swords.

"Now, comrade," said Sir Turquine, "let us wait awhile, and answer me what I shall ask thee."

"Say on," said Lancelot.

"Thou art," said Turquine, "the best man I ever met, and seemest like one that I hate above all other knights that live; but if thou be not he, I will make peace with thee, and for sake of thy great valor, will deliver all the three score prisoners and four who lie within my dungeons, and thou and I will be companions evermore. Tell me, then, thy name."

"Thou sayest well," replied Sir Lancelot; "but who is he thou hatest so above all others?"

"His name," said Turquine, "is Sir Lancelot of the Lake; and he slew my brother Sir Carados, at the dolorous tower; wherefore, if ever I shall meet with him, one of us two shall slay the other; and thereto I have sworn by a great oath. And to discover and destroy him I have slain a hundred knights, and crippled utterly as many more, and many have died in my prisons; and now, as I have told thee, I have many more therein, who all shall be delivered, if thou tell me thy name, and it be not Sir Lancelot."

"Well," said Lancelot, "I am that knight, son of King Ban of Benwick, and Knight of the Round Table; so now I defy thee to do thy best!"

"Aha!" said Turquine, with a shout, "is it then so at last! Thou art more welcome to my sword than ever knight or lady was to feast, for never shall we part till one of us be dead."

Then did they hurtle together like two wild bulls, slashing and lashing with their shields and swords, and sometimes falling both on to the ground. For two more hours they fought so, and at the last Sir Turquine grew very faint, and gave a little back, and bare his shield full low for weariness. When Sir Lancelot saw him thus, he leaped upon him fiercely as a lion, and took him by the crest of his helmet, and dragged him to his knees; and then he tore his helmet off and smote his neck asunder.

Then he arose, and went to the damsel who had brought him to Sir Turquine, and said, "I am ready, fair lady, to go with thee upon thy service, but I have no horse."

"Fair sir," said she, "take ye this horse of the wounded knight whom Turquine but just now was carrying to his prisons, and send that knight on to deliver all the prisoners."

So Sir Lancelot went to the knight and prayed him for the loan of his horse.

"Fair lord," said he, "ye are right welcome, for to-day ye have saved both me and my horse; and I see that ye are the best knight in all the world, for in my sight have ye slain the mightiest man and the best knight, except thyself, I ever saw."

"Sir," said Sir Lancelot, "I thank thee well; and now go into yonder castle, where thou shalt find many noble knights of the Round Table, for I have seen their shields hung on the trees around. On yonder tree alone there are Sir Key's, Sir Brandel's, Sir Marhaus', Sir Galind's, and Sir Aliduke's, and many more; and also my two kinsmen's shields, Sir Ector de Maris' and Sir Lionel's. And I pray you greet them all from me, Sir Lancelot of the Lake, and tell them that I bid them help themselves to any treasures they can find within the castle; and that I pray my brethren, Lionel and Ector, to go to King Arthur's court and stay there till I come. And by the high feast at Pentecost I must be there; but now I must ride forth with this damsel to fulfill my promise."

So, as they went, the damsel told him, "Sir, we are now near the place where the foul knight haunteth, who robbeth and distresseth all ladies and gentlewomen traveling past this way, against whom I have sought thy aid."

Then they arranged that she should ride on foremost, and Sir Lancelot should follow under cover of the trees by the roadside, and if he saw her come to any mishap, he should ride forth and deal with him that troubled her. And as the damsel rode on at a soft ambling pace, a knight and page burst forth from the roadside and forced the damsel from her horse, till she cried out for help.

Then came Sir Lancelot rushing through the wood as fast as he might fly, and all the branches of the trees crackled and waved around him. "O thou false knight and traitor to all knighthood!" shouted he, "who taught thee to distress fair ladies thus?"

The foul knight answered nothing, but drew out his sword and rode at Sir Lancelot, who threw his spear away and drew his own sword likewise, and struck him such a mighty blow as clave his head down to the throat. "Now hast thou the wages thou long hast earned!" said he; and so departed from the damsel.

Then for two days he rode in a great forest, and had but scanty food and lodging, and on the third day he rode over a long bridge, when suddenly there started up a passing foul churl, and smote his horse across the nose, so that he started and turned back, rearing with pain. "Why ridest thou over here without my leave?" said he.

"Why should I not?" said Sir Lancelot; "there is no other way to ride."

"Thou shalt not pass by here," cried out the churl, and dashed at him with a great club full of iron spikes, till Sir Lancelot was fain to draw his sword and smite him dead upon the earth.

At the end of the bridge was a fair village, and all the people came and cried, "Ah, sir! a worse deed for thyself thou never didst, for thou hast slain the chief porter of the castle yonder!" But he let them talk as they pleased, and rode straight forward to the castle.

There he alighted, and tied his horse to a ring in the wall; and going in, he saw a wide green court, and thought it seemed a noble place to fight in. And as he looked about, he saw many people watching him from doors and windows, making signs of warning, and saying, "Fair knight, thou art unhappy." In the next moment came upon him two great giants, well armed save their heads, and with two horrible clubs in their hands. Then he put his shield before him, and with it warded off one giant's stroke, and clove the other with his sword from the head downward to the chest. When the first giant saw that, he ran away mad with fear; but Sir Lancelot ran after him, and smote him through the shoulder, and shore him down his back, so that he fell dead.

Then he walked onward to the castle hall, and saw a band of sixty ladies and young damsels coming forth, who knelt to him, and thanked him for their freedom. "For, sir," said they, "the most of us have been prisoners here these seven years; and have been kept at all manner of work to earn our meat, though we be all great gentlewomen born. Blessed be the time that thou wast born, for never did a knight a deed of greater worship than thou hast this day, and thereto will we all bear witness in all times and places! Tell us, therefore, noble knight, thy name and court, that we may tell them to our friends!" And when they heard it, they all cried aloud, "Well may it be so, for we knew that no knight save thou shouldst ever overcome those giants; and many a long day have we sighed for thee; for the giants feared no other name among all knights but thine."

Then he told them to take the treasures of the castle as a reward for their grievances; and to return to their homes, and so rode away into many strange and wild countries. And at last, after many days, by chance he came, near the night time, to a fair mansion, wherein he found an old gentlewoman, who gave him and his horse good cheer. And when bed time was come, his host brought him to a chamber over a gate, and there he unarmed, and went to bed and fell asleep.

But soon thereafter came one riding in great haste, and knocking vehemently at the gate below, which when Sir Lancelot heard, he rose and looked out of the window, and, by the moonlight, saw three knights come riding fiercely after one man, and lashing on him all at once with their swords, while the one knight nobly fought them all.

Then Sir Lancelot quickly armed himself, and getting through the window, let himself down by a sheet into the midst of them, crying out, "Turn ye on me, ye cowards, and leave fighting with that knight!" Then they all left Sir Key, for the first knight was he, and began to fall upon Sir Lancelot furiously. And when Sir Key would have come forward to assist him, Sir Lancelot refused, and cried, "Leave me alone to deal with them." And presently, with six great strokes, he felled them all.

Then they cried out, "Sir knight, we yield us unto thee, as to a man of might!"

"I will not take your yielding!" said he; "yield ye to Sir Key, the seneschal, or I will have your lives."

"Fair knight," said they, "excuse us in that thing, for we have chased Sir Key thus far, and should have overcome him but for thee."

"Well," said Sir Lancelot, "do as ye will, for ye may live or die; but, if ye live, ye shall be holden to Sir Key."

Then they yielded to him; and Sir Lancelot commanded them

to go unto King Arthur's court at the next Pentecost, and say, Sir Key had sent them prisoners to Queen Guinevere. And this they sware to do upon their swords.

Then Sir Lancelot knocked at the gate with his sword-hilt till his hostess came and let him in again, and Sir Key also. And when the light came, Sir Key knew Sir Lancelot, and knelt and thanked him for his courtesy, and gentleness, and kindness. "Sir," said he, "I have done no more than what I ought to do, and ye are welcome; therefore let us now take rest."

So when Sir Key had supped, they went to sleep, and Sir Lancelot and he slept in the same bed. On the morrow, Sir Lancelot rose early, and took Sir Key's shield and armor and set forth. When Sir Key arose, he found Sir Lancelot's armor by his bedside, and his own arms gone. "Now, by my faith," thought he, "I know that he will grieve some knights of our king's court; for those who meet him will be bold to joust with him, mistaking him for me, while I, dressed in his shield and armor, shall surely ride in peace."

Then Sir Lancelot, dressed in Sir Key's apparel, rode long in a great forest, and came at last to a low country, full of rivers and fair meadows, and saw a bridge before him, whereon were three silk tents of divers colors, and to each tent was hung a white shield, and by each shield stood a knight. So Sir Lancelot went by without speaking a word. And when he had passed, the three knights said it was the proud Sir Key, "who thinketh no knight equal to himself, although the contrary is full often proved upon him."

"By my faith!" said one of them, named Gaunter, "I will ride after and attack him for all his pride, and ye shall watch my speed."

Then, taking shield and spear, he mounted and rode after Sir Lancelot, and cried, "Abide, proud knight, and turn, for thou shalt not pass free!"

So Sir Lancelot turned, and each one put his spear in rest and came with all his might against the other. And Sir Gaunter's spear brake short, but Sir Lancelot smote him down, both horse and man.

When the other knights saw this, they said, "Yonder is not Sir Key, but a bigger man."

"I dare wager my head," said Sir Gilmere, "yonder knight hath slain Sir Key, and taken his horse and harness."

"Be it so, or not," said Sir Reynold, the third brother; "let us now go to our brother Gaunter's rescue; we shall have enough to do to match that knight, for, by his stature, I believe it is Sir Lancelot or Sir Tristram."

Anon, they took their horses and galloped after Sir Lancelot; and Sir Gilmere first assailed him, but was smitten down forthwith, and lay stunned on the earth. Then said Sir Reynold, "Sir knight, thou art a strong man, and, I believe, hast slain my two brothers, wherefore my heart is sore against thee; yet, if I might with honor, I would avoid thee. Nevertheless, that cannot be, so keep thyself." And so they hurtled together with all their might, and each man shivered his spear to pieces; and then they drew their swords and lashed out eagerly.

And as they fought, Sir Gaunter and Sir Gilmere presently arose and mounted once again, and came down at full tilt upon Sir Lancelot. But, when he saw them coming, he put forth all his strength, and struck Sir Reynold off his horse. Then, with two other strokes, he served the others likewise.

Anon, Sir Reynold crept along the ground, with his head all bloody, and came towards Sir Lancelot. "It is enough," said Lancelot, "I was not far from thee when thou wast made a knight, Sir Reynold, and know thee for a good and valiant man, and was full loth to slay thee."

"Gramercy for thy gentleness!" said Sir Reynold. "I and my brethren will straightway yield to thee when we know thy name, for well we know that thou art not Sir Key."

"As for that," said Sir Lancelot, "be it as it may, but ye shall yield to Queen Guinevere at the next Feast of Pentecost as prisoners, and say that Sir Key sent ye."

Then they swore to him it should be done as he commanded. And so Sir Lancelot passed on, and the three brethren helped each other's wounds as best they might.

Then rode Sir Lancelot forward into a deep forest, and came upon four knights of King Arthur's court, under an oak tree—

Sir Sagramour, Sir Ector, Sir Gawain, and Sir Ewaine. And when they spied him, they thought he was Sir Key. "Now by my faith," said Sir Sagramour, "I will prove Sir Key's might!" and taking his spear he rode towards Sir Lancelot.

But Sir Lancelot was aware of him, and, setting his spear in rest, smote him so sorely, that horse and man fell to the earth.

"Lo!" cried Sir Ector, "I see by the buffet that knight hath given our fellow he is stronger than Sir Key. Now will I try what I can do against him!" So Sir Ector took his spear, and galloped at Sir Lancelot; and Sir Lancelot met him as he came, and smote him through shield and shoulder, so that he fell, but his own spear was not broken.

"By my faith," cried Sir Ewaine, "yonder is a strong knight, and must have slain Sir Key, and taken his armor! By his strength, I see it will be hard to match him." So saying he rode towards Sir Lancelot, who met him halfway and struck him so fiercely, that at one blow he overthrew him also.

"Now," said Sir Gawain, "will I encounter him." So he took a good spear in his hand, and guarded himself with his shield. And he and Sir Lancelot rode against each other, with their horses at full speed, and furiously smote each other on the middle of their shields; but Sir Gawain's spear broke short asunder, and Sir Lancelot charged so mightily upon him, that his horse and he both fell, and rolled upon the ground.

"Ah," said Sir Lancelot, smiling, as he rode away from the four knights, "heaven give joy to him who made this spear, for never held I better in my hand."

But the four knights said to each other, "Truly one spear hath felled us all."

"I dare lay my life," said Sir Gawain, "it is Sir Lancelot. I know him by his riding."

So they all departed for the court.

And as Sir Lancelot rode still in the forest, he saw a black bloodhound, running with its head towards the ground, as if it tracked a deer. And following after it, he came to a great pool of blood. But the hound, ever and anon looking behind, ran through a great marsh, and over a bridge, towards an old manor house. So Sir Lancelot followed, and went into the hall, and saw a dead knight lying there, whose wounds the hound licked. And a lady stood behind him, weeping and wringing her hands, who cried, "O knight! too great is the sorrow which thou hast brought me!"

"Why say ye so?" replied Sir Lancelot; "for I never harmed this knight, and am full sorely grieved to see thy sorrow."

"Nay, sir," said the lady, "I see it is not thou hast slain my husband, for he that truly did that deed is deeply wounded, and shall never more recover."

"What is thy husband's name?" said Sir Lancelot.

"His name," she answered, "was Sir Gilbert—one of the best knights in all the world; but I know not his name who hath slain him."

"God send thee comfort," said Sir Lancelot, and departed again into the forest.

And as he rode, he met with a damsel who knew him, who cried out, "Well found, my lord! I pray ye of your knighthood help my brother, who is sore wounded and ceases not to bleed, for he fought this day with Sir Gilbert, and slew him, but was himself well nigh slain. And there is a sorceress, who dwelleth in a castle hard by, and she this day hath told me that my brother's wound shall never be made whole until I find a knight to go into the Chapel Perilous, and bring from thence a sword and the bloody cloth in which the wounded knight was wrapped."

"This is a marvelous thing!" said Sir Lancelot; "but what is your brother's name?"

"His name, sir," she replied, "is Sir Meliot de Logres."

"He is a Fellow of the Round Table," said Sir Lancelot, "and truly will I do my best to help him."

"Then, sir," said she, "follow this way, and it will bring ye to the Chapel Perilous. I will abide here till God send ye hither again; for if ye speed not, there is no living knight who may achieve that adventure."

So Sir Lancelot departed, and when he came to the Chapel Perilous he alighted, and tied his horse to the gate. And as soon as he was within the churchyard, he saw on the front of the chapel many shields of knights whom he had known, turned upside down. Then saw he in the pathway thirty mighty knights, taller than any men whom he had ever seen, all armed in black armor, with their swords drawn; and they gnashed their teeth upon him as he came. But he put his shield before him, and took his sword in hand, ready to do battle with them. And when he would have cut his way through them, they scattered on every side and let him pass. Then he went into the chapel, and saw therein no light but of a dim lamp burning. Then he was aware of a corpse in the midst of the chapel, covered with a silken cloth, and so stooped down and cut off a piece of the cloth, whereat the earth beneath him trembled. Then saw he a sword lying by the dead knight, and taking it in his hand, he hied him from the chapel. As soon as he was in the churchyard again, all the thirty knights cried out to him with fierce voices, "Sir Lancelot! lay that sword from thee, or thou diest!"

"Whether I live or die," said he, "ye shall fight for it ere ye take it from me."

With that they let him pass.

And further on, beyond the chapel, he met a fair damsel, who said, "Sir Lancelot, leave that sword behind thee, or thou diest."

"I will not leave it," said Sir Lancelot, "for any asking."

"Then, gentle knight," said the damsel, "I pray thee kiss me once."

"Nay," said Sir Lancelot, "that God forbid!"

"Alas!" cried she, "I have lost all my labor! but hadst thou kissed me, thy life's days had been all done!"

"Heaven save me from thy subtle crafts!" said Sir Lancelot; and therewith took his horse and galloped forth.

And when he was departed, the damsel sorrowed greatly, and died in fifteen days. Her name was Ellawes, the sorceress.

Then came Sir Lancelot to Sir Meliot's sister, who, when she saw him, clapped her hands and wept for joy, and took him to the castle hard by, where Sir Meliot was. And when Sir Lancelot saw Sir Meliot, he knew him, though he was pale as ashes for loss of blood. And Sir Meliot, when he saw Sir Lancelot, kneeled to him and cried aloud, "O lord, Sir Lancelot! help me!"

And thereupon, Sir Lancelot went to him and touched his wounds with the sword, and wiped them with the piece of bloody cloth. And immediately he was as whole as though he had been never wounded. Then was there great joy between him and Sir Meliot; and his sister made Sir Lancelot good cheer. So on the morrow, he took his leave, that he might go to King Arthur's court, "for," said he, "it draweth nigh the Feast of Pentecost, and there, by God's grace, shall ye then find me."

And riding through many strange countries, over marshes and valleys, he came at length before a castle. As he passed by he heard two little bells ringing, and looking up, he saw a falcon flying overhead, with bells tied to her feet, and long strings dangling from them. And as the falcon flew past an elm-tree, the strings caught in the boughs, so that she could fly no further.

In the meanwhile, came a lady from the castle, and cried, "Oh, Sir Lancelot! as thou art the flower of all knights in the world, help me to get my hawk, for she hath slipped away from me, and if she be lost, my lord my husband is so hasty, he will surely slay me!"

"What is thy lord's name?" said Sir Lancelot.

"His name," said she, "is Sir Phelot, a knight of the King of Northgales."

"Fair lady," said Sir Lancelot, "since you know my name, and require me, on my knighthood, to help you, I will do what I can to get your hawk."

And thereupon alighting, he tied his horse to the same tree, and prayed the lady to unarm him. So when he was unarmed, he climbed up and reached the falcon, and threw it to the lady.

Then suddenly came down, out of the wood, her husband, Sir Phelot, all armed, with a drawn sword in his hand, and said, "Oh, Sir Lancelot! now have I found thee as I would have thee!" and stood at the trunk of the tree to slay him.

"Ah, lady!" cried Sir Lancelot, "why have ye betrayed me?"

"She hath done as I commanded her," said Sir Phelot, "and thine hour is come that thou must die."

"It were shame," said Lancelot, "for an armed to slay an unarmed man."

"Thou hast no other favor from me," said Sir Phelot.

"Alas!" cried Sir Lancelot, "that ever any knight should die weaponless!" And looking overhead, he saw a great bough without leaves, and wrenched it off the tree, and suddenly leaped down. Then Sir Phelot struck at him eagerly, thinking to have slain him, but Sir Lancelot put aside the stroke with the bough, and therewith smote him on the side of the head, till he fell swooning to the ground. And tearing his sword from out his hands, he shore his neck through from the body. Then did the lady shriek dismally, and swooned as though she would die. But Sir Lancelot put on his armor, and with haste took his horse and departed thence, thanking God he had escaped that peril.

And as he rode through a valley, among many wild ways, he saw a knight, with a drawn sword, chasing a lady to slay her. And seeing Sir Lancelot, she cried and prayed to him to come and rescue her.

At that he went up, saying, "Fie on thee, knight! why wilt thou slay this lady? Thou doest shame to thyself and all knights."

"What hast thou to do between me and my wife?" replied the knight. "I will slay her in spite of thee."

"Thou shalt not harm her," said Lancelot, "till we have first fought together."

"Sir," answered the knight, "thou doest ill, for this lady hath betrayed me."

"He speaketh falsely," said the lady, "for he is jealous of me without cause, as I shall answer before Heaven; but as thou art named the most worshipful knight in the world, I pray thee of thy true knighthood to save me, for he is without mercy."

"Be of good cheer," said Sir Lancelot; "it shall not lie within his power to harm thee."

"Sir," said the knight, "I will be ruled as ye will have me."

So Sir Lancelot rode between the knight and the lady. And when they had ridden awhile, the knight cried out suddenly to Sir Lancelot to turn and see what men they were who came riding after them; and while Sir Lancelot, thinking not of treason, turned to look, the knight, with one great stroke, smote off the lady's head.

Then was Sir Lancelot passing wroth, and cried, "Thou traitor! Thou hast shamed me forever!" and, alighting from his horse, he drew his sword to have slain him instantly; but the knight fell on the ground and clasped Sir Lancelot's knees, and cried out for mercy. "Thou shameful knight," answered Lancelot, "thou mayest have no mercy, for thou showedst none, therefore arise and fight with me."

"Nay," said the knight, "I will not rise till thou dost grant me mercy."

"Now will I deal fairly by thee," said Sir Lancelot; "I will unarm me to my shirt, and have my sword only in my hand, and if thou canst slay me thou shalt be quit forever."

"That will I never do," said the knight.

"Then," answered Sir Lancelot, "take this lady and the head, and bear it with thee, and swear to me upon thy sword never to rest until thou comest to Queen Guinevere."

"That will I do," said he.

"Now," said Sir Lancelot, "tell me thy name."

"It is Pedivere," answered the knight.

"In a shameful hour wert thou born," said Sir Lancelot.

So Sir Pedivere departed, bearing with him the dead lady and her head. And when he came to Winchester, where the Queen was with King Arthur, he told them all the truth; and afterwards did great and heavy penance many years, and became an holy hermit.

So, two days before the Feast of Pentecost, Sir Lancelot returned to the court, and King Arthur was full glad of his coming. And when Sir Gawain, Sir Ewaine, Sir Sagramour, and Sir Ector, saw him in Sir Key's armor, they knew well it was he who had smitten them all down with one spear. Anon, came all the knights Sir Turquine had taken prisoners, and gave worship and honor to Sir Lancelot. Then Sir Key told the King how Sir Lancelot had rescued him when he was in near danger of his death; "and," said Sir Key, "he made the knights yield, not to himself, but me. And by Heaven! because Sir Lancelot took my armor and left me his, I rode in peace, and no man would have aught to do with me." Then came the knights who fought with Sir Lancelot at the long bridge and yielded themselves also to Sir Key, but he said nay, he had not fought with them. "It is Sir Lancelot," said he, "that overcame ye." Next came Sir Meliot de Logres, and told King Arthur how Sir Lancelot had saved him from death.

And so all Sir Lancelot's deeds and great adventures were made known; how the four sorceress-queens had him in prison; how he was delivered by the daughter of King Bagdemagus, and what deeds of arms he did at the tournament between the King of North Wales and King Bagdemagus. And so, at that festival, Sir Lancelot had the greatest name of any knight in all the world, and by high and low was he the most honored of all men.

XI. THE ADVENTURES OF
SIR BEAUMAINS OR SIR GARETH

Again King Arthur held the Feast of Pentecost, with all the Table Round, and after his custom sat in the banquet hall, before beginning meat, waiting for some adventure. Then came there to the king a squire and said, "Lord, now may ye go to meat, for here a damsel cometh with some strange adventure." So the king was glad, and sat down to meat.

Anon the damsel came in and saluted him, praying him for succor. "What wilt thou?" said the king. "Lord," answered she, "my mistress is a lady of great renown, but is at this time besieged by a tyrant, who will not suffer her to go out of her castle; and because here in thy court the knights are called the noblest in the world, I come to pray thee for thy succor." "Where dwelleth your lady?" answered the king. "What is her name, and who is he that hath besieged her?" "For her name," replied the damsel, "as yet I may not tell it; but she is a lady of worship and great lands. The tyrant that besiegeth her and wasteth her lands is called the Red Knight of the Redlands." "I know him not," said Arthur. "But I know him, lord," said Sir Gawain, "and he is one of the most perilous knights in all the world. Men say he hath the strength of seven; and from him I myself once hardly escaped with life." "Fair damsel," said the king, "there be here many knights that would gladly do their uttermost to rescue your lady, but unless ye tell me her name, and where she dwelleth, none of my knights shall go with you by my leave."

Now, there was a stripling at the court called Beaumains, who served in the king's kitchen, a fair youth and of great stature. Twelve months before this time he had come to the king as he sat at meat, at Whitsuntide, and prayed three gifts of him. And being asked what gifts, he answered, "As for the first gift I will ask it now, but the other two gifts I will ask on this day twelve months, wheresoever ye hold your high feast." Then said King Arthur, "What is thy first request?" "This, lord," said he, "that thou wilt give me meat and drink enough for twelve months from this time, and then will I ask my other two gifts." And the king seeing that he was a goodly youth, and deeming that he was come of honorable blood, had granted his desire, and given him into the charge of Sir Key, the steward. But Sir Key scorned and mocked the youth, calling Beaumains, because his hands were large and fair, and putting him into the kitchen, where he had served for twelve months as a scullion, and, in spite of all his churlish treatment, had faithfully obeyed Sir Key. But Sir Lancelot and Sir Gawain were angered when they saw Sir Key so churlish to a youth that had so worshipful a bearing, and ofttimes had they given him gold and clothing.

And now at this time came young Beaumains to the king, while the damsel was there, and said, "Lord, now I thank thee well and heartily that I have been twelve months kept in thy kitchen, and have had full sustenance. Now will I ask my two remaining gifts." "Ask," said King Arthur, "on my good faith." "These, lord," said he, "shall be my two gifts—the one, that thou wilt grant me this adventure of the damsel, for to me of right it belongeth; and the other, that thou wilt bid Sir Lancelot make me a knight, for of him only will I have that honor; and I pray that he may ride after me and make me a knight when I require him." "Be it as thou wilt," replied the king. But thereupon the damsel was full wroth, and said, "Shall I have a kitchen page for this adventure?" and so she took horse and departed.

Then came one to Beaumains, and told him that a dwarf with a horse and armor were waiting for him. And all men marveled whence these things came. But when he was on horseback and armed, scarce any one at the court was a goodlier man than he. And coming into the hall, he took his leave of the king and Sir Gawain, and prayed Sir Lancelot to follow him. So he rode after the damsel, and many of the court went out to see him, so richly arrayed and horsed; yet he had neither shield nor spear. Then Sir

Key cried, "I also will ride after the kitchen boy, and see whether he will obey me now." And taking his horse, he rode after him, and said, "Know ye not me, Beaumains?" "Yea," said he, "I know thee for an ungentle knight, therefore beware of me." Then Sir Key put his spear in rest and ran at him, but Beaumains rushed upon him with his sword in his hand, and therewith, putting aside the spear, struck Sir Key so sorely in the side, that he fell down, as if dead. Then he alighted, and took his shield and spear, and bade his dwarf ride upon Sir Key's horse.

By this time, Sir Lancelot had come up, and Beaumains offering to tilt with him, they both made ready. And their horses came together so fiercely that both fell to the earth, full sorely bruised. Then they arose, and Beaumains, putting up his shield before him, offered to fight Sir Lancelot, on foot. So they rushed upon each other, striking, and thrusting, and parrying, for the space of an hour. And Lancelot marveled at the strength of Beaumains, for he fought more like a giant than a man, and his fighting was passing fierce and terrible. So, at the last, he said, "Fight not so sorely, Beaumains; our quarrel is not such that we may not now cease." "True," answered Beaumains; "yet it doth me good to feel thy might, though I have not yet proved my uttermost." "By my faith," said Lancelot, "I had as much as I could do to save myself from you unshamed, therefore be in no doubt of any earthly knight." "May I, then, stand as a proved knight?" said Beaumains. "For that will I be thy warrant," answered Lancelot. "Then, I pray thee," said he, "give me the order of knighthood." "First, then, must thou tell me of thy name and kindred," said Sir Lancelot. "If thou wilt tell them to no other, I will tell thee," answered he. "My name is Gareth of Orkney, and I am own brother to Sir Gawain." "Ah!" said Sir Lancelot, "at that am I full glad; for, truly, I deemed thee to be of gentle blood." So then he knighted Beaumains, and, after that, they parted company, and Sir Lancelot, returning to the court, took up Sir Key on his shield. And hardly did Sir Key escape with his life, from the wound Beaumains had given him; but all men blamed him for his ungentle treatment of so brave a knight.

Then Sir Beaumains rode forward, and soon overtook the damsel; but she said to him, in scorn, "Return again, base kitchen page! What art thou, but a washer-up of dishes!" "Damsel," said he, "say to me what thou wilt, I will not leave thee; for I have undertaken to King Arthur to relieve thy adventure, and I will finish it to the end, or die." "Thou finish my adventure!" said she—"anon, thou shalt meet one, whose face thou wilt not even dare to look at." "I shall attempt it," answered he. So, as they rode thus, into a wood, there met them a man, fleeing, as for his life. "Whither fleest thou?" said Sir Beaumains. "O lord!" he answered, "help me; for, in a valley hard by, there are six thieves, who have taken my lord, and bound him, and I fear will slay him." "Bring me thither," said Sir Beaumains. So they rode to the place, and Sir Beaumains rushed after the thieves, and smote one, at the first stroke, so that he died; and then, with two other blows, slew a second and third. Then fled the other three, and Sir Beaumains rode after them, and overtook and slew them all. Then he returned and unbound the knight. And the knight thanked him, and prayed him to ride to his castle, where he would reward him. "Sir," answered Sir Beaumains, "I will have no reward of thee, for but this day was I made knight by the most noble Sir Lancelot; and besides, I must go with this damsel." Then the knight begged the damsel to rest that night at his castle. So they all rode thither, and ever the damsel scoffed at Sir Beaumains as a kitchen boy, and laughed at him before the knight their host, so that he set his meat before him at a lower table, as though he were not of their company.

And on the morrow, the damsel and Sir Beaumains took their leave of the knight, and thanking him departed. Then they rode on their way till they came to a great forest, through which flowed a river, and there was but one passage over it, whereat stood two knights armed to hinder the way. "Wilt thou match those two knights," said the damsel to Sir Beaumains, "or return again?" "I would not return," said he, "though they were six." Therewith he galloped into the water, and swam his horse into the middle of the stream. And there, in the river, one of the knights met him, and they brake their spears together, and then drew their swords, and smote fiercely at each other. And at the last, Sir Beaumains struck the other mightily upon the helm, so that he fell down stunned into the water, and was drowned. Then Sir Beaumains spurred his horse on to the land, where instantly the other knight fell on him. And they also brake their spears upon each other, and then drew their swords, and fought savagely and long together. And after many blows, Sir Beaumains clove through the knight's skull down to the shoulders. Then rode Sir Beaumains to the damsel, but ever she still scoffed at him, and said, "Alas! that a kitchen page should chance to slay two such brave knights! Thou deemest now that thou hast done a mighty deed, but it is not so; for the first knight's horse stumbled, and thus was he drowned—not by thy strength; and as for the second knight, thou wentest by chance behind him, and didst kill him shamefully." "Damsel," said Sir Beaumains, "say what ye list, I care not so I may win your lady; and wouldst thou give me but fair language, all my care were past; for whatsoever knights I meet, I fear them not." "Thou shalt see knights that shall abate thy boast, base kitchen knave," replied she; "yet say I this for thine advantage, for if thou followest me thou wilt be surely slain, since I see all thou doest is but by chance, and not by thy own prowess." "Well, damsel," said he, "say what ye will, wherever ye go I will follow."

So they rode on until the eventide, and still the damsel evermore kept chiding Sir Beaumains. Then came they to a black space of land, whereon was a black hawthorn tree, and on the tree there hung a black banner, and on the other side was a black shield and spear, and by them a great black horse, covered with silk; and hard by sat a knight armed in black armor, whose name was the Knight of the Blacklands. When the damsel saw him, she cried out to Beaumains, "Flee down the valley, for thy horse is not saddled!" "Wilt thou forever deem me coward?" answered he. With that came the Black Knight to the damsel, and said, "Fair damsel, hast thou brought this knight from Arthur's court to be thy champion?" "Not so, fair knight," said she; "he is but a kitchen knave." "Then wherefore cometh he in such array?" said he; "it is a shame that he should bear thee company." "I cannot be delivered from him," answered she: "for in spite of me he rideth with me; and would to Heaven you would put him from me, or now slay him, for he hath slain two knights at the river passage yonder, and done many marvelous deeds through pure mischance." "I marvel," said the Black Knight, "that any man of worship will fight with him." "They know him not," said the damsel, "and think, because he rideth with me, that he is well born." "Truly, he hath a goodly person, and is likely to be a strong man," replied the knight; "but since he is no man of worship, he shall leave his horse and armor with me, for it were a shame for me to do him more harm."

When Sir Beaumains heard him speak thus, he said, "Horse or armor gettest thou none of me, Sir knight, save thou winnest them with thy hands; therefore defend thyself, and let me see what thou canst do." "How sayest thou?" answered the Black Knight. "Now quit this lady also, for it beseemeth not a kitchen knave like thee to ride with such a lady." "I am of higher lineage than thou," said Sir Beaumains, "and will straightway prove it on thy body." Then furiously they drove their horses at each other, and came together as it had been thunder. But the Black Knight's spear brake short, and Sir Beaumains thrust him through the side, and his spear breaking at the head, left its point sticking fast in the Black Knight's body. Yet did the Black Knight draw his sword, and smite at Sir Beaumains with many fierce and bitter blows; but after they had fought an hour and more, he fell down from his horse in a swoon, and forthwith died. Then Sir Beaumains lighted down and armed himself in the Black Knight's armor, and rode on after the damsel. But notwithstanding all his valor, still she scoffed at him, and said, "Away! for thou savorest ever of the kitchen. Alas! that such a knave should by mishap destroy so good a knight; yet once again I counsel thee to flee, for hard by is a knight who shall repay thee!" "It may chance that I am beaten or slain," answered Sir Beaumains, "but I warn thee, fair damsel, that I will not flee away, nor leave thy company, or my quest, for all that ye can say."

Anon, as they rode, they saw a knight come swiftly towards them, dressed all in green, who, calling to the damsel said, "Is that my brother, the Black Knight, that ye have brought with you?" "Nay, and alas!" said she, "this kitchen knave hath slain thy brother through mischance." "Alas!" said the Green Knight, "that such a noble knight as he was should be slain by a knave's hand. Traitor!" cried he to Sir Beaumains, "thou shalt die for this! Sir Pereard was my brother, and a full noble knight." "I defy thee," said Sir Beaumains, "for I slew him knightly and not shamefully." Then the Green Knight rode to a thorn whereon hung a green horn, and, when he blew three notes, there came three damsels forth, who quickly armed him, and brought him a great horse and a green shield and spear. Then did they run at one another with their fullest might, and break their spears asunder; and, drawing their swords, they closed in fight, and sorely smote and wounded each other with many grievous blows.

At last, Sir Beaumains' horse jostled against the Green Knight's horse, and overthrew him. Then both alighted, and, hurtling together like mad lions, fought a great while on foot. But the damsel cheered the Green Knight, and said, "My lord, why wilt thou let a kitchen knave so long stand up against thee?" Hearing these words, he was ashamed, and gave Sir Beaumains such a mighty stroke as clave his shield asunder. When Sir Beaumains heard the damsel's words, and felt that blow, he waxed passing wroth, and gave the Green Knight such a buffet on the helm that he fell on his knees, and with another blow Sir Beaumains threw him on the ground. Then the Green Knight yielded, and prayed him to spare his life. "All thy prayers are vain," said he, "unless this damsel who came with me pray for thee." "That will I never do, base kitchen knave," said she. "Then shall he die," said Beaumains. "Alas! fair lady," said the Green Knight, "suffer me not to die for a word! O, Sir knight," cried he to Beaumains, "give me my life, and I will ever do thee homage; and thirty knights, who owe me service, shall give allegiance to thee." "All availeth not," answered Sir Beaumains, "unless the damsel ask me for thy life"; and thereupon he made as though he would have slain him. Then cried the damsel, "Slay him not; for if thou do thou shalt repent it." "Damsel," said Sir Beaumains, "at thy command, he shall obtain his life. Arise, Sir knight of the green armor, I release thee!" Then the Green Knight knelt at his feet, and did him homage with his words. "Lodge with me this night," said he, "and to-morrow will I guide ye through the forest." So, taking their horses, they rode to his castle, which was hard by.

Yet still did the damsel rebuke and scoff at Sir Beaumains, and would not suffer him to sit at her table. "I marvel," said the Green Knight to her, "that ye thus chide so noble a knight, for truly I know none to match him; and be sure, that whatsoever he appeareth now, he will prove, at the end, of noble blood and royal lineage." But of all this would the damsel take no heed, and ceased not to mock at Sir Beaumains. On the morrow, they arose and heard mass; and when they had broken their fast, took their horses and rode on their way, the Green Knight conveying them through the forest. Then, when he had led them for a while, he said to Sir Beaumains, "My lord, my thirty knights and I shall always be at thy command whensoever thou shalt send for us." "It is well said," replied he; "and when I call upon you, you shall yield yourself and all your knights unto King Arthur." "That will we gladly do," said the Green Knight, and so departed.

And the damsel rode on before Sir Beaumains, and said to him, "Why dost thou follow me, thou kitchen boy? I counsel thee to throw aside thy spear and shield, and flee betimes, for wert thou as mighty as Sir Lancelot or Sir Tristram, thou shouldest not pass a valley near this place, called the Pass Perilous." "Damsel," answered he, "let him that feareth flee; as for me, it were indeed a shameful thing to turn after so long a journey." As he spake, they came upon a tower as white as snow, with mighty battlements, and double moats round it, and over the tower-gate hung fifty shields of divers colors. Before the tower walls, they saw a fair meadow, wherein were many knights and squires in pavilions, for on the morrow there was a tournament at that castle.

Then the lord of the castle, seeing a knight armed at all points, with a damsel and a page, riding towards the tower, came forth to meet them; and his horse and harness, with his shield and spear, were all of a red color. When he came near Sir Beaumains, and saw his armor all of black, he thought him his own brother, the Black Knight, and so cried aloud, "Brother! what do ye here, within these borders?" "Nay!" said the damsel, "it is not thy brother, but a kitchen knave of Arthur's court, who hath slain thy brother, and overcome thy other brother also, the Green Knight." "Now do I defy thee!" cried the Red Knight to Sir Beaumains, and put his spear in rest and spurred his horse. Then both knights turned back a little space, and ran together with all their might, till their horses fell to the earth. Then, with their swords, they fought fiercely for the space of three hours. And at last, Sir Beaumains overcame his foe, and smote him to the ground. Then the Red Knight prayed his mercy, and said, "Slay me not, noble knight, and I will yield to thee with sixty knights that do my bidding." "All avails not," answered Sir Beaumains, "save this damsel pray me to release thee." Then did he lift his sword to slay him; but the damsel cried aloud, "Slay him not, Beaumains, for he is a noble knight." Then Sir Beaumains bade him rise up and thank the damsel, which straightway he did, and afterwards invited them to his castle, and made them goodly cheer.

But notwithstanding all Sir Beaumains' mighty deeds, the damsel ceased not to revile and chide him, at which the Red Knight marveled much; and caused his sixty knights to watch Sir Beaumains, that no villainy might happen to him. And on the morrow, they heard mass and broke their fast, and the Red Knight came before Sir Beaumains, with his sixty knights, and proffered him homage and fealty. "I thank thee," answered he; "and when I call upon thee thou shalt come before my lord King Arthur at his court, and yield yourselves to him." "That will we surely do," said the Red Knight. So Sir Beaumains and the damsel departed.

And as she constantly reviled him and tormented him, he said to her, "Damsel, ye are discourteous thus always to rebuke me, for I have done you service; and for all your threats of knights that shall destroy me, all they who come lie in the dust before me. Now, therefore, I pray you rebuke me no more till you see me beaten or a recreant, and then bid me go from you." "There shall soon meet thee a knight who shall repay thee all thy deeds, thou boaster," answered she, "for, save King Arthur, he is the man of most worship in the world." "It will be the greater honor to encounter him," said Sir Beaumains.

Soon after, they saw before them a city passing fair, and between them and the city was a meadow newly mown, wherein were many goodly tents. "Seest thou yonder blue pavilion?" said the damsel to Sir Beaumains; "it is Sir Perseant's, the lord of that great city, whose custom is, in all fair weather, to lie in this meadow, and joust with his knights."

And as she spake, Sir Perseant, who had espied them coming, sent a messenger to meet Sir Beaumains, and to ask him if he came in war or peace. "Say to thy lord," he answered, "that I care not whether of the twain it be." So when the messenger gave this reply, Sir Perseant came out to fight with Sir Beaumains. And making ready, they rode their steeds against each other; and when their spears were shivered asunder, they fought with their swords. And for more than two hours did they hack and hew at each other, till their shields and hauberks were all dented with many blows, and they themselves were sorely wounded. And at the last, Sir Beaumains smote Sir Perseant on the helm, so that he fell groveling on the earth. And when he unlaced his helm to slay him, the damsel prayed for his life. "That will I grant gladly," answered Sir Beaumains, "for it were pity such a noble knight should die." "Gramercy!" said Sir Perseant, "for now I certainly know that it was thou who slewest my brother, the Black Knight, Sir Pereard; and overcame my brothers, the Green Knight, Sir Pertolope, and the Red Knight, Sir Perimones; and since thou hast overcome me also, I will do thee homage and fealty, and place at thy command one hundred knights to do thy bidding."

But when the damsel saw Sir Perseant overthrown, she marveled greatly at the might of Sir Beaumains, and said, "What manner of man may ye be, for now am I sure that ye be come of noble blood? And truly, never did woman revile knight as I have done thee, and yet ye have ever courteously borne with me, which surely never had been were ye not of gentle blood and lineage."

"Lady," replied Sir Beaumains, "a knight is little worth who may not bear with a damsel; and so whatsoever ye said to me I took no heed, save only that at times when your scorn angered me, it made me all the stronger against those with whom I fought, and thus have ye furthered me in my battles. But whether I be born of gentle blood or no, I have done you gentle service, and peradventure will do better still, ere I depart from you."

"Alas!" said she, weeping at his courtesy, "forgive me, fair Sir Beaumains, all that I have missaid and misdone against you." "With all my heart," said he; "and since you now speak fairly to me, I am passing glad of heart, and methinks I have the strength to overcome whatever knights I shall henceforth encounter."

Then Sir Perseant prayed them to come to his pavilion, and set before them wines and spices, and made them great cheer. So they rested that night; and on the morrow, the damsel and Sir Beaumains rose, and heard mass. And when they had broken their fast, they took their leave of Sir Perseant. "Fair damsel," said he, "whither lead ye this knight?" "Sir," answered she, "to the Castle Dangerous, where my sister is besieged by the Knight of the Redlands." "I know him well," said Sir Perseant, "for the most perilous knight alive—a man without mercy, and with the strength of seven men. God save thee, Sir Beaumains, from him! and enable thee to overcome him, for the Lady Lyones, whom he besiegeth, is as fair a lady as there liveth in this world." "Thou sayest truth, sir," said the damsel; "for I am her sister; and men call me Linet, or the Wild Maiden." "Now, I would have thee know," said Sir Perseant to Sir Beaumains, "that the Knight of the Redlands hath kept that siege more than two years, and prolongeth the time hoping that Sir Lancelot, or Sir Tristram, or Sir Lamoracke, may come and battle with him; for these three knights divide between them all knighthood; and thou if thou mayest match the Knight of the Redlands, shalt well be called the fourth knight of the world." "Sir," said Sir Beaumains, "I would fain have that good fame; and truly, I am come of great and honorable lineage. And so that you and this fair damsel will conceal it, I will tell ye my descent." And when they swore to keep it secret, he told them, "My name is Sir Gareth of Orkney, my father was King Lot, and my mother the Lady Belisent, King Arthur's sister. Sir Gawain, Sir Agravain, and Sir Gaheris, are my brethren, and I am the youngest of them all. But, as yet King Arthur and the court know me not, who I am." When he had thus told them, they both wondered greatly.

And the damsel Linet sent the dwarf forward to her sister, to tell her of their coming. Then did Dame Lyones inquire what manner of man the knight was who was coming to her rescue. And the dwarf told her of all Sir Beaumains' deeds by the way: how he had overthrown Sir Key, and left him for dead; how he had battled with Sir Lancelot, and was knighted of him; how he had fought with, and slain, the thieves; how he had overcome the two knights who kept the river passage; how he had fought with, and slain, the Black Knight; and how he had overcome the Green Knight, the Red Knight, and last of all, the Blue Knight, Sir Perseant. Then was Dame Lyones passing glad, and sent the dwarf back to Sir Beaumains with great gifts, thanking him for his courtesy, in taking such a labor on him for her sake, and praying him to be of good heart and courage. And as the dwarf returned, he met the Knight of the Redlands, who asked him whence he came. "I came here with the sister of my lady of the castle," said the dwarf, "who hath been now to King Arthur's court and brought a knight with her to take her battle on him." "Then is her travail lost," replied the knight; "for, though she had brought Sir Lancelot, Sir Tristram, Sir Lamoracke, or Sir Gawain, I count myself their equal, and who besides shall be so called?" Then the dwarf told the knight what deeds Sir Beaumains had done; but he answered, "I care not for him, whosoever he be, for I shall shortly overcome him, and give him shameful death, as to so many others I have done."

Then the damsel Linet and Sir Beaumains left Sir Perseant, and rode on through a forest to a large plain, where they saw many pavilions, and hard by, a castle passing fair.

But as they came near Sir Beaumains saw upon the branches of some trees which grew there, the dead bodies of forty knights hanging, with rich armor on them, their shields and swords about their necks, and golden spurs upon their heels. "What meaneth this?" said he, amazed. "Lose not thy courage, fair sir," replied the damsel, "at this shameful sight, for all these knights came hither to rescue my sister; and when the Knight of the Redlands had overcome them, he put them to this piteous death, without mercy; and in such wise will he treat thee also unless thou bearest thee more valiantly than they." "Truly he useth shameful customs," said Sir Beaumains; "and it is a marvel that he hath endured so long."

So they rode onward to the castle walls, and found them double-moated, and heard the sea waves dashing on one side the walls. Then said the damsel, "See you that ivory horn hanging upon the sycamore-tree? The Knight of the Redlands hath hung it there, that any knight may blow thereon, and then will he himself come out and fight with him. But I pray thee sound it not till high noontide, for now it is but daybreak, and till noon his strength increases to the might of seven men." "Let that be as it may, fair damsel," answered he, "for were he stronger knight than ever lived, I would not fail him. Either will I defeat him at his mightiest, or die knightly in the field." With that he spurred his horse unto the sycamore, and blew the ivory horn so eagerly, that all the castle rang its echoes. Instantly, all the knights who were in the pavilions ran forth, and those within the castle looked out from the windows, or above the walls. And the Knight of the Redlands, arming himself quickly in blood-red armor, with spear, and shield, and horse's trappings of like color, rode forth into a little valley by the castle walls, so that all in the castle, and at the siege, might see the battle.

"Be of good cheer," said the damsel Linet to Sir Beaumains, "for thy deadly enemy now cometh; and at yonder window is my lady and sister, Dame Lyones." "In good sooth," said Sir Beaumains, "she is the fairest lady I have ever seen, and I would wish no better quarrel than to fight for her." With that, he looked up to the window, and saw the Lady Lyones, who waved her handkerchief to her sister and to him to cheer them. Then called the Knight of the Redlands to Sir Beaumains, "Leave now thy gazing, Sir knight, and turn to me, for I warn thee that lady is mine." "She loveth none of thy fellowship," he answered; "but know this, that I love her, and will rescue her from thee, or die." "Say ye so!"

said the Red Knight. "Take ye no warning from those knights that hang on yonder trees?" "For shame that thou so boastest!" said Sir Beaumains. "Be sure that sight hath raised a hatred for thee that will not lightly be put out, and given me not fear, but rage." "Sir knight, defend thyself," said the Knight of the Redlands, "for we will talk no longer."

Then did they put their spears in rest, and came together at the fullest speed of their horses, and smote each other in the midst of their shields, so that their horses' harness sundered by the shock, and they fell to the ground. And both lay there so long time, stunned, that many deemed their necks were broken. And all men said the strange knight was a strong man, and a noble jouster, for none had ever yet so matched the Knight of the Redlands. Then, in a while, they rose, and putting up their shields before them, drew their swords, and fought with fury, running at each other like wild beasts—now striking such buffets that both reeled backwards, now hewing at each other till they shore the harness off in pieces, and left their bodies naked and unarmed. And thus they fought till noon was past, when, for a time, they rested to get breath, so sorely staggering and bleeding, that many who beheld them wept for pity. Then they renewed the battle—sometimes rushing so furiously together, that both fell to the ground, and anon changing swords in their confusion. Thus they endured, and lashed, and struggled, until eventide, and none who saw knew which was the likeliest to win; for though the Knight of the Redlands was a wily and subtle warrior, his subtlety made Sir Beaumains wilier and wiser too. So once again they rested for a little space, and took their helms off to find breath.

But when Sir Beaumains' helm was off, he looked up to Dame Lyones, where she leaned, gazing and weeping, from her window. And when he saw the sweetness of her smiling, all his heart was light and joyful, and starting up, he bade the Knight of the Redlands make ready. Then did they lace their helms and fight together yet afresh, as though they had never fought before. And at the last, the Knight of the Redlands with a sudden stroke smote Sir Beaumains on the hand, so that his sword fell from it, and with a second stroke upon the helm he drove him to the earth. Then cried aloud the damsel Linet, "Alas! Sir Beaumains, see how my sister weepeth to behold thee fallen!" And when Sir Beaumains heard her words, he sprang upon his feet with strength, and leaping to his sword, he caught it; and with many heavy blows pressed so sorely on the Knight of the Redlands, that in the end he smote his sword from out his hand, and, with a mighty blow upon the head, hurled him upon the ground.

Then Sir Beaumains unlaced his helm, and would have straightway slain him, but the Knight of the Redlands yielded, and prayed for mercy. "I may not spare thee," answered he, "because of the shameful death which thou hast given to so many noble knights." "Yet hold thy hand, Sir knight," said he, "and hear the cause. I loved once a fair damsel, whose brother was slain, as she told me, by a knight of Arthur's court, either Sir Lancelot, or Sir Gawain; and she prayed me, as I truly loved her, and by the faith of my knighthood, to labor daily in deeds of arms, till I should meet with him; and to put all knights of the Round Table whom I should overcome to a villainous death. And this I swore to her." Then prayed the earls, and knights, and barons, who stood round Sir Beaumains, to spare the Red Knight's life. "Truly," replied he, "I am loth to slay him, notwithstanding he hath done such shameful deeds. And inasmuch as what he did was done to please his lady and to gain her love, I blame him less, and for your sakes I will release him. But on this agreement only shall he hold his life—that straightway he depart into the castle, and yield him to the lady there, and make her such amends as she shall ask, for all the trespass he hath done upon her lands; and afterwards, that he shall go unto King Arthur's court, and ask the pardon of Sir Lancelot and Sir Gawain for all the evil he hath done against them." "All this, Sir knight, I swear to do," said the Knight of the Redlands; and therewith he did him homage and fealty.

Then came the damsel Linet to Sir Beaumains and the Knight of the Redlands, and disarmed them, and staunched their wounds. And when the Knight of the Redlands had made amends for all his trespasses, he departed for the court.

Then Sir Beaumains, being healed of his wounds, armed himself, and took his horse and spear and rode straight to the castle of Dame Lyones, for greatly he desired to see her. But when he came to the gate they closed it fast, and pulled the drawbridge up. And as he marveled thereat, he saw the Lady Lyones standing at a window, who said, "Go thy way as yet, Sir Beaumains, for thou shalt not wholly have my love until thou be among the worthiest knights of all the world. Go, therefore, and labor yet in arms for twelve months more, and then return to me." "Alas! fair lady," said Sir Beaumains, "I have scarce deserved this of thee, for sure I am that I have bought thy love with all the best blood in my body." "Be not aggrieved, fair knight," said she, "for none of thy service is forgot or lost. Twelve months will soon be passed in noble deeds; and trust that to my death I shall love thee and not another." With that she turned and left the window.

So Sir Beaumains rode away from the castle very sorrowful at heart, and rode he knew not whither, and lay that night in a poor man's cottage. On the morrow he went forward, and came at noon to a broad lake, and thereby he alighted, being very sad and weary, and rested his head upon his shield, and told his dwarf to keep watch while he slept.

Now, as soon as he had departed, the Lady Lyones repented, and greatly longed to see him back, and asked her sister many times of what lineage he was; but the damsel would not tell her, being bound by her oath to Sir Beaumains, and said his dwarf best knew. So she called Sir Gringamors, her brother, who dwelt with her, and prayed him to ride after Sir Beaumains till he found him sleeping, and then to take his dwarf away and bring him back to her. Anon Sir Gringamors departed, and rode till he came to Sir Beaumains, and found him as he lay sleeping by the water-side. Then stepping stealthily behind the dwarf he caught him in his arms and rode off in haste. And though the dwarf cried loudly to his lord for help, and woke Sir Beaumains, yet, though he rode full quickly after him, he could not overtake Sir Gringamors.

When Dame Lyones saw her brother come back, she was passing glad of heart, and forthwith asked the dwarf his master's lineage. "He is a king's son," said the dwarf, "and his mother is King Arthur's sister. His name is Sir Gareth of Orkney, and he is brother to the good knight, Sir Gawain. But I pray you suffer me to go back to my lord, for truly he will never leave this country till he have me again." But when the Lady Lyones knew her deliverer was come of such a kingly stock, she longed more than ever to see him again.

Now as Sir Beaumains rode in vain to rescue his dwarf, he came to a fair green road and met a poor man of the country, and asked him had he seen a knight on a black horse, riding with a dwarf of a sad countenance behind him. "Yea," said the man, "I met with such a knight an hour agone, and his name is Sir Gringamors. He liveth at a castle two miles from hence; but he is a perilous knight, and I counsel ye not to follow him save ye bear him goodwill." Then Sir Beaumains followed the path which the poor man showed him, and came to the castle. And riding to the gate in great anger, he drew his sword, and cried aloud, "Sir Gringamors, thou traitor! deliver me my dwarf again, or by my knighthood it shall be ill for thee!" Then Sir Gringamors looked out of a window and said, "Sir Gareth of Orkney, leave thy boasting words, for thou wilt not get thy dwarf again." But the Lady Lyones said to her brother, "Nay, brother, but I will that he have his dwarf, for he hath done much for me, and delivered me from the Knight of the Redlands, and well do I love him above all other knights." So Sir Gringamors went down to Sir Gareth and cried him mercy, and prayed him to alight and take good cheer.

Then he alighted, and his dwarf ran to him. And when he was in the hall came the Lady Lyones dressed royally like a princess. And Sir Gareth was right glad of heart when he saw her. Then she told him how she had made her brother take away his dwarf and bring him back to her. And then she promised him her love, and faithfully to cleave to him and none other all the days of her life. And so they plighted their troth to each other. Then Sir Gringamors prayed him to sojourn at the castle, which willing he did. "For," said he, "I have promised to quit the court for twelve months, though sure I am that in the meanwhile I shall be sought and found by my lord King Arthur and many others." So he sojourned long at the castle.

Anon the knights, Sir Perseant, Sir Perimones, and Sir Pertolope, whom Sir Gareth had overthrown, went to King Arthur's court with all the knights who did them service, and told the king they had been conquered by a knight of his named Beaumains. And as they yet were talking, it was told the king there came another great lord with five hundred knights, who, entering in, did homage, and declared himself to be the Knight of the Redlands. "But my true name," said he, "is Ironside, and I am hither sent by one Sir Beaumains, who conquered me, and charged me to yield unto your grace." "Thou art welcome," said King Arthur, "for thou hast been long a foe to me and mine, and truly I am much beholden to the knight who sent thee. And now, Sir Ironside, if thou wilt amend thy life and hold of me, I will entreat thee as a friend, and make thee Knight of the Round Table; but thou mayst no more be a murderer of noble knights." Then the Knight of the Redlands knelt to the king, and told him of his promise to Sir Beaumains to use never more such shameful customs; and how he had so done but at the prayer of a lady whom he loved. Then knelt he to Sir Lancelot and Sir Gawain, and prayed their pardon for the hatred he had borne them.

But the king and all the court marveled greatly who Sir Beaumains was. "For," said the king, "he is a full noble knight." Then said Sir Lancelot, "Truly he is come of honorable blood, else had I not given him the order of knighthood; but he charged me that I should conceal his secret."

Now as they talked thus it was told King Arthur that his sister, the Queen of Orkney, was come to the court with a great retinue of knights and ladies. Then was there great rejoicing, and the king rose and saluted his sister. And her sons, Sir Gawain, Sir Agravain, and Sir Gaheris knelt before her and asked her blessing, for during fifteen years last past they had not seen her. Anon she said, "Where is my youngest son, Sir Gareth? for I know that he was here a twelve-month with you, and that ye made a kitchen knave of him." Then the king and all the knights knew that Sir

Beaumains and Sir Gareth were the same. "Truly," said the king, "I knew him not." "Nor I," said Sir Gawain and both his brothers. Then said the king, "God be thanked, fair sister, that he is proved as worshipful a knight as any now alive, and by the grace of Heaven he shall be found forthwith if he be anywhere within these seven realms." Then said Sir Gawain and his brethren, "Lord, if ye will give us leave we will go seek him." But Sir Lancelot said, "It were better that the king should send a messenger to Dame Lyones and pray her to come hither with all speed, and she will counsel where ye shall find him." "It is well said," replied the king; and sent a messenger quickly unto Dame Lyones.

When she heard the message she promised she would come forthwith, and told Sir Gareth what the messenger had said, and asked him what to do. "I pray you," said he, "tell them not where I am, but when my lord King Arthur asketh for me, advise him thus—that he proclaim a tournament before this castle on Assumption Day, and that the knight who proveth best shall win yourself and all your lands." So the Lady Lyones departed and came to King Arthur's court, and there was right nobly welcomed. And when they asked her where Sir Gareth was, she said she could not tell. "But, lord," said she, "with thy goodwill I will proclaim a tournament before my castle on the Feast of the Assumption, whereof the prize shall be myself and all my lands. Then if it be proclaimed that you, lord, and your knights will be there, I will find knights on my side to fight you and yours, and thus am I sure ye will hear tidings of Sir Gareth." "Be it so done," replied the king.

So Sir Gareth sent messengers privily to Sir Perseant and Sir Ironside, and charged them to be ready on the day appointed, with their companies of knights to aid him and his party against the king. And when they were arrived he said, "Now be ye well assured that we shall be matched with the best knights of the world, and therefore must we gather all the good knights we can find."

So proclamation was made throughout all England, Wales, Scotland, Ireland, and Cornwall, and in the out isles and other countries, that at the Feast of the Assumption of our Lady, next coming, all knights who came to joust at Castle Perilous should

155

make choice whether they would side with the king or with the castle. Then came many good knights on the side of the castle. Sir Epinogris, the son of the King of Northumberland, and Sir Palomedes the Saracen, and Sir Grummore Grummorsum, a good knight of Scotland, and Sir Brian des Iles, a noble knight, and Sir Carados of the Tower Dolorous, and Sir Tristram, who as yet was not a knight of the Round Table, and many others. But none among them knew Sir Gareth, for he took no more upon him than any mean person.

And on King Arthur's side there came the King of Ireland and the King of Scotland, the noble prince Sir Galahaut, Sir Gawain and his brothers Sir Agravain and Sir Gaheris, Sir Ewaine, Sir Tor, Sir Perceval, and Sir Lamoracke, Sir Lancelot also and his kindred, Sir Lionel, Sir Ector, Sir Bors and Sir Bedivere, likewise Sir Key and the most part of the Table Round. The two queens also, Queen Guinevere and the Queen of Orkney, Sir Gareth's mother, came with the king. So there was a great array both within and without the castle, with all manner of feasting and minstrelsy.

Now before the tournament began, Sir Gareth privily prayed Dame Lyones, Sir Gringamors, Sir Ironside, and Sir Perseant, that they would in nowise disclose his name, nor make more of him than of any common knight. Then said Dame Lyones, "Dear lord, I pray thee take this ring, which hath the power to change the wearer's clothing into any color he may will, and guardeth him from any loss of blood. But give it me again, I pray thee, when the tournament is done, for it greatly increaseth my beauty whensoever I wear it." "Gramercy, mine own lady," said Sir Gareth, "I wished for nothing better, for now I may be certainly disguised as long as I will." Then Sir Gringamors gave Sir Gareth a bay courser that was a passing good horse, with sure armor, and a noble sword, won by his father from a heathen tyrant. And then every knight made him ready for the tournament.

So on the day of the Assumption, when mass and matins were said, the heralds blew their trumpets and sounded for the tourney. Anon came out the knights of the castle and the knights of King Arthur, and matched themselves together.

Then Sir Epinogris, son of the King of Northumberland, a knight of the castle, encountered Sir Ewaine, and both broke off their spears short to their hands. Then came Sir Palomedes from the castle, and met Sir Gawain, and they so hardly smote each other, that both knights and horses fell to the earth. Then Sir Tristram, from the castle, encountered with Sir Bedivere, and smote him to the earth, horse and man. Then the Knight of the Redlands and Sir Gareth met with Sir Bors and Sir Bleoberis; and the Knight of the Redlands and Sir Bors smote together so hard that their spears burst, and their horses fell groveling to the ground. And Sir Bleoberis brake his spear upon Sir Gareth, but himself was hurled upon the ground. When Sir Galihodin saw that, he bade Sir Gareth keep him, but Sir Gareth lightly smote him to the earth. Then Sir Galihud got a spear to avenge his brother, but was served in like manner. And Sir Dinadam, and his brother La-cote-male-taile, and Sir Sagramour le Desirous, and Dodinas le Savage, he bore down all with one spear.

When King Anguish of Ireland saw this, he marveled what that knight could be who seemed at one time green and at another blue; for so at every course he changed his color that none might know him. Then he ran towards him and encountered him, and Sir Gareth smote the king from his horse, saddle and all. And in like manner he served the King of Scotland, and King Urience of Gore, and King Bagdemagus.

Then Sir Galahaut, the noble prince, cried out, "Knight of the many colors! thou hast jousted well; now make thee ready to joust with me." When Sir Gareth heard him, he took a great spear and met him swiftly. And the prince's spear broke off, but Sir Gareth smote him on the left side of the helm, so that he reeled here and there, and had fallen down had not his men recovered him. "By my faith," said King Arthur, "that knight of the many colors is a good knight. I pray thee, Sir Lancelot du Lake, encounter with him." "Lord," said Sir Lancelot, "by thy leave I will forbear. I find it in my heart to spare him at this time, for he hath done enough work for one day; and when a good knight doth so well it is no knightly part to hinder him from this honor. And peradventure his quarrel is here to-day, and he may be the best beloved of the Lady Lyones of all that be here; for I see well he paineth and forceth himself to do great deeds. Therefore, as for me, this day he shall have the honor; for though I were able to put him from it, I would not." "You speak well and truly," said the king.

Then after the tilting, they drew swords, and there began a great tournament, and there Sir Lancelot did marvelous deeds of arms, for first he fought with both Sir Tristram and Sir Carados, albeit they were the most perilous in all the world. Then came Sir Gareth and put them asunder, but would not smite a stroke against Sir Lancelot, for by him he had been knighted. Anon Sir Gareth's helm had need of mending, and he rode aside to see to it and to drink water, for he was sore athirst with all his mighty feats of strength. And while he drank, his dwarf said to him, "Give me your ring, lest ye lose it while ye drink." So Sir Gareth took it off. And when he had finished drinking, he rode back eagerly to the field, and in his haste forgot to take the ring again. Then all the people saw that he wore yellow armor. And King Arthur told a herald, "Ride and espy the cognizance of that brave knight, for I have asked many who he is, and none can tell me."

Then the herald rode near, and saw written round about his helmet in letters of gold, "Sir Gareth of Orkney." And instantly the herald cried his name aloud, and all men pressed to see him.

But when he saw he was discovered, he pushed with haste through all the crowd, and cried to his dwarf, "Boy, thou hast beguiled me foully in keeping my ring; give it me again, that I may be hidden." And as soon as he had put it on, his armor changed again, and no man knew where he had gone. Then he passed forth from the field; but Sir Gawain, his brother, rode after him.

And when Sir Gareth had ridden far into the forest, he took off his ring, and sent it back by the dwarf to the Lady Lyones, praying her to be true and faithful to him while he was away.

Then rode Sir Gareth long through the forest, till night fell, and coming to a castle he went up to the gate, and prayed the porter to let him in. But churlishly he answered "that he should not lodge there." Then said Sir Gareth, "Tell thy lord and lady that

I am a knight of King Arthur's court, and for his sake I pray their shelter." With that the porter went to the duchess who owned the castle. "Let him in straightway," cried she; "for the king's sake he shall not be harborless!" and went down to receive him. When Sir Gareth saw her coming, he saluted her, and said, "Fair lady, I pray you give me shelter for this night, and if there be here any champion or giant with whom I must needs fight, spare me till to-morrow, when I and my horse shall have rested, for we are full weary." "Sir knight," she said, "thou speakest boldly; for the lord of this castle is a foe to King Arthur and his court, and if thou wilt rest here to-night thou must agree, that wheresoever thou mayest meet my lord, thou must yield to him as a prisoner." "What is thy lord's name, lady?" said Sir Gareth. "The Duke de la Rowse," said she. "I will promise thee," said he, "to yield to him, if he promise to do me no harm; but if he refuse, I will release myself with my sword and spear."

"It is well," said the duchess; and commanded the drawbridge to be let down. So he rode into the hall and alighted. And when he had taken off his armor, the duchess and her ladies made him passing good cheer. And after supper his bed was made in the hall, and there he rested that night. On the morrow he rose and heard mass, and having broken his fast, took his leave and departed.

And as he rode past a certain mountain there met him a knight named Sir Bendelaine, and cried unto him, "Thou shalt not pass unless thou joust with me or be my prisoner!" "Then will we joust," replied Sir Gareth. So they let their horses run at full speed, and Sir Gareth smote Sir Bendelaine through his body so sorely that he scarcely reached his castle ere he fell dead. And as Sir Gareth presently came by the castle, Sir Bendelaine's knights and servants rode out to revenge their lord. And twenty of them fell on him at once, although his spear was broken. But drawing his sword he put his shield before him. And though they brake their spears upon him, one and all, and sorely pressed on him, yet ever he defended himself like a noble knight. Anon, finding they could not overcome him, they agreed to slay his horse; and having killed it with their spears, they set upon Sir Gareth as he fought on foot.

But every one he struck he slew, and drave at them with fearful blows, till he had slain them all but four, who fled. Then taking the horse of one of those that lay there dead, he rode upon his way.

Anon he came to another castle and heard from within a sound as of many women moaning and weeping. Then said he to a page who stood without, "What noise is this I hear?" "Sir knight," said he, "there be within thirty ladies, the widows of thirty knights who have been slain by the lord of this castle. He is called the Brown Knight without pity, and is the most perilous knight living, wherefore I warn thee to flee." "That will I never do," said Sir Gareth, "for I fear him not." Then the page saw the Brown Knight coming and said to Gareth, "Lo! my lord is near."

So both knights made them ready and galloped their horses towards each other, and the Brown Knight brake his spear upon Sir Gareth's shield; but Sir Gareth smote him through the body so that he fell dead. At that he rode into the castle and told the ladies he had slain their foe. Then were they right glad of heart and made him all the cheer they could, and thanked him out of measure. But on the morrow as he went to mass he found the ladies weeping in the chapel upon divers tombs that were there. And he knew that in those tombs their husbands lay. Then he bade them be comforted, and with noble and high words he desired and prayed them all to be at Arthur's court on the next Feast of Pentecost.

So he departed and rode past a mountain where was a goodly knight waiting, who said to him, "Abide, Sir knight, and joust with me!" "How are ye named?" said Sir Gareth. "I am the Duke de la Rowse," answered he. "In good sooth," then said Sir Gareth, "not long ago I lodged within your castle, and there promised I would yield to you whenever we might meet." "Art thou that proud knight," said the duke, "who was ready to fight with me? Guard thyself therefore and make ready." So they ran together, and Sir Gareth smote the duke from his horse. Then they alighted and drew their swords, and fought full sorely for the space of an hour; and at the last Sir Gareth smote the duke to the earth and would have slain him, but he yielded. "Then must ye go," said Sir Gareth, "to my lord King Arthur at the next Feast of Pentecost and say that I, Sir Gareth, sent ye." "As ye will be it," said the duke; and gave him up his shield for pledge.

And as Sir Gareth rode alone he saw an armed knight coming towards him. And putting the duke's shield before him he rode fast to tilt with him; and so they ran together as it had been thunder, and brake their spears upon each other. Then fought they fiercely with their swords, and lashed together with such mighty strokes that blood ran to the ground on every side. And after they had fought together for two hours and more, it chanced the damsel Linet passed that way; and when she saw them, she cried out, "Sir Gawain and Sir Gareth, leave your fighting, for ye are brethren!" At that they threw away their shields and swords, and took each other in their arms, and wept a great while ere they could speak. And each gave to the other the honor of the battle, and there was many a kind word between them. Then said Sir Gawain, "O my brother, for your sake have I had great sorrow and labor! But truly I would honor you though ye were not my brother, for ye have done great worship to King Arthur and his court, and sent more knights to him than any of the Table Round, except Sir Lancelot."

Then the damsel Linet staunched their wounds, and their horses being weary she rode her palfrey to King Arthur and told him of this strange adventure. When she had told her tidings, the king himself mounted his horse and bade all come with him to meet them. So a great company of lords and ladies went forth to meet the brothers. And when King Arthur saw them he would have spoken hearty words, but for gladness he could not. And both Sir Gawain and Sir Gareth fell down at their uncle's knees and did him homage, and there was passing great joy and gladness among them all.

Then said the king to the damsel Linet, "Why cometh not the Lady Lyones to visit her knight, Sir Gareth, who hath had such travail for her love?" "She knoweth not, my lord, that he is here," replied the damsel, "for truly she desireth greatly to see him." "Go ye and bring her hither," said the king. So the damsel rode to tell her sister where Sir Gareth was, and when she heard it she rejoiced full heartily and came with all the speed she could. And when Sir Gareth saw her, there was great joy and comfort between them.

Then the king asked Sir Gareth whether he would have that lady for his wife? "My lord," replied Sir Gareth, "know well that I love her above all ladies living." "Now, fair lady," said King Arthur, "what say ye?" "Most noble king," she answered, "my lord, Sir Gareth, is my first love and shall be my last, and if I may not have him for my husband I will have none." Then said the king to them, "Be well assured that for my crown I would not be the cause of parting your two hearts."

Then was high preparation made for the marriage, for the king desired it should be at the Michaelmas next following, at Kinkenadon-by-the-Sea.

So Sir Gareth sent out messages to all the knights whom he had overcome in battle that they should be there upon his marriage-day.

Therefore, at the next Michaelmas, came a goodly company to Kinkenadon-by-the-Sea. And there did the Archbishop of Canterbury marry Sir Gareth and the Lady Lyones with all solemnity. And all the knights whom Sir Gareth had overcome were at the feast; and every manner of revels and games was held with music and minstrelsy. And there was a great jousting for three days. But because of his bride the king would not suffer Sir Gareth to joust. Then did King Arthur give great lands and fair, with store of gold, to Sir Gareth and his wife, that so they might live royally together to their lives' end.

XII. THE ADVENTURES OF SIR TRISTRAM

Again King Arthur held high festival at Caerleon, at Pentecost, and gathered round him all the fellowship of the Round Table, and so, according to his custom, sat and waited till some adventure should arise, or some knight return to court whose deeds and perils might be told.

Anon he saw Sir Lancelot and a crowd of knights coming through the doors and leading in their midst the mighty knight, Sir Tristram. As soon as King Arthur saw him, he rose up and went through half the hall, and held out both his hands and cried, "Right welcome to thee, good Sir Tristram, as welcome art thou as any knight that ever came before into this court. A long time have I wished for thee amongst my fellowship." Then all the knights and barons rose up with one accord and came around, and cried out, "Welcome." Queen Guinevere came also, and many ladies with her, and all with one voice said the same.

Then the king took Sir Tristram by the hand and led him to the Round Table and said, "Welcome again for one of the best and gentlest knights in all the world; a chief in war, a chief in peace, a chief in field and forest, a chief in the ladies' chamber—right heartily welcome to this court, and mayest thou long abide in it."

When he had so said he looked at every empty seat until he came to what had been Sir Marhaus', and there he found written in gold letters, "This is the seat of the noble knight, Sir Tristram." Whereat they made him, with great cheer and gladness, a Fellow of the Round Table.

Now the story of Sir Tristram was as follows:—

There was a king of Lyonesse, named Meliodas, married to the sister of King Mark of Cornwall, a right fair lady and a good. And so it happened that King Meliodas hunting in the woods was taken by enchantment and made prisoner in a castle. When his

163

wife Elizabeth heard it she was nigh mad with grief, and ran into the forest to seek out her lord. But after many days of wandering and sorrow she found no trace of him, and laid her down in a deep valley and prayed to meet her death. And so indeed she did, but ere she died she gave birth in the midst of all her sorrow to child, a boy, and called him with her latest breath Tristram; for she said, "His name shall show how sadly he hath come into this world."

Therewith she gave up her ghost, and the gentlewoman who was with her took the child and wrapped it from the cold as well as she was able, and lay down with it in her arms beneath the shadow of a tree hard by, expecting death to come to her in turn.

But shortly after came a company of lords and barons seeking for the queen, and found the lady and the child and took them home. And on the next day came King Meliodas, whom Merlin had delivered, and when he heard of the queen's death his sorrow was greater than tongue can tell. And anon he buried her solemnly and nobly, and called the child Tristram as she had desired.

Then for seven years King Meliodas mourned and took no comfort, and all that time young Tristram was well nourished; but in a while he wedded with the daughter of Howell, King of Brittany, who, that her own children might enjoy the kingdom, cast about in her mind how she might destroy Tristram. So on a certain day she put poison in a silver cup, where Tristram and her children were together playing, that when he was athirst he might drink of it and die. But so it happened that her own son saw the cup, and, thinking it must hold good drink, he climbed and took it, and drank deeply of it, and suddenly thereafter burst and fell down dead.

When the queen heard that, her grief was very great, but her anger and envy were fiercer than before, and soon again she put more poison in the cup. And by chance one day her husband finding it when thirsty, took it up and was about to drink therefrom, when, seeing him, she sprang up with a mighty cry and dashed it from his hands.

At that King Meliodas, wondering greatly, called to mind the sudden death of his young child, and taking her fiercely by the hand he cried:

"Traitress, tell me what drink is in this cup or I will slay thee in a moment;" and therewith pulling out his sword he swore by a great oath to slay her if she straightway told him not the truth.

"Ah, mercy, lord," said she, and fell down at his feet; "mercy, and I will tell thee all."

And then she told him of her plot to murder Tristram, so that her own sons might enjoy the kingdom.

"The law shall judge thee," said the king.

And so anon she was tried before the barons, and condemned to be burnt to death.

But when the fire was made, and she brought out, came Tristram kneeling at his father's feet and besought of him a favor.

"Whatsoever thou desirest I will give thee," said the king.

"Give me the life, then, of the queen, my step-mother," said he.

"Thou doest wrong to ask it," said Meliodas; "for she would have slain thee with her poisons if she could, and chiefly for thy sake she ought to die."

"Sir," said he, "as for that, I beseech thee of thy mercy to forgive it her, and for my part may God pardon her as I do; and so I pray thee grant me my boon, and for God's sake hold thee to thy promise."

"If it must be so," said the king, "take thou her life, for to thee I give it, and go and do with her as thou wilt."

Then went young Tristram to the fire and loosed the queen from all her bonds and delivered her from death.

And after a great while by his good means the king again forgave and lived in peace with her, though never more in the same lodgings.

Anon was Tristram sent abroad to France in care of one named Governale. And there for seven years he learned the language of the land, and all knightly exercises and gentle crafts, and especially was he foremost in music and in hunting, and was a harper beyond all others. And when at nineteen years of age he came back to his father, he was as lusty and strong of body and as noble of heart as ever man was seen.

Now shortly after his return it befell that King Anguish of Ireland sent to King Mark of Cornwall for the tribute due to Ireland, but which was now seven years behindhand. To whom King Mark sent answer, if he would have it he must send and fight for it, and they would find a champion to fight against it.

So King Anguish called for Sir Marhaus, his wife's brother, a good knight of the Round Table, who lived then at his court, and sent him with a knightly retinue in six great ships to Cornwall. And, casting anchor by the castle of Tintagil, he sent up daily to King Mark for the tribute or the champion. But no knight there would venture to assail him, for his fame was very high in all the realm for strength and hardihood.

Then made King Mark a proclamation throughout Cornwall, that if any knight would fight Sir Marhaus he should stand at the king's right hand forevermore, and have great honor and riches all the rest of his days. Anon this news came to the land of Lyonesse, and when young Tristram heard it he was angry and ashamed to think no knight of Cornwall durst assail the Irish champion. "Alas," said he, "that I am not a knight, that I might match this Marhaus! I pray you give me leave, sir, to depart to King Mark's court and beg him of his grace to make me knight."

"Be ruled by thy own courage," said his father.

So Tristram rode away forthwith to Tintagil to King Mark, and went up boldly to him and said, "Sir, give me the order of knighthood and I will fight to the uttermost with Sir Marhaus of Ireland."

"What are ye, and whence come ye?" said the king, seeing he was but a young man, though strong and well made both in body and limb.

"My name is Tristram," said he, "and I was born in the country of Lyonesse."

"But know ye," said the king, "this Irish knight will fight with none who be not come of royal blood and near of kin to kings or queens, as he himself is, for his sister is the Queen of Ireland."

Then said Tristram, "Let him know that I am come both on my father's and my mother's side of blood as good as his, for my father is King Meliodas and my mother was that Queen Elizabeth, thy sister, who died in the forest at my birth."

When King Mark heard that he welcomed him with all his heart, and knighted him forthwith, and made him ready to go forth as soon as he would choose, and armed him royally in armor covered with gold and silver.

Then he sent Sir Marhaus word, "That a better man than he should fight with him, Sir Tristram of Lyonesse, son of King Meliodas and of King Mark's own sister." So the battle was ordained to be fought in an island near Sir Marhaus' ships, and there Sir Tristram landed on the morrow, with Governale alone attending him for squire, and him he sent back to the land when he had made himself ready.

When Sir Marhaus and Sir Tristram were thus left alone, Sir Marhaus said, "Young knight Sir Tristram, what doest thou here? I am full sorry for thy rashness, for ofttimes have I been assailed in vain, and by the best knights of the world. Be warned in time, return to them that sent thee."

"Fair knight, and well-proved knight," replied Sir Tristram, "be sure that I shall never quit this quarrel till one of us be overcome. For this cause have I been made knight, and thou shalt know before we part that though as yet unproved, I am a king's son and firstborn of a queen. Moreover I have promised to deliver Cornwall from this ancient burden, or to die. Also, thou shouldst have known, Sir Marhaus, that thy valor and thy might are but the better reasons why I should assail thee; for whether I win or lose I shall gain honor to have met so great a knight as thou art."

Then they began the battle, and tilted at their hardest against each other, so that both knights and horses fell to the earth. But Sir Marhaus' spear smote Sir Tristram a great wound in the side. Then, springing up from their horses, they lashed together with their swords like two wild boars. And when they had stricken together a great while they left off strokes and lunged at one another's breasts and visors; but seeing this availed not they hurtled together again to bear each other down.

Thus fought they more than half the day, till both were sorely spent and blood ran from them to the ground on every side. But by this time Sir Tristram remained fresher than Sir Marhaus and better winded, and with a mighty stroke he smote him such a buffet as cut through his helm into his brain-pan, and there his sword stuck in so fast that thrice Sir Tristram pulled ere he could get it from his head. Then fell Sir Marhaus down upon his knees, and the edge of Sir Tristram's sword broke off into his brain-pan. And suddenly when he seemed dead, Sir Marhaus rose and threw his sword and shield away from him and ran and fled into his ship. And Tristram cried out after him, "Aha! Sir knight of the Round Table, dost thou withdraw thee from so young a knight? it is a shame to thee and all thy kin; I would rather have been hewn into a hundred pieces than have fled from thee."

But Sir Marhaus answered nothing, and sorely groaning fled away.

"Farewell, Sir knight, farewell," laughed Tristram, whose own voice now was hoarse and faint with loss of blood; "I have thy sword and shield in my safe keeping, and will wear them in all places where I ride on my adventures, and before King Arthur and the Table Round."

Then was Sir Marhaus taken back to Ireland by his company; and as soon as he arrived his wounds were searched, and when they searched his head they found therein a piece of Tristram's sword; but all the skill of surgeons was in vain to move it out. So anon Sir Marhaus died.

But the queen, his sister, took the piece of sword-blade and put it safely by, for she thought that some day it might help her to revenge her brother's death.

Meanwhile, Sir Tristram, being sorely wounded, sat down softly on a little mound and bled passing fast; and in that evil case was found anon by Governale and King Mark's knights. Then they gently took him up and brought him in a barge back to the land, and lifted him into a bed within the castle, and had his wounds dressed carefully.

But for a great while he lay sick, and was likely to have died of the first stroke Sir Marhaus had given him with the spear, for the point of it was poisoned. And, though the wisest surgeons and leeches—both men and women—came from every part, yet could he be by no means cured. At last came a wise lady, and said plainly that Sir Tristram never should be healed, until he went and stayed in that same country when the poison came. When this was understood, the king sent Sir Tristram in a fair and goodly ship to Ireland, and by fortune he arrived fast by a castle where the king and queen were. And as the ship was being anchored, he sat upon his bed and harped a merry lay, and made so sweet a music as was never equaled.

When the king heard that the sweet harper was a wounded knight, he sent for him, and asked his name. "I am of the country of Lyonesse," he answered, "and my name is Tramtrist;" for he dared not tell his true name lest the vengeance of the queen should fall upon him for her brother's death.

"Well," said King Anguish, "thou art right welcome here, and shalt have all the help this land can give thee; but be not anxious if I am at times cast down and sad, for but lately in Cornwall the best knight in the world, fighting for my cause, was slain; his name was Sir Marhaus, a knight of King Arthur's Round Table." And then he told Sir Tristram all the story of Sir Marhaus' battle, and Sir Tristram made pretense of great surprise and sorrow, though he knew all far better than the king himself.

Then was he put in charge of the king's daughter, La Belle Isault, to be healed of his wound, and she was as fair and noble a lady as men's eyes might see. And so marvelously was she skilled in medicine, that in a few days she fully cured him; and in return Sir Tramtrist taught her the harp; so, before long, they two began to love each other greatly.

But at that time a heathen knight, Sir Palomedes, was in Ireland, and much cherished by the king and queen. He also loved mightily La Belle Isault, and never wearied of making her great gifts, and seeking for her favor, and was ready even to be christened for her sake. Sir Tramtrist therefore hated him out of measure, and Sir Palomedes was full of rage and envy against Tramtrist.

And so it befell that King Anguish proclaimed a great tournament to be held, the prize whereof should be a lady called the Lady of the Launds, of near kindred to the king: and her the winner of the tournament should wed in three days afterwards, and possess all her lands. When La Belle Isault told Sir Tramtrist of this tournament, he said, "Fair lady! I am yet a feeble knight, and but for thee had been a dead man now: what wouldest thou I should do? Thou knowest well I may not joust."

"Ah, Tramtrist," said she, "why wilt thou not fight in this tournament? Sir Palomedes will be there, and will do his mightiest; and therefore be thou there, I pray thee, or else he will be winner of the prize."

"Madam," said Tramtrist, "I will go, and for thy sake will do my best; but let me go unknown to all men; and do thou, I pray thee, keep my counsel, and help me to a disguise."

So on the day of jousting came Sir Palomedes, with a black shield, and overthrew many knights. And all the people wondered at his prowess; for on the first day he put to the worse Sir Gawain, Sir Gaheris, Sir Agravaine, Sir Key, and many more from far and near. And on the morrow he was conqueror again, and overthrew the king with a hundred knights and the King of Scotland. But presently Sir Tramtrist rode up to the lists, having been let out at a privy postern of the castle, where none could see. La Belle Isault had dressed him in white armor and given him a white horse and shield, and so he came suddenly into the field as it had been a bright angel.

As soon as Sir Palomedes saw him he ran at him with a great spear in rest, but Sir Tramtrist was ready, and at the first encounter hurled him to the ground. Then there arose a great cry that the knight with the black shield was overthrown. And Palomedes, sorely hurt and shamed, sought out a secret way and would have left the field; but Tramtrist watched him, and rode after him, and bade him stay, for he had not yet done with him. Then did Sir Palomedes turn with fury, and lash at Sir Tramtrist with his sword; but at the first stroke Sir Tramtrist smote him to the earth, and cried, "Do now all my commands, or take thy death." Then he yielded to Sir Tristram's mercy, and promised to forsake La Belle Isault, and for twelve months to wear no arms or armor. And rising up, he cut his armor off him into shreds with rage and madness,

170

and turned and left the field: and Sir Tramtrist also left the lists, and rode back to the castle through the postern gate.

Then was Sir Tramtrist long cherished by the King and Queen of Ireland, and ever with La Belle Isault. But on a certain day, while he was bathing, came the queen with La Belle Isault by chance into his chamber, and saw his sword lie naked on the bed: anon she drew it from the scabbard and looked at it a long while, and both thought it a passing fair sword; but within a foot and a half of the end there was a great piece broken out, and while the queen was looking at the gap, she suddenly remembered the piece of sword-blade that was found in the brain-pan of her brother Sir Marhaus.

Therewith she turned and cried, "By my faith, this is the felon knight who slew thy uncle!" And running to her chamber she sought in her casket for the piece of iron from Sir Marhaus' head and brought it back, and fitted it in Tristram's sword; and surely did it fit therein as closely as it had been but yesterday broke out.

Then the queen caught the sword up fiercely in her hand, and ran into the room where Sir Tristram was yet in his bath, and making straight for him, had run him through the body, had not his squire, Sir Hebes, got her in his arms, and pulled the sword away from her.

Then ran she to the king, and fell upon her knees before him, saying, "Lord and husband, thou hast here in thy house that felon knight who slew my brother Marhaus!"

"Who is it?" said the king.

"It is Sir Tramtrist!" said she, "whom Isault hath healed."

"Alas!" replied the king, "I am full grieved thereat, for he is a good knight as ever I have seen in any field; but I charge thee leave thou him, and let me deal with him."

Then the king went to Sir Tramtrist's chamber and found him all armed and ready to mount his horse, and said to him, "Sir Tramtrist, it is not to prove me against thee I come, for it were shameful of thy host to seek thy life. Depart in peace, but tell me first thy name, and whether thou slewest my brother, Sir Marhaus."

Then Sir Tristram told him all the truth, and how he had hid his name, to be unknown in Ireland; and when he had ended, the king declared he held him in no blame. "Howbeit, I cannot for mine honor's sake retain thee at this court, for so I should displease my barons, and my wife, and all her kin."

"Sir," said Sir Tristram, "I thank thee for the goodness thou hast shown me here, and for the great goodness my lady, thy daughter, hath shown me; and it may chance to be more for thy advantage if I live than if I die; for wheresoever I may be, I shall ever seek thy service, and shall be my lady thy daughter's servant in all places, and her knight in right and wrong, and shall never fail to do for her as much as knight can do."

Then Sir Tristram went to La Belle Isault, and took his leave of her. "O gentle knight," said she, "full of grief am I at your departing, for never yet I saw a man to love so well."

"Madam," said he, "I promise faithfully that all my life I shall be your knight."

Then Sir Tristram gave her a ring, and she gave him another, and after that he left her, weeping and lamenting, and went among the barons, and openly took his leave of them all, saying, "Fair lords, it so befalleth that I now must depart hence; therefore, if there be any here whom I have offended or who is grieved with me, let him now say it, and before I go I will amend it to the utmost of my power. And if there be but one who would speak shame of me behind my back, let him say it now or never, and here is my body to prove it on—body against body."

And all stood still and said no word, though some there were of the queen's kindred who would have assailed him had they dared.

So Sir Tristram departed from Ireland and took the sea and came with a fair wind to Tintagil. And when the news came to King Mark that Sir Tristram was returned, healed of his wound, he was passing glad, and so were all his barons. And when he had visited the king his uncle, he rode to his father, King Meliodas, and there had all the heartiest welcome that could be made him. And both the king and queen gave largely to him of their lands and goods.

Anon he came again to King Mark's court, and there lived in

great joy and pleasure, till within a while the king grew jealous of his fame, and of the love and favor shown him by all damsels. And as long as King Mark lived, he never after loved Sir Tristram, though there was much fair speech between them.

Then it befell upon a certain day that the good knight Sir Bleoberis de Ganis, brother to Sir Blamor de Ganis, and nigh cousin to Sir Lancelot of the Lake, came to King Mark's court and asked of him a favor. And though the king marveled, seeing he was a man of great renown, and a knight of the Round Table, he granted him all his asking. Then said Sir Bleoberis, "I will have the fairest lady in your court, at my own choosing."

"I may not say thee nay," replied the king; "choose therefore, but take all the issues of thy choice."

So when he had looked around, he chose the wife of Earl Segwarides, and took her by the hand, and set her upon horseback behind his squire, and rode forth on his way.

Presently thereafter came in the earl, and rode out straightway after him in rage. But all the ladies cried out shame upon Sir Tristram that he had not gone, and one rebuked him foully and called him coward knight, that he would stand and see a lady forced away from his uncle's court. But Sir Tristram answered her, "Fair lady, it is not my place to take part in this quarrel while her lord and husband is here to do it. Had he not been at this court, peradventure I had been her champion. And if it so befall that he speed ill, then may it happen that I speak with that foul knight before he pass out of this realm."

Anon ran in one of Sir Segwarides' squires, and told that his master was sore wounded, and at the point of death. When Sir Tristram heard that, he was soon armed and on his horse, and Governale, his servant, followed him with shield and spear.

And as he rode, he met his cousin Sir Andret, who had been commanded by King Mark to bring home to him two knights of King Arthur's court who roamed the country thereabouts seeking adventures.

"What tidings?" said Sir Tristram.

"God help me, never worse," replied his cousin; "for those I went to bring have beaten and defeated me, and set my message at naught."

"Fair cousin," said Sir Tristram, "ride ye on your way, perchance if I should meet them ye may be revenged."

So Sir Andret rode into Cornwall, but Sir Tristram rode after the two knights who had misused him, namely, Sir Sagramour le Desirous, and Sir Dodinas le Savage. And before long he saw them but a little way before him.

"Sir," said Governale, "by my advice thou wilt leave them alone, for they be two well-proved knights of Arthur's court."

"Shall I not therefore rather meet them!" said Sir Tristram, and, riding swiftly after them, he called to them to stop, and asked them whence they came, and whither they were going, and what they were doing in those marches.

Sir Sagramour looked haughtily at Sir Tristram, and made mocking of his words, and said, "Fair knight, be ye a knight of Cornwall?"

"Wherefore askest thou that?" said Tristram.

"Truly, because it is full seldom seen," replied Sir Sagramour, "that Cornish knights are valiant with their arms as with their tongues. It is but two hours since there met us such a Cornish knight, who spoke great words with might and prowess, but anon, with little mastery, he was laid on earth, as I trow wilt thou be also."

"Fair lords," said Sir Tristram, "it may chance I be a better man than he; but, be that as it may, he was my cousin, and for his sake I will assail ye both; one Cornish knight against ye two."

When Sir Dodinas le Savage heard this speech, he caught at his spear and said, "Sir knight, keep well thyself;" and then they parted and came together as it had been thunder, and Sir Dodinas' spear split asunder; but Sir Tristram smote him with so full a stroke as hurled him over his horse's crupper, and nearly brake his neck. Sir Sagramour, seeing his fellow's fall, marveled who this new knight be, and dressed his spear, and came against Sir Tristram as a whirlwind; but Sir Tristram smote him a mighty buffet, and rolled him with his horse down on the ground; and in the falling he brake his thigh.

174

Then, looking at them both as they lay groveling on the grass, Sir Tristram said, "Fair knights, will ye joust any more? Are there no bigger knights in King Arthur's court? Will ye soon again speak shame of Cornish knights?"

"Thou hast defeated us, in truth," replied Sir Sagramour, "and on the faith of knighthood I require thee tell us thy right name?"

"Ye charge me by a great thing," said Sir Tristram, "and I will answer ye."

And when they heard his name the two knights were right glad that they had met Sir Tristram, for his deeds were known through all the land, and they prayed him to abide in their company.

"Nay," said he, "I must find a fellow-knight of yours, Sir Bleoberis de Ganis, whom I seek."

"God speed you well," said the two knights; and Sir Tristram rode away.

Soon he saw before him in a valley Sir Bleoberis with Sir Segwarides' wife riding behind his squire upon a palfrey. At that he cried out aloud, "Abide, Sir knight of King Arthur's court, bring back again that lady or deliver her to me."

"I will not," said Bleoberis, "for I dread no Cornish knight."

"Why," said Sir Tristram, "may not a Cornish knight do well as any other? This day, but three miles back, two knights of thy own court met me, and found one Cornish knight enough for both before we parted."

"What were their names?" said Sir Bleoberis.

"Sir Sagramour le Desirous and Sir Dodinas le Savage," said Sir Tristram.

"Ah," said Sir Bleoberis, amazed; "hast thou then met with them? By my faith, they were two good knights and men of worship, and if thou hast beat both thou must needs be a good knight; but for all that, thou shalt beat me also ere thou hast this lady."

"Defend thee, then," cried out Sir Tristram, and came upon him swiftly with his spear in rest. But Sir Bleoberis was as swift as he, and each bore down the other, horse and all, on to the earth.

Then they sprang clear of their horses, and lashed together full eagerly and mightily with their swords, tracing and traversing on the right hand and on the left more than two hours, and sometimes rushing together with such fury that they both lay groveling on the ground. At last Sir Bleoberis started back and said, "Now, gentle knight, hold hard awhile, and let us speak together."

"Say on," said Sir Tristram, "and I will answer thee."

"Sir," said Sir Bleoberis, "I would know thy name, and court, and country."

"I have no shame to tell them," said Sir Tristram. "I am King Meliodas' son, and my mother was sister to King Mark, from whose court I now come. My name is Sir Tristram de Lyonesse."

"Truly," said Sir Bleoberis, "I am right glad to hear it, for thou art he that slew Sir Marhaus hand-to-hand, fighting for the Cornish tribute; and overcame Sir Palomedes at the great Irish tournament, where also thou didst overthrow Sir Gawain and his nine companions."

"I am that knight," said Sir Tristram, "and now I pray thee tell me thy name."

"I am Sir Bleoberis de Ganis, cousin of Sir Lancelot of the Lake, one of the best knights in all the world," he answered.

"Thou sayest truth," said Sir Tristram; "for Sir Lancelot, as all men know, is peerless in courtesy and knighthood, and for the great love I bear to his name I will not willingly fight more with thee his kinsman."

"In good faith, sir," said Sir Bleoberis, "I am as loth to fight thee more; but since thou hast followed me to win this lady, I proffer thee kindness, courtesy, and gentleness; this lady shall be free to go with which of us she pleaseth best."

"I am content," said Sir Tristram, "for I doubt not she will come to me."

"That shalt thou shortly prove," said he, and called his squire, and set the lady in the midst between them, who forthwith walked to Sir Bleoberis and elected to abide with him. Which, when Sir Tristram saw, he was in wondrous anger with her, and felt that he could scarce for shame return to King Mark's court. But Sir Bleoberis said, "Hearken to me, good knight, Sir Tristram, because King Mark gave me free choice of any gift, and because

176

this lady chose to go with me, I took her; but now I have fulfilled my quest and my adventure, and for thy sake she shall be sent back to her husband at the abbey where he lieth."

So Sir Tristram rode back to Tintagil, and Sir Bleoberis to the abbey where Sir Segwarides lay wounded, and there delivered up his lady, and departed as a noble knight.

After this adventure Sir Tristram abode still at his uncle's court, till in the envy of his heart King Mark devised a plan to be rid of him. So on a certain day he desired him to depart again for Ireland, and there demand La Belle Isault on his behalf, to be his queen—forever had Sir Tristram praised her beauty and her goodness, till King Mark desired to wed her for himself. Moreover, he believed his nephew surely would be slain by the queen's kindred if he once were found again in Ireland.

But Sir Tristram, scorning fear, made ready to depart, and took with him the noblest knights that could be found, arrayed in the richest fashion.

And when they were come to Ireland, upon a certain day Sir Tristram gave his uncle's message, and King Anguish consented thereto.

But when La Belle Isault was told the tidings she was very sorrowful and loth—yet made she ready to set forth with Sir Tristram, and took with her Dame Bragwaine, her chief gentlewoman. Then the queen gave Dame Bragwaine, and Governale, Sir Tristram's servant, a little flask, and charged them that La Belle Isault and King Mark should both drink of it on their marriage day, and then should they surely love each other all their lives.

Anon, Sir Tristram and Isault, with a great company, took the sea and departed. And so it chanced that one day sitting in their cabin they were athirst, and saw a little flask of gold which seemed to hold good wine. So Sir Tristram took it up, and said, "Fair lady, this looketh to be the best of wines, and your maid, Dame Bragwaine, and my servant, Governale, have kept it for themselves." Thereat they both laughed merrily, and drank each after other from the flask, and never before had they tasted any wine which seemed so good and sweet. But by the time they had finished drinking they loved each other so well that their love nevermore might leave them for weal or woe. And thus it came to pass that though Sir Tristram might never wed La Belle Isault, he did the mightiest deeds of arms for her sake only all his life.

Then they sailed onwards till they came to a castle called Pluere, where they would have rested. But anon there ran forth a great company and took them prisoners. And when they were in prison, Sir Tristram asked a knight and lady whom they found therein wherefore they were so shamefully dealt with; "for," said he, "it was never the custom of any place of honor that I ever came unto to seize a knight and lady asking shelter and thrust them into prison, and a full evil and discourteous custom is it."

"Sir," said the knight, "know ye not that this is called the Castle Pluere, or the weeping castle, and that it is an ancient custom here that whatsoever knight abideth in it must needs fight the lord of it, Sir Brewnor, and he that is the weakest shall lose his head. And if the lady he hath with him be less fair than the lord's wife, she shall lose her head; but if she be fairer, then must the lady of the castle lose her head."

"Now Heaven help me," said Sir Tristram, "but this is a foul and shameful custom. Yet have I one advantage, for my lady is the fairest that doth live in all the world, so that I nothing fear for her; and as for me, I will full gladly fight for my own head in a fair field."

Then said the knight, "Look ye be up betimes to-morrow, and make you ready and your lady."

And on the morrow came Sir Brewnor to Sir Tristram, and put him and Isault forth out of prison, and brought him a horse and armor, and bade him make ready, for all the commons and estates of that lordship waited in the field to see and judge the battle.

Then Sir Brewnor, holding his lady by the hand, all muffled, came forth, and Sir Tristram went to meet him with La Belle Isault beside him, muffled also. Then said Sir Brewnor, "Sir knight, if thy lady be fairer than mine, with thy sword smite off my lady's head; but if my lady be fairer than thine, with my sword I will smite off thy lady's head. And if I overcome thee thy lady shall be mine, and thou shalt lose thy head."

"Sir knight," replied Sir Tristram, "this is a right foul and felon custom, and rather than my lady shall lose her head will I lose my own."

"Nay," said Sir Brewnor, "but the ladies shall be now compared together and judgment shall be had."

"I consent not," cried Sir Tristram, "for who is here that will give rightful judgment? Yet doubt not that my lady is far fairer than thine own, and that will I prove and make good." Therewith Sir Tristram lifted up the veil from off La Belle Isault, and stood beside her with his naked sword drawn in his hand.

Then Sir Brewnor unmuffled his lady and did in like manner. But when he saw La Belle Isault he knew that none could be so fair, and all there present gave their judgment so. Then said Sir Tristram, "Because thou and thy lady have long used this evil custom, and have slain many good knights and ladies, it were a just thing to destroy thee both."

"In good sooth," said Sir Brewnor, "thy lady is fairer than mine, and of all women I never saw any so fair. Therefore, slay my lady if thou wilt, and I doubt not but I shall slay thee and have thine."

"Thou shalt win her," said Sir Tristram, "as dearly as ever knight won lady; and because of thy own judgment and of the evil custom that thy lady hath consented to, I will slay her as thou sayest."

And therewithal Sir Tristram went to him and took his lady from him, and smote off her head at a stroke.

"Now take thy horse," cried out Sir Brewnor, "for since I have lost my lady I will win thine and have thy life."

So they took their horses and came together as fast as they could fly, and Sir Tristram lightly smote Sir Brewnor from his horse. But he rose right quickly, and when Sir Tristram came again he thrust his horse through both the shoulders, so that it reeled and fell. But Sir Tristram was light and nimble, and voided his horse, and rose up and dressed his shield before him, though meanwhile, ere he could draw out his sword, Sir Brewnor gave him three or four grievous strokes. Then they rushed furiously together like two wild boars, and fought hurtling and hewing here and there for nigh two hours, and wounded each other full sorely. Then at the last Sir Brewnor rushed upon Sir Tristram and took him in his arms to throw him, for he trusted greatly in his strength. But Sir Tristram was at that time called the strongest and biggest knight of the world; for he was bigger than Sir Lancelot, though Sir Lancelot was better breathed. So anon he thrust Sir Brewnor groveling to the earth, and then unlaced his helm and struck off his head. Then all they that belonged to the castle came and did him homage and fealty, and prayed him to abide there for a season and put an end to that foul custom.

But within a while he departed and came to Cornwall, and there King Mark was forthwith wedded to La Belle Isault with great joy and splendor.

And Sir Tristram had high honor, and ever lodged at the king's court. But for all he had done him such services King Mark hated him, and on a certain day he set two knights to fall upon him as he rode in the forest. But Sir Tristram lightly smote one's head off, and sorely wounded the other, and made him bear his fellow's body to the king. At that the king dissembled and hid from Sir Tristram that the knights were sent by him; yet more than ever he hated him in secret, and sought to slay him.

So on a certain day, by the assent of Sir Andret, a false knight, and forty other knights, Sir Tristram was taken prisoner in his sleep and carried to a chapel on the rocks above the sea to be cast down. But as they were about to cast him in, suddenly he brake his bonds asunder, and rushing at Sir Andret, took his sword and smote him down therewith. Then, leaping down the rocks where none could follow, he escaped them. But one shot after him and wounded him full sorely with a poisoned arrow in the arm.

Anon, his servant Governale, with Sir Lambegus, sought him and found him safe among the rocks, and told him that King Mark had banished him and all his followers to avenge Sir Andret's death. So they took ship and came to Brittany.

Now Sir Tristram, suffering great anguish from his wound,

180

was told to seek Isoude, the daughter of the King of Brittany, for she alone could cure such wounds. Wherefore he went to King Howell's court, and said, "Lord, I am come into this country to have help from thy daughter, for men tell me none but she may help me." And Isoude gladly offering to do her best, within a month he was made whole.

While he abode still at that court, an earl named Grip made war upon King Howell, and besieged him; and Sir Kay Hedius, the king's son, went forth against him, but was beaten in battle and sore wounded. Then the king praying Sir Tristram for his help, he took with him such knights as he could find, and on the morrow, in another battle, did such deeds of arms that all the land spake of him. For there he slew the earl with his own hands, and more than a hundred knights besides.

When he came back King Howell met him, and saluted him with every honor and rejoicing that could be thought of, and took him in his arms, and said, "Sir Tristram, all my kingdom will I resign to thee."

"Nay," answered he, "God forbid, for truly am I beholden to you forever for your daughter's sake."

Then the king prayed him to take Isoude in marriage, with a great dower of lands and castles. To this Sir Tristram presently consenting anon they were wedded at the court.

But within a while Sir Tristram greatly longed to see Cornwall, and Sir Kay Hedius desired to go with him. So they took ship; but as soon as they were at sea the wind blew them upon the coast of North Wales, nigh to Castle Perilous, hard by a forest wherein were many strange adventures ofttimes to be met. Then said Sir Tristram to Sir Kay Hedius, "Let us prove some of them ere we depart." So they took their horses and rode forth.

When they had ridden a mile or more, Sir Tristram spied a goodly knight before him well armed, who sat by a clear fountain with a strong horse near him, tied to an oak-tree. "Fair sir," said he, when they came near, "ye seem to be a knight errant by your arms and harness, therefore make ready now to joust with one of us, or both."

181

Thereat the knight spake not, but took his shield and buckled it round his neck, and leaping on his horse caught a spear from his squire's hand.

Then said Sir Kay Hedius to Sir Tristram, "Let me assay him."

"Do thy best," said he.

So the two knights met, and Sir Kay Hedius fell sorely wounded in the breast.

"Thou hast well jousted," cried Sir Tristram to the knight; "now make ready for me!"

"I am ready," answered he, and encountered him, and smote him so heavily that he fell down from his horse. Whereat, being ashamed, he put his shield before him, and drew his sword, crying to the strange knight to do likewise. Then they fought on foot for well nigh two hours, till they were both weary.

At last Sir Tristram said, "In all my life I never met a knight so strong and well-breathed as ye be. It were a pity we should further hurt each other. Hold thy hand, fair knight, and tell me thy name."

"That will I," answered he, "if thou wilt tell me thine."

"My name," said he, "is Sir Tristram of Lyonesse."

"And mine, Sir Lamoracke of Gaul."

Then both cried out together, "Well met;" and Sir Lamoracke said, "Sir for your great renown, I will that ye have all the worship of this battle, and therefore will I yield me unto you." And therewith he took his sword by the point to yield him.

"Nay," said Sir Tristram, "ye shall not do so, for well I know ye do it of courtesy, and not of dread." And therewith he offered his sword to Sir Lamoracke, saying, "Sir, as an overcome knight, I yield me unto you as unto the man of noblest powers I have ever met with."

"Hold," said Sir Lamoracke, "let us now swear together nevermore to fight against each other."

Then did they swear as he said.

Then Sir Tristram returned to Sir Kay Hedius, and when he was whole of his wounds, they departed together in a ship, and landed on the coast of Cornwall. And when they came ashore, Sir Tristram eagerly sought news of La Belle Isault. And one told him in mistake that she was dead. Whereat, for sore and grievous sorrow, he fell down in a swoon, and so lay for three days and nights.

When he awoke therefrom he was crazed, and ran into the forest and abode there like a wild man many days; whereby he waxed lean and weak of body, and would have died, but that a hermit laid some meat beside him as he slept. Now in that forest was a giant named Tauleas, who, for fear of Tristram, had hid himself within a castle, but when they told him he was mad, came forth and went at large again. And on a certain day he saw a knight of Cornwall, named Sir Dinaunt, pass by with a lady, and when he had alighted by a well to rest, the giant leaped out from his ambush, and took him by the throat to slay him. But Sir Tristram, as he wandered through the forest, came upon them as they struggled; and when the knight cried out for help, he rushed upon the giant, and taking up Sir Dinaunt's sword, struck off therewith the giant's head, and straightway disappeared among the trees.

Anon, Sir Dinaunt took the head of Tauleas, and bare it with him to the court of King Mark, whither he was bound, and told of his adventures. "Where had ye this adventure?" said King Mark.

"At a fair fountain in thy forest," answered he.

"I would fain see that wild man," said the king.

So within a day or two he commanded his knights to a great hunting in the forest. And when the king came to the well, he saw a wild man lying there asleep, having a sword beside him; but he knew not that it was Sir Tristram. Then he blew his horn, and summoned all his knights to take him gently up and bear him to the court.

And when they came thereto they bathed and washed him, and brought him somewhat to his right mind. Now La Belle Isault knew not that Sir Tristram was in Cornwall; but when she heard that a wild man had been found in the forest, she came to see him. And so sorely was he changed, she knew him not. "Yet," said she to Dame Bragwaine, "in good faith I seem to have beheld him ofttimes before."

As she thus spoke a little hound, which Sir Tristram had given her when she first came to Cornwall, and which was ever with her, saw Sir Tristram lying there, and leapt upon him, licking his hands and face, and whined and barked for joy.

"Alas," cried out La Belle Isault, "it is my own true knight, Sir Tristram."

And at her voice Sir Tristram's senses wholly came again, and wellnigh he wept for joy to see his lady living.

But never would the hound depart from Tristram; and when King Mark and other knights came up to see him, it sat upon his body and bayed at all who came too near. Then one of the knights said, "Surely this is Sir Tristram; I see it by the hound."

"Nay," said the king, "it cannot be," and asked Sir Tristram on his faith who he was.

"My name," said he, "is Sir Tristram of Lyonesse, and now ye may do what ye list with me."

Then the king said, "It repents me that ye are recovered," and sought to make his barons slay him. But most of them would not assent thereto, and counseled him instead to banish Tristram for ten years again from Cornwall, for returning without orders from the king. So he was sworn to depart forthwith.

And as he went towards the ship a knight of King Arthur, named Sir Dinadan, who sought him, came and said, "Fair knight, ere that you pass out of this country, I pray you joust with me!"

"With a good will," said he.

Then they ran together, and Sir Tristram lightly smote him from his horse. Anon he prayed Sir Tristram's leave to bear him company, and when he had consented they rode together to the ship.

Then was Sir Tristram full of bitterness of heart, and said to all the knights who took him to the shore, "Greet well King Mark and all mine enemies from me, and tell them I will come again when I may. Well am I now rewarded for slaying Sir Marhaus, and delivering this kingdom from its bondage, and for the perils wherewithal I brought La Belle Isault from Ireland to the king, and rescued her at the Castle Pluere, and for the slaying of the giant Tauleas, and all the other deeds that I have done for Cornwall and

King Mark." Thus angrily and passing bitterly he spake, and went his way.

And after sailing awhile the ship stayed at a landing-place upon the coast of Wales; and there Sir Tristram and Sir Dinadan alighted, and on the shore they met two knights, Sir Ector and Sir Bors. And Sir Ector encountered with Sir Dinadan and smote him to the ground; but Sir Bors would not encounter with Sir Tristram, "For," said he, "no Cornish knights are men of worship." Thereat Sir Tristram was full wroth, but presently there met them two more knights, Sir Bleoberis and Sir Driant; and Sir Bleoberis proffered to joust with Sir Tristram, who shortly smote him down.

"I had not thought," cried out Sir Bors, "that any Cornish knight could do so valiantly."

Then Sir Tristram and Sir Dinadan departed, and rode into a forest, and as they rode a damsel met them, who for Sir Lancelot's sake was seeking any noble knights to rescue him. For Queen Morgan le Fay, who hated him, had ordered thirty men-at-arms to lie in ambush for him as he passed, with the intent to kill him. So the damsel prayed them to rescue him.

Then said Sir Tristram, "Bring me to that place, fair damsel."

But Sir Dinadan cried out, "It is not possible for us to meet with thirty knights! I will take no part in such a hardihood, for to match one or two or three knights is enough; but to match fifteen I will never assay."

"For shame," replied Sir Tristram, "do but your part."

"That will I not," said he; "wherefore, I pray ye, lend me your shield, for it is of Cornwall, and because men of that country are deemed cowards, ye are but little troubled as ye ride with knights to joust with."

"Nay," said Sir Tristram, "I will never give my shield up for her sake who gave it me; but if thou wilt not stand by me to-day I will surely slay thee; for I ask no more of thee than to fight one knight, and if thy heart will not serve thee that much, thou shalt stand by and look on me and them."

"Would God that I had never met with ye!" cried Sir Dinadan; "but I promise to look on and do all that I may to save myself."

Anon they came to where the thirty knights lay waiting, and Sir Tristram rushed upon them, saying, "Here is one who fights for love of Lancelot!" Then slew he two of them at the first onset with his spear, and ten more swiftly after with his sword. At that Sir Dinadan took courage, and assailed the others with him, till they turned and fled.

But Sir Tristram and Sir Dinadan rode on till nightfall, and meeting with a shepherd, asked him if he knew of any lodging thereabouts.

"Truly, fair lords," said he, "there is good lodging in a castle hard by, but it is a custom there that none shall lodge therein save ye first joust with two knights, and as soon as ye be within, ye shall find your match."

"That is an evil lodging," said Sir Dinadan; "lodge where ye will, I will not lodge there."

"Shame on thee!" said Sir Tristram; "art thou a knight at all?"

Then he required him on his knighthood to go with him, and they rode together to the castle. As soon as they were near, two knights came out and ran full speed against them; but both of them they overthrew, and went within the castle, and had noble cheer. Now, when they were unarmed and ready to take rest, there came to the castle-gate two knights, Sir Palomedes and Sir Gaheris, and desired the custom of the castle.

"I would far rather rest than fight," said Sir Dinadan.

"That may not be," replied Sir Tristram, "for we must needs defend the custom of the castle, seeing we have overcome its lords; therefore, make ready."

"Alas that I ever came into your company," said Sir Dinadan.

So they made ready, and Sir Gaheris encountered Sir Tristram and fell before him; but Sir Palomedes overthrew Sir Dinadan. Then would all fight on foot save Sir Dinadan, for he was sorely bruised and frighted by his fall. And when Sir Tristram prayed him to fight, "I will not," answered he, "for I was wounded by those thirty knights with whom we fought this morning; and as to you, ye are in truth like one gone mad, and who would cast himself away! There be but two knights in the world so mad, and the other is Sir Lancelot, with whom I once rode forth, who kept me evermore at battling so that for a quarter of a year thereafter I lay in my bed. Heaven defend me again from either of your fellowships!"

"Well," said Sir Tristram, "if it must be, I will fight them both."

Therewith he drew his sword and assailed Sir Palomedes and Sir Gaheris together; but Sir Palomedes said, "Nay, but it is a shame for two to fight with one." So he bade Sir Gaheris stand by, and he and Sir Tristram fought long together; but in the end Sir Tristram drave him backward, whereat Sir Gaheris and Sir Dinadan with one accord sundered them. Then Sir Tristram prayed the two knights to lodge there; but Dinadan departed and rode away into a priory hard by, and there he lodged that night.

And on the morrow came Sir Tristram to the priory to find him, and seeing him so weary that he could not ride, he left him, and departed. At that same priory was lodged Sir Pellinore, who asked Sir Dinadan Sir Tristram's name, but could not learn it, for Sir Tristram had charged that he should remain unknown. Then said Sir Pellinore, "Since ye will not tell it me, I will ride after him and find it myself."

"Beware, Sir knight," said Sir Dinadan, "ye will repent it if ye follow him."

But Sir Pellinore straightway mounted and overtook him, and cried to him to joust; whereat Sir Tristram forthwith turned and smote him down; and wounded him full sorely in the shoulder.

On the day after, Sir Tristram met a herald, who told him of a tournament proclaimed between King Carados of Scotland, and the King of North Wales, to be held at the Maiden's Castle. Now King Carados sought Sir Lancelot to fight there on his side, and the King of North Wales sought Sir Tristram. And Sir Tristram purposed to be there. So as he rode, he met Sir Key, the seneschal, and Sir Sagramour, and Sir Key proffered to joust with him. But he refused, desiring to keep himself unwearied for the tourney. Then Sir Key cried, "Sir knight of Cornwall, joust with me, or yield as recreant." When Sir Tristram heard that, he fiercely turned and set his spear in rest, and spurred his horse towards him. But when Sir

Key saw him so madly coming on, he in his turn refused, whereat Sir Tristram called him coward, till for shame he was compelled to meet him. Then Sir Tristram lightly smote him down, and rode away. But Sir Sagramour pursued him, crying loudly to joust with him also. So Sir Tristram turned and quickly overthrew him likewise, and departed.

Anon a damsel met him as he rode, and told him of a knight adventurous who did great harm thereby, and prayed him for his help. But as he went with her he met Sir Gawain, who knew the damsel for a maiden of Queen Morgan le Fay. Knowing, therefore, that she needs must have evil plots against Sir Tristram, Sir Gawain demanded of him courteously whither he went.

"I know not whither," said he, "save as this damsel leadeth me."

"Sir," said Sir Gawain, "ye shall not ride with her, for she and her lady never yet did good to any;" and, drawing his sword, he said to the damsel, "Tell me now straightway for what cause thou leadest this knight, or else shalt thou die; for I know of old thy lady's treason."

"Mercy, Sir Gawain," cried the damsel, "and I will tell thee all." Then she told him that Queen Morgan had ordained thirty fair damsels to seek out Sir Lancelot and Sir Tristram, and by their wiles persuade them to her castle, where she had thirty knights in wait to slay them.

"Oh shame!" cried Sir Gawain, "that ever such foul treason should be wrought by a queen, and a king's sister." Then said he to Sir Tristram, "Sir knight, if ye will stand with me, we will together prove the malice of these thirty knights."

"I will not fail you," answered he, "for but few days since I had to do with thirty knights of that same queen, and trust we may win honor as lightly now as then."

So they rode together, and when they came to the castle, Sir Gawain cried aloud, "Queen Morgan le Fay, send out thy knights that we may fight with them."

Then the queen urged her knights to issue forth, but they durst not, for they well knew Sir Tristram, and feared him greatly.

So Sir Tristram and Sir Gawain went on their way, and as they rode they saw a knight, named Sir Brewse-without-pity, chasing a lady, with intent to slay her. Then Sir Gawain prayed Sir Tristram to hold still and let him assail that knight. So he rode up between Sir Brewse and the lady, and cried, "False knight, turn thee to me and leave that lady." Then Sir Brewse turned and set his spear in rest, and rushed against Sir Gawain and overthrew him, and rode his horse upon him as he lay, which when Sir Tristram saw, he cried, "Forbear that villainy," and galloped at him. But when Sir Brewse saw by the shield it was Sir Tristram, he turned and fled. And though Sir Tristram followed swiftly after him, yet he was so well horsed that he escaped.

Anon Sir Tristram and Sir Gawain came nigh the Maiden's Castle, and there an old knight named Sir Pellonnes gave them lodging. And Sir Persides, the son of Sir Pellonnes, a good knight, came out to welcome them. And, as they stood talking at a bay window of the castle, they saw a goodly knight ride by on a black horse, and carrying a black shield. "What knight is that?" asked Tristram.

"One of the best knights in all the world," said Sir Persides.

"Is he Sir Lancelot?" said Sir Tristram.

"Nay," answered Sir Persides, "it is Sir Palomedes, who is yet unchristened."

Within a while one came and told them that a knight with a black shield had smitten down thirteen knights. "Let us go and see this jousting," said Sir Tristram. So they armed themselves and went down. And when Sir Palomedes saw Sir Persides, he sent a squire to him and proffered him to joust. So they jousted, and Sir Persides was overthrown. Then Sir Tristram made ready to joust, but ere he had his spear in rest, Sir Palomedes took him at advantage, and struck him on the shield so that he fell. At that Sir Tristram was wroth out of measure and sore ashamed, wherefore he sent a squire and prayed Sir Palomedes to joust once again. But he would not, saying, "Tell thy master to revenge himself to-morrow at the Maiden's Castle, where he shall see me again."

So on the morrow Sir Tristram commanded his servant to give him a black shield with no cognizance thereon, and he and Sir Persides rode into the tournament and joined King Carados' side.

Then the knights of the King of North Wales came forth, and there was a great fighting and breaking of spears, and overthrow of men and horses.

Now King Arthur sat above in a high gallery to see the tourney and give the judgment, and Sir Lancelot sat beside him. Then came against Sir Tristram and Sir Persides, two knights with them of North Wales, Sir Bleoberis and Sir Gaheris; and Sir Persides was smitten down and nigh slain, for four horsemen rode over him. But Sir Tristram rode against Sir Gaheris and smote him from his horse, and when Sir Bleoberis next encountered him, he overthrew him also. Anon they horsed themselves again, and with them came Sir Dinadan, whom Sir Tristram forthwith smote so sorely, that he reeled off his saddle. Then cried he, "Ah! Sir knight, I know ye better than ye deem, and promise nevermore to come against ye." Then rode Sir Bleoberis at him the second time, and had a buffet that felled him to the earth. And soon thereafter the king commanded to cease for that day, and all men marveled who Sir Tristram was, for the prize of the first day was given him in the name of the Knight of the Black Shield.

Now Sir Palomedes was on the side of the King of North Wales, but knew not Sir Tristram again. And, when he saw his marvelous deeds, he sent to ask his name. "As to that," said Sir Tristram, "he shall not know at this time, but tell him he shall know when I have broken two spears upon him, for I am the knight he smote down yesterday, and whatever side he taketh, I will take the other."

So when they told him that Sir Palomedes would be on King Carados' side—for he was kindred to King Arthur—"Then will I be on the King of North Wales' side," said he, "but else would I be on my lord King Arthur's."

Then on the morrow, when King Arthur was come, the heralds blew unto the tourney. And King Carados jousted with the King of a Hundred Knights and fell before him, and then came in King Arthur's knights and bare back those of North Wales. But anon Sir Tristram came to aid them and bare back the battle, and fought so mightily that none could stand against him, for he smote down on the right and on the left, so that all the knights and common people shouted his praise.

"Since I bare arms," said King Arthur, "never saw I a knight do more marvelous deeds."

Then the King of the Hundred Knights and those of North Wales set upon twenty knights who were of Sir Lancelot's kin, who fought all together, none failing the others. When Sir Tristram beheld their nobleness and valor, he marveled much. "Well may he be valiant and full of prowess," said he, "who hath such noble knights for kindred." So, when he had looked on them awhile, he thought it shame to see two hundred men assailing twenty, and riding to the King of a Hundred Knights, he said, "I pray thee, Sir king, leave your fighting with those twenty knights, for ye be too many and they be too few. For ye shall gain no honor if ye win, and that I see verily ye will not do unless ye slay them; but if ye will not stay, I will ride with them and help them."

"Nay," said the king, "ye shall not do so; for full gladly I will do your courtesy," and with that he withdrew his knights.

Then Sir Tristram rode his way into the forest, that no man might know him. And King Arthur caused the heralds to blow that the tourney should end that day, and he gave the King of North Wales the prize, because Sir Tristram was on his side. And in all the field there was such a cry that the sound thereof was heard two miles away—"The knight with the black shield hath won the field."

"Alas!" said King Arthur, "where is that knight? it is shame to let him thus escape us." Then he comforted his knights, and said, "Be not dismayed, my friends, howbeit ye have lost the day; be of good cheer; to-morrow I myself will be in the field, and fare with you." So they all rested that night.

And on the morrow the heralds blew unto the field. So the King of North Wales and the King of a Hundred Knights encountered with King Carados and the King of Ireland, and overthrew them. With that came King Arthur, and did mighty deeds of arms, and overthrew the King of North Wales and his fellows, and put twenty valiant knights to the worse. Anon came in Sir Palomedes, and made great fight upon King Arthur's side. But Sir Tristram rode furiously against him, and Sir Palomedes was thrown from his horse. Then cried King Arthur, "Knight of the Black Shield, keep thyself." And as he spake he came upon him, and smote him from his saddle to the ground, and so passed on to other knights. Then Sir Palomedes having now another horse rushed at Sir Tristram, as he was on foot, thinking to run over him. But he was aware of him, and stepped aside, and grasped Sir Palomedes by the arms, and pulled him off his horse. Then they rushed together with their swords, and many stood still to gaze on them. And Sir Tristram smote Sir Palomedes with three mighty strokes upon the helm, crying at each stroke, "Take this for Sir Tristram's sake," and with that Sir Palomedes fell to the earth.

Anon the King of North Wales brought Sir Tristram another horse, and Sir Palomedes found one also. Then did they joust again with passing rage, for both by now were like mad lions. But Sir Tristram avoided his spear, and seized Sir Palomedes by the neck, and pulled him from his saddle, and bore him onward ten spears' length, and so let him fall. Then King Arthur drew forth his sword and smote the spear asunder, and gave Sir Tristram two or three sore strokes ere he could get at his own sword. But when he had it in his hand he mightily assailed the king. With that eleven knights of Lancelot's kin went forth against him, but he smote them all down to the earth, so that men marveled at his deeds.

And the cry was now so great that Sir Lancelot got a spear in his hand, and came down to assay Sir Tristram, saying, "Knight with the black shield, make ready." When Sir Tristram heard him he leveled his spear, and both stooping their heads, they ran together mightily, as it had been thunder. And Sir Tristram's spear brake short, but Sir Lancelot struck him with a deep wound in the side and broke his spear, yet overthrew him not. Therewith Sir Tristram, smarting at his wound, drew forth his sword, and rushing at Sir Lancelot, gave him mighty strokes upon the helm, so that the sparks flew from it, and Sir Lancelot stooped his head down to the saddle-bow. But then Sir Tristram turned and left the field, for he felt his wound so grievous that he deemed he should soon die. Then did Sir Lancelot hold the field against all comers, and put the King of North Wales and his party to the worse. And because he was the last knight in the field the prize was given him.

But he refused to take it, and when the cry was raised, "Sir Lancelot hath won the day," he cried out, "Nay, but Sir Tristram is the victor, for he first began and last endured, and so hath he done each day." And all men honored Lancelot more for his knightly words than if he had taken the prize.

This was the tournament ended, and King Arthur departed to Caerleon, for the Whitsun feast was now nigh come, and all the knights adventurous went their ways. And many sought Sir Tristram in the forest whither he had gone, and at last Sir Lancelot found him, and brought him to King Arthur's court, as hath been told already.

SIR GALAHAD AND THE QUEST OF THE HOLY GRAIL

XIII. THE KNIGHTS GO TO SEEK THE GRAIL

After these things Merlin fell into a dotage of love for a damsel of the lady of the lake, and would let her have no rest, but followed her in every place. And ever she encouraged him, and made him welcome till she had learned all his crafts that she desired to know.

Then upon a time she went with him beyond the sea to the land of Benwicke, and as they went he showed her many wonders, till at length she was afraid, and would fain have been delivered from him.

And as they were in the forest of Broceliande, they sat together under an oak-tree, and the damsel prayed to see all that charm whereby men might be shut up yet alive in rocks or trees. But he refused her a long time, fearing to let her know, yet in the end, her prayers and kisses overcame him, and he told her all. Then did she make him great cheer, but anon, as he lay down to sleep, she softly rose, and walked about him waving her hands and muttering the charm, and presently enclosed him fast within the tree whereby he slept. And therefrom nevermore he could by any means come out for all the crafts that he could do. And so she departed and left Merlin.

At the vigil of the next Feast of Pentecost, when all the Knights of the Round Table were met together at Camelot, and had heard mass, and were about to sit down to meat, there rode into the hall a fair lady on horseback, who went straight up to King Arthur where he sat upon his throne, and reverently saluted him.

"God be with thee, fair damsel," quoth the king; "what desirest thou of me?"

"I pray thee tell me, lord," she answered, "where Sir Lancelot is."

"Yonder may ye see him," said King Arthur.

Then went she to Sir Lancelot and said, "Sir, I salute thee in

197

King Pelles' name, and require thee to come with me into the forest hereby."

Then asked he her with whom she dwelt, and what she wished of him.

"I dwell with King Pelles," said she, "whom Balin erst so sorely wounded when he smote the dolorous stroke. It is he who hath sent me to call thee."

"I will go with thee gladly," said Sir Lancelot, and bade his squire straightway saddle his horse and bring his armor.

Then came the queen to him and said, "Sir Lancelot, will ye leave me thus at this high feast?"

"Madam," replied the damsel, "by dinner-time to-morrow he shall be with you."

"If I thought not," said the queen, "he should not go with thee by my goodwill."

Then Sir Lancelot and the lady rode forth till they came to the forest, and in a valley thereof found an abbey of nuns, whereby a squire stood ready to open the gates. When they had entered, and descended from their horses, a joyful crowd pressed round Sir Lancelot and heartily saluted him, and led him to the abbess's chamber, and unarmed him. Anon he saw his cousins likewise there, Sir Bors and Sir Lionel, who also made great joy at seeing him, and said, "By what adventure art thou here, for we thought to have seen thee at Camelot to-morrow?"

"A damsel brought me here," said he, "but as yet I know not for what service."

As they thus talked twelve nuns came in, who brought with them a youth so passing fair and well made, that in all the world his match could not be found. His name was Galahad, and though he knew him not, nor Lancelot him, Sir Lancelot was his father.

"Sir," said the nuns, "we bring thee here this child whom we have nourished from his youth, and pray thee to make him a knight, for from no worthier hand can he receive that order."

Then Sir Lancelot, looking on the youth, saw that he was seemly and demure as a dove, with every feature good and noble, and thought he never had beheld a better fashioned man of his years. "Cometh this desire from himself?" said he.

"Yea," answered Galahad and all the nuns.

"To-morrow, then, in reverence for the feast, he shall have his wish," said Sir Lancelot.

And the next day at the hour of prime, he knighted him, and said, "God make of thee as good a man as He hath made thee beautiful."

Then with Sir Lionel and Sir Bors he returned to the court, and found all gone to the minster to hear service. When they came into the banquet-hall each knight and baron found his name written in some seat in letters of gold, as "here ought to sit Sir Lionel," "here ought to sit Sir Gawain,"—and so forth. And in the Perilous Seat, at the high center of the table, a name was also written, whereat they marveled greatly, for no living man had ever yet dared sit upon that seat, save one, and him a flame leaped forth and drew down under earth, so that he was no more seen.

Then came Sir Lancelot and read the letters in that seat, and said, "My counsel is that this inscription be now covered up until the knight be come who shall achieve this great adventure." So they made a veil of silk and put it over the letters.

In the meanwhile came Sir Gawain to the court and told the king he had a message to him from beyond the sea, from Merlin.

"For," said he, "as I rode through the forest of Broceliande but five days since, I heard the voice of Merlin speaking to me from the midst of an oak-tree, whereat, in great amazement, I besought him to come forth. But he, with many groans, replied he never more might do so, for that none could free him, save the damsel of the Lake, who had enclosed him there by his own spells which he had taught her. 'But go,' said he, 'to King Arthur, and tell him, that he now prepare his knights and all his Table Round to seek the Sangreal, for the time is come when it shall be achieved.'"

When Sir Gawain had spoken thus, King Arthur sat pensive in spirit, and mused deeply of the Holy Grail and what saintly knight should come who might achieve it.

Anon he bade them hasten to set on the banquet. "Sir," said

Sir Key, the seneschal, "if we go now to meat ye will break the ancient custom of your court, for never have ye dined at this high feast till ye have seen some strange adventure."

"Thou sayest truly," said the king, "but my mind was full of wonders and musings, till I bethought me not of mine old custom."

As they stood speaking thus, a squire ran in and cried, "Lord, I bring thee marvelous tidings."

"What be they?" said King Arthur.

"Lord," said he, "hereby at the river is a marvelous great stone, which I myself saw swim down hither-wards upon the water, and in it there is set a sword, and ever the stone heaveth and swayeth on the water, but floateth down no further with the stream."

"I will go and see it," said the king. So all the knights went with him, and when they came to the river, there surely found they a mighty stone of red marble floating on the water, as the squire had said, and therein stuck a fair and rich sword, on the pommel whereof were precious stones wrought skillfully with gold into these words: "No man shall take me hence but he by whose side I should hang, and he shall be the best knight in the world."

When the king read this, he turned round to Sir Lancelot, and said, "Fair sir, this sword ought surely to be thine, for thou art the best knight in all the world."

But Lancelot answered soberly, "Certainly, sir, it is not for me; nor will I have the hardihood to set my hand upon it. For he that toucheth it and faileth to achieve it shall one day be wounded by it mortally. But I doubt not, lord, this day will show the greatest marvels that we yet have seen, for now the time is fully come, as Merlin hath forewarned us, when all the prophecies about the Sangreal shall be fulfilled."

Then stepped Sir Gawain forward and pulled at the sword, but could not move it, and after him Sir Percival, to keep him fellowship in any peril he might suffer. But no other knight durst be so hardy as to try.

"Now may ye go to your dinner," said Sir Key, "for a marvelous adventure ye have had."

So all returned from the river, and every knight sat down in his

200

own place, and the high feast and banquet then was sumptuously begun, and all the hall was full of laughter and loud talk and jests, and running to and fro of squires who served their knights, and noise of jollity and mirth.

Then suddenly befell a wondrous thing, for all the doors and windows of the hall shut violently of themselves, and made thick darkness; and presently there came a fair and gentle light from out the Perilous Seat, and filled the palace with its beams. Then a dead silence fell on all the knights, and each man anxiously beheld his neighbor.

But King Arthur rose and said, "Lords and fair knights, have ye no fear, but rejoice; we have seen strange things to-day, but stranger yet remain. For now I know we shall to-day see him who may sit in the Siege Perilous, and shall achieve the Sangreal. For as ye all well know, that holy vessel, wherefrom at the Supper of our Lord before His death He drank the wine with His disciples, hath been held ever since the holiest treasure of the world, and wheresoever it hath rested peace and prosperity have rested with it on the land. But since the dolorous stroke which Balin gave King Pelles none have seen it, for Heaven, wroth with that presumptuous blow, hath hid it none know where. Yet somewhere in the world it still may be, and may be it is left to us, and to this noble order of the Table Round, to find and bring it home, and make of this our realm the happiest in the earth. Many great quests and perilous adventures have ye all taken and achieved, but this high quest he only shall attain who hath clean hands and a pure heart, and valor and hardihood beyond all other men."

While the king spoke there came in softly an old man robed all in white, leading with him a young knight clad in red from top to toe, but without armor or shield, and having by his side an empty scabbard.

The old man went up to the king, and said, "Lord, here I bring thee this young knight of royal lineage, and of the blood of Joseph of Arimathea, by whom the marvels of thy court shall fully be accomplished."

The king was right glad at his words, and said, "Sir, ye be right heartily welcome, and the young knight also."

Then the old man put on Sir Galahad (for it was he) a crimson robe trimmed with fine ermine, and took him by the hand and led him to the Perilous Seat, and lifting up the silken cloth which hung upon it, read these words written in gold letters, "This is the seat of Sir Galahad, the good knight."

"Sir," said the old man, "this place is thine."

Then sat Sir Galahad down firmly and surely, and said to the old man, "Sir, ye may now go your way, for ye have done well and truly all ye were commanded, and commend me to my grandsire, King Pelles, and say that I shall see him soon." So the old man departed with a retinue of twenty noble squires.

But all the knights of the Round Table marveled at Sir Galahad, and at his tender age, and at his sitting there so surely in the Perilous Seat.

Then the king led Sir Galahad forth from the palace, to show him the adventure of the floating stone. "Here," said he, "is as great a marvel as I ever saw, and right good knights have tried and failed to gain that sword."

"I marvel not thereat," said Galahad, "for this adventure is not theirs, but mine; and for the certainty I had thereof, I brought no sword with me, as thou mayst see here by this empty scabbard."

Anon he laid his hand upon the sword, and lightly drew it from the stone, and put it in his sheath, and said, "This sword was that enchanted one which erst belonged to the good knight, Sir Balin, wherewith he slew through piteous mistake his brother Balan; who also slew him at the same time: all which great woe befell him through the dolorous stroke he gave my grandsire, King Pelles, the wound whereof is not yet whole, nor shall be till I heal him."

As he stood speaking thus, they saw a lady riding swiftly down the river's bank towards them, on a white palfrey, who, saluting the king and queen, said, "Lord king, Nacien the hermit sendeth thee word that to thee shall come to-day the greatest honor and worship that hath yet ever befallen a king of Britain; for this day shall the Sangreal appear in thy house."

With that the damsel took her leave, and departed the same way she came.

"Now," said the king, "I know that from to-day the quest of the Sangreal shall begin, and all ye of the Round Table will be scattered so that nevermore shall I see ye again together as ye are now; let me then see a joust and tournament amongst ye for the last time before ye go."

So they all took their harness and met together in the meadows by Camelot, and the queen and all her ladies sat in a tower to see.

Then Sir Galahad, at the prayer of the king and queen, put on a coat of light armor, and a helmet, but shield he would take none, and grasping a lance, he drove into the middle of the press of knights, and began to break spears marvelously, so that all men were full of wonder. And in so short a time he had surmounted and exceeded the rest, save Sir Lancelot and Sir Percival, that he took the chief worship of the field.

Then the king and all the court and fellowship of knights went back to the palace, and so to evensong in the great minster, a royal and goodly company, and after that sat down to supper in the hall, every knight in his own seat, as they had been before.

Anon suddenly burst overhead the cracking and crying of great peals of thunder, till the palace walls were shaken sorely, and they thought to see them riven all to pieces.

And in the midst of the blast there entered in a sunbeam, clearer by seven times than ever they saw day, and a marvelous great glory fell upon them all. Then each knight, looking on his neighbor, found his face fairer than he had ever seen, and so—all standing on their feet—they gazed as dumb men on each other, not knowing what to say.

Then entered into the hall the Sangreal, borne aloft without hands through the midst of the sunbeam, and covered with white samite, so that none might see it. And all the hall was filled with perfume and incense, and every knight was fed with the food he best loved. And when the holy vessel had been thus borne through the hall, it suddenly departed, no man saw whither.

When they recovered breath to speak, King Arthur first rose up, and yielded thanks to God and to our Lord.

Then Sir Gawain sprang up and said, "Now have we all been fed by miracle with whatsoever food we thought of or desired; but with our eyes we have not seen the blessed vessel whence it came, so carefully and preciously it was concealed. Therefore, I make a vow, that from to-morrow I shall labor twelve months and a day in quest of the Sangreal, and longer if need be; nor will I come again into this court until mine eyes have seen it evidently."

When he had spoken thus, knight after knight rose up and vowed himself to the same quest, till the most part of the Round Table had thus sworn.

But when King Arthur heard them all, he could not refrain his eyes from tears, and said, "Sir Gawain, Sir Gawain, thou hast set me in great sorrow, for I fear me my true fellowship shall never meet together here again; and surely never Christian king had such a company of worthy knights around his table at one time."

And when the queen and her ladies and gentlewomen heard the vows, they had such grief and sorrow as no tongue could tell; and Queen Guinevere cried out, "I marvel that my lord will suffer them to depart from him." And many of the ladies who loved knights would have gone with them, but were forbidden by the hermit Nacien, who sent this message to all who had sworn themselves to the quest: "Take with ye no lady nor gentlewoman, for into so high a service as ye go in, no thought but of our Lord and heaven may enter."

On the morrow morning all the knights rose early, and when they were fully armed, save shields and helms, they went in with the king and queen to service in the minster. Then the king counted all who had taken the adventure on themselves, and found them a hundred and fifty knights of the Round Table; and so they all put on their helms, and rode away together in the midst of cries and lamentations from the court, and from the ladies, and from all the town.

But the queen went alone to her chamber, that no man might see her sorrow; and Sir Lancelot followed her to say farewell.

When she saw him she cried out, "Oh, Sir Lancelot, thou hast betrayed me; thou hast put me to death thus to depart and leave my lord the king."

"Ah, madam," said he, "be not displeased or angry, for I shall come again as soon as I can with honor."

"Alas!" said she, "that ever I saw thee; but He that suffered death upon the cross for all mankind be to thee safety and good conduct, and to all thy company."

Then Sir Lancelot saluted her and the king, and went forth with the rest, and came with them that night to Castle Vagon, where they abode, and on the morrow they departed from each other on their separate ways, every knight taking the way that pleased him best.

Now Sir Galahad went forth without a shield, and rode so four days without adventure; and on the fourth day, after evensong, he came to an abbey of white monks, where he was received in the house, and led into a chamber. And there he was unarmed, and met two knights of the Round Table, King Bagdemagus, and Sir Uwaine.

"Sirs," said Sir Galahad, "what adventure hath brought ye here?"

"Within this place, as we are told," they answered, "there is a shield no man may bear around his neck without receiving sore mischance, or death within three days."

"To-morrow," said King Bagdemagus, "I shall attempt the adventure; and if I fail, do thou, Sir Galahad, take it up after me."

"I will willingly," said he; "for as ye see I have no shield as yet."

So on the morrow they arose and heard mass, and afterwards King Bagdemagus asked where the shield was kept. Then a monk led him behind the altar, where the shield hung, as white as any snow, and with a blood-red cross in the midst of it.

"Sir," said the monk, "this shield should hang from no knight's neck unless he be the worthiest in the world. I warn ye, therefore, knights; consider well before ye dare to touch it."

"Well," said King Bagdemagus, "I know well that I am far from the best knight in all the world, yet shall I make the trial"; and so he took the shield, and bore it from the monastery.

"If it please thee," said he to Sir Galahad, "abide here till thou hearest how I speed."

"I will abide thee," said he.

Then taking with him a squire who might return with any tidings to Sir Galahad, the king rode forth; and before he had gone two miles, he saw in a fair valley a hermitage, and a knight who came forth dressed in white armor, horse and all, who rode fast against him. When they encountered, Bagdemagus brake his spear upon the White Knight's shield, but was himself struck through the shoulder with a sore wound, and hurled down from his horse. Then the White Knight alighting, came and took the white shield from the king, and said, "Thou hast done great folly, for this shield ought never to be borne but by one who hath no living peer." And turning to the squire, he said, "Bear thou this shield to the good knight, Sir Galahad, and greet him well from me."

"In whose name shall I greet him?" said the squire.

"Take thou no heed of that," he answered; "it is not for thee or any earthly man to know."

"Now tell me, fair sir, at the least," said the squire, "why may this shield be never borne except its wearer come to injury or death?"

"Because it shall belong to no man save its rightful owner, Galahad," replied the knight.

Then the squire went to his master, and found him wounded nigh to death, wherefore he fetched his horse, and bore him back with him to the abbey. And there they laid him in a bed, and looked to his wounds; and when he had lain many days grievously sick, he at the last barely escaped with his life.

"Sir Galahad," said the squire, "the knight who overthrew King Bagdemagus sent you greeting, and bade you bear this shield."

"Now blessed be God and fortune," said Sir Galahad, and hung the shield about his neck, and armed him, and rode forth.

Anon he met the White Knight by the hermitage, and each saluted courteously the other.

"Sir," said Sir Galahad, "this shield I bear hath surely a full marvelous history."

"Thou sayest rightly," answered he. "That shield was made in the days of Joseph of Arimathea, the gentle knight who took our Lord down from the cross. He, when he left Jerusalem with his kindred, came to the country of King Evelake, who warred continually with one Tollome; and when, by the teaching of Joseph, King Evelake became a Christian, this shield was made for him in our Lord's name; and through its aid King Tollome was defeated. For when King Evelake met him next in battle, he hid it in a veil, and suddenly uncovering it, he showed his enemies the figure of a bleeding man nailed to a cross, at sight of which they were discomfited and fled. Presently after that, a man whose hand was smitten off touched the cross upon the shield, and had his hand restored to him; and many other miracles it worked. But suddenly the cross that was upon it vanished away. Anon both Joseph and King Evelake came to Britain, and by the preaching of Joseph the people were made Christians. And when at length he lay upon his death-bed, King Evelake begged of him some token ere he died. Then, calling for his shield, he dipped his finger in his own blood, for he was bleeding fast, and none could staunch the wound, and marked that cross upon it, saying, 'This cross shall ever show as bright as now, and the last of my lineage shall wear this shield about his neck, and go forth to all the marvelous deeds he will achieve.'"

When the White Knight had thus spoken he vanished suddenly away, and Sir Galahad returned to the abbey.

As he alighted, came a monk, and prayed him to go see a tomb in the churchyard, wherefrom came such a great and hideous noise, that none could hear it but they went nigh mad, or lost all strength. "And, sir," said he, "I deem it is a fiend."

"Lead me thither," said Sir Galahad.

When they were come near the place, "Now," said the monk, "go thou to the tomb, and lift it up."

And Galahad, nothing afraid, quickly lifted up the stone, and forthwith came out a foul smoke, and from the midst thereof leaped up the loathliest figure that ever he had seen in the likeness of man; and Galahad blessed himself, for he knew it was a fiend of hell. Then he heard a voice crying out, "Oh, Galahad, I cannot tear thee as I would; I see so many angels round thee, that I may not come at thee."

Then the fiend suddenly disappeared with a marvelous great cry; and Sir Galahad, looking in the tomb, saw there a body all armed, with a sword beside it. "Now, fair brother," said he to the monk, "let us remove this cursed body, which is not fit to lie in a churchyard, for when it lived, a false and perjured Christian man dwelt in it. Cast it away, and there shall come no more hideous noises from the tomb."

"And now must I depart," he added, "for I have much in hand, and am upon the holy quest of the Sangreal, with many more good knights."

So he took his leave, and rode many journeys backwards and forwards as adventure would lead him; and at last one day he departed from a castle without first hearing mass, which was it ever his custom to hear before he left his lodging. Anon he found a ruined chapel on a mountain, and went in and kneeled before the altar, and prayed for wholesome counsel what to do; and as he prayed he heard a voice, which said, "Depart, adventurous knight, unto the Maiden's Castle, and redress the violence and wrongs there done!"

Hearing these words he cheerfully arose, and mounted his horse, and rode but half a mile, when he saw before him a strong castle, with deep ditches round it, and a fair river running past. And seeing an old churl hard by, he asked him what men called that castle.

"Fair sir," said he, "it is the Maiden's Castle."

"It is a cursed place," said Galahad, "and all its masters are but felons, full of mischief and hardness and shame."

"For that good reason," said the old man, "thou wert well-advised to turn thee back."

"For that same reason," quoth Sir Galahad, "will I the more certainly ride on."

Then, looking at his armor carefully, to see that nothing failed him, he went forward, and presently there met him seven damsels, who cried out, "Sir knight, thou ridest in great peril, for thou hast two waters to pass over."

"Why should I not pass over them?" said he, and rode straight on.

Anon he met a squire, who said, "Sir knight, the masters of this castle defy thee, and bid thee go no further, till thou showest them thy business here."

"Fair fellow," said Sir Galahad, "I am come here to destroy their wicked customs."

"If that be thy purpose," answered he, "thou wilt have much to do."

"Go thou," said Galahad, "and hasten with my message."

In a few minutes after rode forth furiously from the gateways of the castle seven knights, all brothers, and crying out, "Knight, keep thee," bore down all at once upon Sir Galahad. But thrusting forth his spear, he smote the foremost to the earth, so that his neck was almost broken, and warded with his shield the spears of all the others, which every one brake off from it, and shivered into pieces. Then he drew out his sword, and set upon them hard and fiercely, and by his wondrous force drave them before him, and chased them to the castle gate, and there he slew them.

At that came out to him an ancient man, in priest's vestments, saying, "Behold, sir, here, the keys of this castle."

Then he unlocked the gates, and found within a multitude of people, who cried out, "Sir knight, ye be welcome, for long have we waited thy deliverance," and told him that the seven felons he had slain had long enslaved the people round about, and killed all knights who passed that way, because the maiden whom they had robbed of the castle had foretold that by one knight they should themselves be overthrown.

"Where is the maiden?" asked Sir Galahad.

"She lingereth below in a dungeon," said they.

So Sir Galahad went down and released her, and restored her her inheritance; and when he had summoned the barons of the country to do her homage, he took his leave, and departed.

Presently thereafter, as he rode, he entered a great forest, and in a glade thereof met two knights, disguised, who proffered him to joust. These were Sir Lancelot, his father, and Sir Percival, but neither knew the other. So he and Sir Lancelot encountered first, and Sir Galahad smote down his father. Then drawing his sword, for his spear was broken, he fought with Sir Percival, and struck so mightily that he clave Sir Percival's helm, and smote him from his horse.

Now hard by where they fought there was a hermitage, where dwelt a pious woman, a recluse, who, when she heard the sound, came forth, and seeing Sir Galahad ride, she cried, "God be with thee, the best knight in the world; had yonder knights known thee as well as I do, they would not have encountered with thee."

When Sir Galahad heard that, fearing to be made known, he forthwith smote his horse with his spurs, and departed at a great pace.

Sir Lancelot and Sir Percival heard her words also, and rode fast after him, but within a while he was out of their sight. Then Sir Percival rode back to ask his name of the recluse; but Sir Lancelot went forward on his quest, and following any path his horse would take, he came by-and-by after nightfall to a stone cross hard by an ancient chapel. When he had alighted and tied his horse up to a tree, he went and looked in through the chapel door, which was all ruinous and wasted, and there within he saw an altar, richly decked with silk, whereon there stood a fair candlestick of silver, bearing six great lights. And when Sir Lancelot saw the light, he tried to get within the chapel, but could find no place. So, being passing weary and heavy, he came again to his horse, and when he had unsaddled him, and set him free to pasture, he unlaced his helm, and ungirded his sword, and laid him down to sleep upon his shield before the cross.

And while he lay between waking and sleeping, he saw come by him two white palfreys bearing a litter, wherein a sick knight lay, and the palfreys stood still by the cross. Then Sir Lancelot heard the sick man say, "O sweet Lord, when shall this sorrow leave me, and the holy vessel pass by me, wherethrough I shall be blessed? for I have long endured."

With that Sir Lancelot saw the chapel open, and the candlestick with the six tapers come before the cross, but he could see none who bare it. Then came there also a table of silver, and thereon the holy vessel of the Sangreal. And when the sick knight saw that, he sat up, and lifting both his hands, said, "Fair Lord, sweet Lord, who art here within this holy vessel, have mercy on me, that I may be whole"; and therewith he crept upon his hands and knees so nigh, that he might touch the vessel; and when he had kissed it, he leaped up, and stood and cried aloud, "Lord God, I thank Thee, for I am made whole." Then the Holy Grail departed with the table and the silver candlestick into the chapel, so that Sir Lancelot saw it no more, nor for his sins' sake could he follow it. And the knight who was healed went on his way.

Then Sir Lancelot awake, and marveled whether he had seen aught but a dream. And as he marveled, he heard a voice saying, "Sir Lancelot, thou art unworthy, go thou hence, and withdraw thee from this holy place." And when he heard that, he was passing heavy, for he bethought him of his sins.

So he departed weeping, and cursed the day of his birth, for the words went into his heart, and he knew wherefore he was thus driven forth. Then he went to seek his arms and horse, but could not find them; and then he called himself the wretchedest and most unhappy of all knights, and said, "My sin hath brought me unto great dishonor: for when I sought earthly honors, I achieved them ever; but now I take upon me holy things, my guilt doth hinder me, and shameth me; therefore had I no power to stir or speak when the holy blood appeared before me."

So thus he sorrowed till it was day, and he heard the birds sing; then was he somewhat comforted, and departing from the cross on foot, he came into a wild forest, and to a high mountain, and there he found a hermitage; and, kneeling before the hermit down upon both his knees, he cried for mercy for his wicked works, and prayed him to hear his confession. But when he told his name, the hermit marveled to see him in so sore a case, and said, "Sir, ye ought to thank God more than any knight living, for He hath given thee more honor than any; yet for thy presumption, while in deadly sin to come into the presence of His flesh and blood, He suffered thee neither to see nor follow it. Wherefore, believe that all thy strength and manhood will avail thee little, when God is against thee."

Then Sir Lancelot wept and said, "Now know I well ye tell me truth."

Then he confessed to him, and told him all his sins, and how he had for fourteen years served but Queen Guinevere only, and forgotten God, and done great deeds of arms for her, and not for Heaven, and had little or nothing thanked God for the honor that he won. And then Sir Lancelot said, "I pray you counsel me."

"I will counsel thee," said he: "never more enter into that queen's company when ye can avoid it."

So Sir Lancelot promised him.

"Look that your heart and your mouth accord," said the good man, "and ye shall have more honor and more nobleness than ever ye have had."

Then were his arms and horse restored to him, and so he took his leave, and rode forth, repenting greatly.

Now Sir Percival had ridden back to the recluse, to learn who that knight was whom she had called the best in the world. And when he had told her that he was Sir Percival, she made passing great joy of him, for she was his mother's sister, wherefore she opened her door to him, and made him good cheer. And on the morrow she told him of her kindred to him, and they both made great rejoicing. Then he asked her who that knight was, and she told him, "He it is who on Whit Sunday last was clad in the red robe, and bare the red arms; and he hath no peer, for he worketh all by miracle, and shall be never overcome by any earthly hands."

"By my goodwill," said Sir Percival, "I will never after these tidings have to do with Sir Galahad but in the way of kindness; and I would fain learn where I may find him."

"Fair nephew," said she, "ye must ride to the Castle of Goth, where he hath a cousin; by him ye may be lodged, and he will teach you the way to go; but if he can tell you no tidings, ride straight to the Castle of Carbonek, where the wounded king is lying, for there shall ye surely hear true tidings of him."

So Sir Percival departed from his aunt, and rode till evensong time, when he was ware of a monastery closed round with walls and deep ditches, where he knocked at the gate, and anon was let in. And there he had good cheer that night, and on the morrow heard mass. And beside the altar where the priest stood, was a rich bed of silk and cloth of gold; and on the bed there lay a man passing old, having a crown of gold upon his head, and all his body was full of great wounds, and his eyes almost wholly blind; and ever he held up his hands and said, "Sweet Lord, forget not me!"

Then Sir Percival asked one of the brethren who he was.

"Sir," said the good man, "ye have heard of Joseph of Arimathea, how he was sent of Jesus Christ into this land to preach and teach the Christian faith. Now, in the city of Sarras he converted a king named Evelake, and this is he. He came with Joseph to this land, and ever desired greatly to see the Sangreal; so on a time he came nigh thereto, and was struck almost blind. Then he cried out for mercy, and said, 'Fair Lord, I pray thee let me never die until a good knight of my blood achieve the Sangreal, and I may see and kiss him.' When he had thus prayed, he heard a voice that said, 'Thy prayers be heard and answered, for thou shalt not die till that knight kiss thee; and when he cometh shall thine eyes be opened and thy wounds be healed.' And now hath he lived here for three hundred winters in a holy life, and men say a certain knight of King Arthur's court shall shortly heal him."

Thereat Sir Percival marveled greatly, for he well knew who that knight should be; and so, taking his leave of the monk, departed.

Then he rode on till noon, and came into a valley where he met twenty men-at-arms bearing a dead knight on a bier. And they cried to him, "Whence comest thou?"

"From King Arthur's court," he answered.

Then they all cried together, "Slay him," and set upon him.

But he smote down the first man to the ground, and his horse upon him; whereat seven of them all at once assailed him, and others slew his horse. Thus he had been either taken or slain, but

213

by good chance Sir Galahad was passing by that way, who, seeing twenty men attacking one, cried, "Slay him not," and rushed upon them; and, as fast as his horse could drive, he encountered with the foremost man, and smote him down. Then, his spear being broken, he drew forth his sword and struck out on the right hand and on the left, at each blow smiting down a man, till the remainder fled, and he pursued them.

Then Sir Percival, knowing that it was Sir Galahad, would fain have overtaken him, but could not, for his horse was slain. Yet followed he on foot as fast as he could go; and as he went there met him a yeoman riding on a palfrey, and leading in his hand a great black steed. So Sir Percival prayed him to lend him the steed, that he might overtake Sir Galahad. But he replied, "That can I not do, fair sir, for the horse is my master's, and should I lend it he would slay me." So he departed, and Sir Percival sat down beneath a tree in heaviness of heart. And as he sat, anon a knight went riding past on the black steed which the yeoman had led. And presently after came the yeoman back in haste, and asked Sir Percival if he had seen a knight riding his horse.

"Yea," said Sir Percival.

"Alas," said the yeoman, "he hath reft him from me by strength, and my master will slay me."

Then he besought Sir Percival to take his hackney and follow, and get back his steed. So he rode quickly, and overtook the knight, and cried, "Knight, turn again." Whereat he turned and set his spear, and smote Sir Percival's hackney in the breast, so that it fell dead, and then went on his way. Then cried Sir Percival after him, "Turn now, false knight, and fight with me on foot"; but he would not, and rode out of sight.

Then was Sir Percival passing wroth and heavy of heart, and lay down to rest beneath a tree, and slept till midnight. When he awoke he saw a woman standing by him, who said to him right fiercely, "Sir Percival, what doest thou here?"

"I do neither good nor evil," said he.

"If thou wilt promise me," said she, "to do my will whenever

214

I shall ask thee, I will bring thee here a horse that will bear thee wheresoever thou desirest."

At that he was full glad, and promised as she asked. Then anon she came again, with a great black steed, strong and well appareled. So Sir Percival mounted, and rode through the clear moonlight, and within less than an hour had gone a four days' journey, till he came to a rough water that roared; and his horse would have borne him into it, but Sir Percival would not suffer him, yet could he scarce restrain him. And seeing the water so furious, he made the sign of the cross upon his forehead, whereat the horse suddenly shook him off, and with a terrible sound leaped into the water and disappeared, the waves all burning up in flames around him. Then Sir Percival knew it was a fiend which had brought him the horse; so he commended himself to God, and prayed that he might escape temptations, and continued in prayer till it was day.

Then he saw that he was on a wild mountain, nigh surrounded on all sides by the sea, and filled with wild beasts; and going on into a valley, he saw a serpent carrying a young lion by the neck. With that came another lion, crying and roaring after the serpent, and anon overtook him, and began to battle with him. And Sir Percival helped the lion, and drew his sword, and gave the serpent such a stroke that it fell dead. Threat the lion fawned upon him like a dog, licking his hands, and crouching at his feet, and at night lay down by him and slept at his side.

And at noon the next day Sir Percival saw a ship come sailing before a strong wind upon the sea towards him, and he rose and went towards it. And when it came to shore, he found it covered with white samite, and on the deck there stood an old man dressed in priest's robes, who said, "God be with you, fair sir; whence come ye?"

"I am a knight of King Arthur's court," said he, "and follow the quest of the Sangreal; but here have I lost myself in this wilderness."

"Fear nothing," said the old man, "for I have come from a strange country to comfort thee."

Then he told Sir Percival it was a fiend of hell upon which he had ridden to the sea, and that the lion, whom he had delivered from the serpent, meant the Church. And Sir Percival rejoiced at these tidings, and entered into the ship, which presently sailed from the shore into the sea.

Now when Sir Bors rode forth from Camelot to seek the Sangreal, anon he met a holy man riding on an ass, and courteously saluted him.

"Who are ye, son?" said the good man.

"I am a knight," said he, "in quest of the Sangreal, and would fain have thy counsel, for he shall have much earthly honor who may bring it to a favorable end."

"That is truth," said the good man, "for he shall be the best knight of the world; yet know that none shall gain it save by sinless living."

So they rode to his hermitage together, and there he prayed Sir Bors to abide that night, and anon they went into the chapel, and Sir Bors was confessed. And they eat bread and drank water together.

"Now," said the hermit, "I pray thee eat no other food till thou sit at the table where the Sangreal shall be." Thereto Sir Bors agreed.

"Also," said the hermit, "it were wise that ye should wear a sackcloth garment next your skin, for penance"; and in this also did Sir Bors as he was counseled. And afterwards he armed himself and took his leave.

Then rode he onwards all that day, and as he rode he saw a passing great bird sit in an old dry tree, whereon no leaves were left; and many little birds lay round the great one, nigh dead with hunger. Then did the big bird smite himself with his own bill, and bled till he died amongst his little ones, and they recovered life in drinking up his blood. When Sir Bors saw this he knew it was a token, and rode on full of thought. And about eventide he came to a tower, whereto he prayed admission, and he was received gladly by the lady of the castle. But when a supper of many meats and dainties was set before him, he remembered his vow, and bade a squire to bring him water, and therein he dipped his bread, and ate.

Then said the lady, "Sir Bors, I fear ye like not my meat."

"Yea, truly," said he; "God thank thee, madam; but I may eat no other meat this day."

After supper came a squire, and said, "Madam, bethink thee to provide a champion for thee to-morrow for the tourney, or else shall thy sister have thy castle."

At that the lady wept, and made great sorrow. But Sir Bors prayed her to be comforted, and asked her why the tournament was held. Then she told him how she and her sister were the daughters of King Anianse, who left them all his lands between them; and how her sister was the wife of a strong knight, named Sir Pridan le Noir, who had taken from herself all her lands, save the one tower wherein she dwelt. "And now," said she, "this also will they take, unless I find a champion by to-morrow."

Then said Sir Bors, "Be comforted; to-morrow I will fight for thee"; whereat she rejoiced not a little, and sent word to Sir Pridan that she was provided and ready. And Sir Bors lay on the floor, and in no bed, nor ever would do otherwise till he had achieved his quest.

On the morrow he arose and clothed himself, and went into the chapel, where the lady met him, and they heard mass together. Anon he called for his armor, and went with a goodly company of knights to the battle. And the lady prayed him to refresh himself ere he should fight, but he refused to break his fast until the tournament were done. So they all rode together to the lists, and there they saw the lady's eldest sister, and her husband, Sir Pridan le Noir. And a cry was made by the heralds that, whichever should win, his lady should have all the other's lands.

Then the two knights departed asunder a little space, and came together with such force, that both their spears were shivered, and their shields and hauberks pierced through; and both fell to the ground sorely wounded, with their horses under them. But swiftly they arose, and drew their swords, and smote each other on the head with many great and heavy blows, till the blood ran down their bodies; and Sir Pridan was a full good knight, so that Sir Bors had more ado than he had thought for to overcome him.

But at last Sir Pridan grew a little faint; that instantly perceived

Sir Bors, and rushed upon him the more vehemently, and smote him fiercely, till he rent off his helm, and then gave him great strokes upon his visage with the flat of his sword, and bade him yield or be slain.

And then Sir Pridan cried him mercy, and said, "For God's sake slay me not, and I will never war against thy lady more." So Sir Bors let him go, and his wife fled away with all her knights.

Then all those who had held lands of the lady of the tower came and did homage to her again, and swore fealty. And when the country was at peace Sir Bors departed, and rode forth into a forest until it was midday, and there befell him a marvelous adventure.

For at a place where two ways parted, there met him two knights, bearing Sir Lionel, his brother, all naked, bound on a horse, and as they rode, they beat him sorely with thorns, so that the blood trailed down in more than a hundred places from his body; but for all this he uttered no word or groan, so great he was of heart. As soon as Sir Bors knew his brother, he put his spear in rest to run and rescue him; but in the same moment heard a woman's voice cry close beside him in the wood, "St. Mary, succor thy maid"; and, looking round, he saw a damsel whom a felon knight dragged after him into the thickets; and she, perceiving him, cried piteously for help, and adjured him to deliver her as he was a sworn knight. Then was Sir Bors sore troubled, and knew not what to do, for he thought within himself, "If I let my brother be, he will be murdered; but if I help not the maid, she is shamed forever, and my vow compelleth me to set her free; wherefore must I first help her, and trust my brother unto God."

So, riding to the knight who held the damsel, he cried out, "Sir knight, lay your hand off that maid, or else ye be but dead."

At that the knight set down the maid, and dropped his shield, and drew forth his sword against Sir Bors, who ran at him, and smote him through both shield and shoulder, and threw him to the earth; and when he pulled his spear forth, the knight swooned. Then the maid thanked Sir Bors heartily, and he set her on the knight's horse, and brought her to her men-at-arms, who presently came riding after her. And they made much joy, and besought him to come to her father, a great lord, and he should be right welcome. But "truly," said he, "I may not at this time, for I have a great adventure yet to do"; and commending them to God, he departed in great haste to find his brother.

So he rode, seeking him by the track of the horses a great while. Anon he met a seeming holy man riding upon a strong black horse, and asked him, had he seen pass by that way a knight led bound and beaten with thorns by two others.

"Yea, truly, such an one I saw," said the man; "but he is dead, and lo! his body is hard by in a bush."

Then he showed him a newly slain body lying in a thick bush, which seemed indeed to be Sir Lionel. Then made Sir Bors such mourning and sorrow that by-and-by he fell into a swoon upon the ground. And when he came to himself again, he took the body in his arms and put it on his horse's saddle, and bore it to a chapel hard by, and would have buried it. But when he made the sign of the cross, he heard a full great noise and cry as though all the fiends of hell had been about him, and suddenly the body and the chapel and the old man vanished all away. Then he knew that it was the devil who had thus beguiled him, and that his brother yet lived.

Then held he up his hands to heaven, and thanked God for his own escape from hurt, and rode onwards; and anon, as he passed by an hermitage in a forest, he saw his brother sitting armed by the door. And when he saw him he was filled with joy, and lighted from his horse, and ran to him and said, "Fair brother, when came ye hither?"

But Sir Lionel answered, with an angry face, "What vain words be these, when for you I might have been slain? Did ye not see me bound and led away to death, and left me in that peril to go succoring a gentlewoman, the like whereof no brother ever yet hath done? Now, for thy false misdeed, I do defy thee, and ensure thee speedy death."

Then Sir Bors prayed his brother to abate his anger, and said, "Fair brother, remember the love that should be between us twain."

But Sir Lionel would not hear, and prepared to fight, and mounted his horse and came before him, crying, "Sir Bors, keep thee from me, for I shall do to thee as a felon and a traitor; therefore, start upon thy horse, for if thou wilt not, I will run upon thee as thou standest."

But for all his words Sir Bors would not defend himself against his brother. And anon the fiend stirred up Sir Lionel to such rage, that he rushed over him and overthrew him with his horse's hoofs, so that he lay swooning on the ground. Then would he have rent off his helm and slain him, but the hermit of that place ran out, and prayed him to forbear, and shielded Sir Bors with his body.

Then Sir Lionel cried out, "Now, God so help me, sir priest, but I shall slay thee else thou depart, and him too after thee."

And when the good man utterly refused to leave Sir Bors, he smote him on the head until he died, and then he took his brother by the helm and unlaced it, to have stricken off his head, and so he would have done, but suddenly was pulled off backwards by a knight of the Round Table, who, by the will of Heaven, was passing by that place—Sir Colgrevance by name.

"Sir Lionel," he cried, "will ye slay your brother, one of the best knights of all the world? That ought no man to suffer."

"Why," said Sir Lionel, "will ye hinder me and meddle in this strife? beware, lest I shall slay both thee and him."

And when Sir Colgrevance refused to let them be, Sir Lionel defied him, and gave him a great stroke through the helmet, whereat Sir Colgrevance drew his sword, and smote again right manfully. And so long they fought together that Sir Bors awoke from his swoon, and tried to rise and part them, but had no strength to stand upon his feet.

Anon Sir Colgrevance saw him, and cried out to him for help, for now Sir Lionel had nigh defeated him. When Sir Bors heard that, he struggled to his feet, and put his helmet on, and took his sword. But before he could come to him, Sir Lionel had smitten off Sir Colgrevance's helm, and thrown him to the earth and slain him. Then turned he to his brother as a man possessed by fiends, and gave him such a stroke as bent him nearly double.

But Sir Bors prayed him for God's sake to quit that battle, "For if it befell us that we either slew the other we should die for care of that sin."

"Never will I spare thee if I master thee," cried out Sir Lionel.

Then Sir Bors drew his sword all weeping, and said, "Now, God have mercy on me, though I defend my life against my brother"; with that he lifted up his sword to strike, but suddenly he heard a mighty voice, "Put up thy sword, Sir Bors, and flee, or thou shalt surely slay him." And then there fell upon them both a fiery cloud, which flamed and burned their shields, and they fell to the earth in sore dread.

Anon Sir Bors rose to his feet, and saw that Sir Lionel had taken no harm. Then came the voice again, and said, "Sir Bors, go hence and leave thy brother, and ride thou forward to the sea, for there Sir Percival abideth thee."

Then he said to his brother, "Brother, forgive me all my trespass against thee."

And Sir Lionel answered, "God forgive it thee, as I do."

Then he departed and rode to the sea, and on the strand he found a ship all covered with white samite, and as soon as he had entered thereinto, it put forth from the shore. And in the midst of the ship there stood an armed knight, whom he knew to be Sir Percival. Then they rejoiced greatly over each other, and said, "We lack nothing now but the good knight Sir Galahad."

Now when Sir Galahad had rescued Sir Percival from the twenty knights he rode into a vast forest. And after many days it befell that he came to a castle whereat was a tournament. And the knights of the castle were put to the worse; which when he saw, he set his spear in rest and ran to help them, and smote down many of their adversaries. And as it chanced, Sir Gawain was amongst the stranger knights, and when he saw the white shield with the red cross, he knew it was Sir Galahad, and proffered to joust with him. So they encountered, and having broken their spears, they drew their swords, and Sir Galahad smote Sir Gawain so sorely on the helm that he clove it through, and struck on slanting to the earth, carving the horse's shoulder in twain, and Sir Gawain fell to the earth. Then Sir Galahad beat back all who warred against the castle, yet would he not wait for thanks, but rode away that no man might know him.

And he rested that night at a hermitage, and when he was asleep, he heard a knocking at the door. So he rose, and found a damsel there, who said, "Sir Galahad, I will that ye arm you, and mount upon your horse and follow me, for I will show you within these three days the highest adventure that ever any knight saw."

Anon Sir Galahad armed him, and took his horse, and commended himself to God, and bade the gentlewoman go, and he would follow where she liked.

So they rode onwards to the sea as fast as their horses might gallop, and at night they came to a castle in a valley, inclosed by running water, and by strong and high walls, whereinto they entered and had great cheer, for the lady of the castle was the damsel's mistress.

And when he was unarmed, the damsel said to her lady, "Madam, shall we abide here this night?"

"Nay," said she, "but only till he hath dined and slept a little."

So he ate and slept a while, till the maid called him, and armed him by torchlight; and when he had saluted the lady of the castle, the damsel and Sir Galahad rode on.

Anon they came to the seaside, and lo! the ship, wherein were Sir Percival and Sir Bors, abode by the shore. Then they cried, "Welcome, Sir Galahad, for we have awaited thee long."

Then they rejoiced to see each other, and told of all their adventures and temptations. And the damsel went into the ship with them, and spake to Sir Percival: "Sir Percival, know ye not who I am?"

And he replied, "Nay, certainly, I know thee not."

Then said she, "I am thy sister, the daughter of King Pellinore, and am sent to help thee and these knights, thy fellows, to achieve the quest which ye all follow."

So Sir Percival rejoiced to see his sister, and they departed from the shore. And after a while they came upon a whirlpool, where their ship could not live. Then saw they another greater ship hard by and went towards it, but saw neither man nor woman therein.

And on the end of it these words were written, "Thou who shalt enter me, beware that thou be in steadfast belief, for I am Faith; and if thou doubtest, I cannot help thee." Then were they all adread, but, commending themselves to God, they entered in.

As soon as they were on board they saw a fair bed, whereon lay a crown of silk, and at the foot was a fair and rich sword drawn from its scabbard half a foot and more. The pommel was of precious stones of many colors, every color having a different virtue, and the scales of the haft were of two ribs of different beasts. The one was bone of a serpent from Calidone forest, named the serpent of the fiend; and its virtue saveth all men who hold it from weariness. The other was of a fish that haunteth the floods of Euphrates, named Ertanax; and its virtue causeth whoever holdeth it to forget all other things, whether of joy or pain, save the thing he seeth before him.

"In the name of God," said Sir Percival, "I shall assay to handle this sword"; and set his hand to it, but could not grasp it. "By my faith," said he, "now have I failed."

Sir Bors set his hand to it, and failed also.

Then came Sir Galahad, and saw these letters written red as blood, "None shall draw me forth save the hardiest of all men; but he that draweth me shall never be shamed or wounded to death." "By my faith," said Sir Galahad, "I would draw it forth, but dare not try."

"Ye may try safely," said the gentlewoman, Sir Percival's sister, "for be ye well assured the drawing of this sword is forbid to all but you. For this was the sword of David, King of Israel, and Solomon his son made for it this marvelous pommel and this wondrous sheath, and laid it on this bed till thou shouldest come and take it up; and though before thee some have dared to raise it, yet have they all been maimed or wounded for their daring."

"Where," said Sir Galahad, "shall we find a girdle for it?"

"Fair sir," said she, "dismay you not"; and therewith took from out a box a girdle, nobly wrought with golden thread, set full of precious stones and with a rich gold buckle. "This girdle, lords," said she, "is made for the most part of mine own hair, which, while I was yet in the world, I loved full well; but when I knew that this adventure was ordained me, I cut off and wove as ye now see."

Then they all prayed Sir Galahad to take the sword, and so anon he gripped it in his fingers; and the maiden girt it round his waist, saying, "Now reck I not though I die, for I have made thee the worthiest knight of all the world."

"Fair damsel," said Sir Galahad, "ye have done so much that I shall be your knight all the days of my life."

Then the ship sailed a great way on the sea, and brought them to land near the Castle of Carteloise. When they were landed came a squire and asked them, "Be ye of King Arthur's court?"

"We are," said they.

"In an evil hour are ye come," said he, and went back swiftly to the castle.

Within a while they heard a great horn blow, and saw a multitude of well-armed knights come forth, who bade them yield or die. At that they ran together, and Sir Percival smote one to the earth and mounted his horse, and so likewise did Sir Bors and Sir Galahad, and soon had they routed all their enemies and alighted on foot, and with their swords slew them downright, and entered into the castle.

Then came there forth a priest, to whom Sir Galahad kneeled and said, "In sooth, good father, I repent me of this slaughter; but we were first assailed, or else it had not been."

"Repent ye not," said the good man, "for if ye lived as long as the world lasted ye could do no better deed, for these were all the felon sons of a good knight, Earl Hernox, whom they have thrown into a dungeon, and in his name have slain priests and clerks, and beat down chapels far and near."

Then Sir Galahad prayed the priest to bring him to the earl; who, when he saw Sir Galahad, cried out, "Long have I waited for thy coming, and now I pray thee hold me in thine arms that I may die in peace."

And therewith, when Sir Galahad had taken him in his arms, his soul departed from his body.

Then came a voice in the hearing of them all, "Depart now, Sir Galahad, and go quickly to the maimed king, for he hath long abided to receive health from thy hand."

So the three knights departed, and Sir Percival's sister with them, and came to a vast forest, and saw before them a white hart, exceeding fair, led by four lions; and marveling greatly at that sight, they followed.

Anon they came to a hermitage and a chapel, whereunto the hart entered, and the lions with it. Then a priest offered mass, and presently they saw the hart change into the figure of a man, most sweet and comely to behold; and the four lions also changed and became a man, an eagle, a lion, and an ox. And suddenly all those five figures vanished without sound. Then the knights marveled greatly, and fell upon their knees, and when they rose they prayed the priest to tell them what that sight might mean.

"What saw ye, sirs?" said he, "for I saw nothing." Then they told him.

"Ah, lords!" said he, "ye are full welcome; now know I well ye be the knights who shall achieve the Sangreal, for unto them alone such mysteries are revealed. The hart ye saw is One above all men, white and without blemish, and the four lions with Him are the four evangelists."

When they heard that they heartily rejoiced, and thanking the priest, departed.

Anon, as they passed by a certain castle, an armed knight suddenly came after them, and cried out to the damsel, "By the holy cross, ye shall not go till ye have yielded to the custom of the castle."

"Let her go," said Sir Percival, "for a maiden, wheresoever she cometh, is free."

"Whatever maiden passeth here," replied the knight, "must give a dishful of her blood from her right arm."

"It is a foul and shameful custom," cried Sir Galahad and both his fellows, "and sooner will we die than let this maiden yield thereto."

"Then shall ye die," replied the knight, and as he spake there came out from a gate hard by, ten or twelve more, and encountered with them, running upon them vehemently with a great cry. But the three knights withstood them, and set their hands to their swords, and beat them down and slew them.

At that came forth a company of threescore knights, all armed. "Fair lords," said Sir Galahad, "have mercy on yourselves and keep from us."

"Nay, fair lords," they answered, "rather be advised by us, and yield ye to our custom."

"It is an idle word," said Galahad, "in vain ye speak it."

"Well," said they, "will ye die?"

"We be not come thereto as yet," replied Sir Galahad.

Then did they fall upon each other, and Sir Galahad drew forth his sword, and smote on the right hand and on the left, and slew so mightily that all who saw him thought he was a monster and no earthly man. And both his comrades helped him well, and so they held the field against that multitude till it was night. Then came a good knight forward from the enemy and said, "Fair knights, abide with us to-night and be right welcome; by the faith of our bodies as we are true knights, to-morrow ye shall rise unharmed, and meanwhile maybe ye will, of your own accord, accept the custom of the castle when ye know it better."

So they entered and alighted and made great cheer. Anon, they asked them whence that custom came. "The lady of this castle is a leper," said they, "and can be no way cured save by the blood of a pure virgin and a king's daughter; therefore to save her life are we her servants bound to stay every maid that passeth by, and try if her blood may not cure our mistress."

Then said the damsel, "Take ye of my blood as much as ye will, if it may avail your lady."

And though the three knights urged her not to put her life in that great peril, she replied, "If I die to heal another's body, I shall get health to my soul," and would not be persuaded to refuse.

So on the morrow she was brought to the sick lady, and her arm was bared, and a vein thereof was opened, and the dish filled with her blood. Then the sick lady was anointed therewith, and anon she was whole of her malady. With that Sir Percival's sister lifted up her hand and blessed her, saying, "Madam, I am come to my death to make you whole; for God's love pray for me"; and thus saying she fell down in a swoon.

Then Sir Galahad, Sir Percival, and Sir Bors started to lift her up and staunch her blood, but she had lost too much to live. So when she came to herself she said to Sir Percival, "Fair brother, I must die for the healing of this lady, and now, I pray thee, bury me not here, but when I am dead put me in a boat at the next haven and let me float at venture on the sea. And when ye come to the city of Sarras, to achieve the Sangreal, shall ye find me waiting by a tower, and there I pray thee bury me, for there shall Sir Galahad and ye also be laid." Thus having said, she died.

Then Sir Percival wrote all the story of her life and put it in her right hand, and so laid her in a barge and covered it with silk. And the wind arising drove the barge from land, and all the knights stood watching it till it was out of sight.

Anon they returned to the castle, and forthwith fell a sudden tempest of thunder and lightning and rain, as if the earth were broken up: and half the castle was thrown down. Then came a voice to the three knights which said, "Depart ye now asunder till ye meet again where the maimed king is lying." So they parted and rode divers ways.

Now after Sir Lancelot had left the hermit, he rode a long while till he knew not whither to turn, and so he lay down to sleep, if haply he might dream whither to go.

And in his sleep a vision came to him saying, "Lancelot, rise up and take thine armor, and enter the first ship that thou shalt find."

When he awoke he obeyed the vision, and rode till he came to the sea-shore, and found there a ship without sails or oars, and as soon as he was in it he smelt the sweetest savor he had ever known, and seemed filled with all things he could think of or desire. And looking round he saw a fair bed, and thereon a gentlewoman lying dead, who was Sir Percival's sister. And as Sir Lancelot looked on her he spied the writing in her right hand, and, taking it, he read therein her story. And more than a month thereafter he abode in that ship and was nourished by the grace of Heaven, as Israel was fed with manna in the desert.

And on a certain night he went ashore to pass the time, for he was somewhat weary, and, listening, he heard a horse come towards him, from which a knight alighted and went up into the ship; who, when he saw Sir Lancelot, said, "Fair sir, ye be right welcome to mine eyes, for I am thy son Galahad, and long time I have sought for thee." With that he kneeled and asked his blessing, and took off his helm and kissed him, and the great joy there was between them no tongue can tell.

Then for half a year they dwelt together in the ship, and served God night and day with all their powers, and went to many unknown islands, where none but wild beasts haunted, and there found many strange and perilous adventures.

And upon a time they came to the edge of a forest, before a cross of stone, and saw a knight armed all in white, leading a white horse. Then the knight saluted them, and said to Galahad, "Ye have been long time enough with your father; now, therefore, leave him and ride this horse till ye achieve the Holy Quest."

Then went Sir Galahad to his father and kissed him full courteously, and said, "Fair father, I know not when I shall see thee again."

And as he took his horse a voice spake in their hearing, "Ye shall meet no more in this life."

"Now, my son, Sir Galahad," said Sir Lancelot, "since we must so part and see each other never more, I pray the High Father of Heaven to preserve both you and me."

Then they bade farewell, and Sir Galahad entered the forest, and Sir Lancelot returned to the ship, and the wind rose and drove him more than a month through the sea, whereby he slept but little, yet ever prayed that he might see the Sangreal.

So it befell upon a certain midnight, the moon shining clear, he came before a fair and rich castle, whereof the postern gate was open towards the sea, having no keeper save two lions in the entry.

Anon Sir Lancelot heard a voice: "Leave now thy ship and go within the castle, and thou shalt see a part of thy desire."

Then he armed and went towards the gate, and coming to the lions he drew out his sword, but suddenly a dwarf rushed out and smote him on the arm, so that he dropt his sword, and heard again the voice, "Oh, man of evil faith, and poor belief, wherefore trustest thou thine arms above thy Maker?" Then he put up his sword and signed the cross upon his forehead, and so passed by the lions without hurt.

And going in, he found a chamber with the door shut, which in vain he tried to open. And listening thereat he heard a voice within, which sang so sweetly that it seemed no earthly thing, "Joy and honor be to the Father of Heaven!" Then he kneeled down at the door, for he knew well the Sangreal was there within.

Anon the door was opened without hands, and forthwith came thereout so great a splendor as if all the torches of the world had been alight together. But when he would have entered in, a voice forbade him; wherefore he drew back, and looked, standing upon the threshold of the door. And there he saw a table of silver, and the holy vessel covered with red samite, and many angels round it holding burning candles and a cross and all the ornaments of the altar.

Then a priest stood up and offered mass, and when he took the vessel up, he seemed to sink beneath that burden. At that Sir Lancelot cried, "O Father, take it not for sin that I go in to help the priest, who hath much need thereof." So saying, he went in, but when he came towards the table he felt a breath of fire which issued out therefrom and smote him to the ground, so that he had no power to rise.

Then felt he many hands about him, which took him up and laid him down outside the chapel door. There lay he in a swoon all through that night, and on the morrow certain people found him senseless, and bore him to an inner chamber and laid him on a bed. And there he rested, living, but moving no limbs, twenty-four days and nights.

On the twenty-fifth day he opened his eyes and saw those standing round, and said, "Why have ye waked me? for I have seen marvels that no tongue can tell, and more than any heart can think."

Then he asked where he was, and they told him, "In the Castle of Carbonek."

"Tell your lord, King Pelles," said he, "that I am Sir Lancelot."

At that they marveled greatly, and told their lord it was Sir Lancelot who had lain there so long.

Then was King Pelles wondrous glad and went to see him, and prayed him to abide there for a season. But Sir Lancelot said, "I know well that I have now seen as much as mine eyes may behold of the Sangreal; wherefore I will return to my own country." So he took leave of King Pelles, and departed towards Logris.

Now after Sir Galahad had parted from Sir Lancelot, he rode many days, till he came to the monastery where the blind King Evelake lay, whom Sir Percival had seen. And on the morrow, when he had heard mass, Sir Galahad desired to see the king, who cried out, "Welcome, Sir Galahad, servant of the Lord! long have I abided thy coming. Take me now in thine arms, that I may die in peace."

At that Sir Galahad embraced him; and when he had so done the king's eyes were opened, and he said, "Fair Lord Jesus, suffer me now to come to Thee"; and anon his soul departed.

Then they buried him royally, as a king should be; and Sir Galahad went on his way.

Within a while he came to a chapel in a forest, in the crypt whereof he saw a tomb which always blazed and burnt. And asking the brethren what that might mean, they told him, "Joseph of Arimathea's son did found this monastery, and one who wronged him hath lain here these three hundred and fifty years and burneth evermore, until that perfect knight who shall achieve the Sangreal doth quench the fire."

Then said he, "I pray ye bring me to the tomb."

And when he touched the place immediately the fire was quenched, and a voice came from the grave and cried, "Thanks be to God, who now hath purged me of my sin, and draweth me from earthly pains into the joys of paradise."

Then Sir Galahad took the body in his arms and bore it to the abbey, and on the morrow put it in the earth before the high altar.

Anon he departed from thence and rode five days in a great forest; and after that he met Sir Percival, and a little further on Sir Bors. When they had told each other their adventures, they rode together to the Castle of Carbonek: and there King Pelles gave them hearty welcome, for he knew they should achieve the Holy Quest.

As soon as they were come into the castle, a voice cried in the midst of the chamber, "Let them who ought not now to sit at the table of the Lord rise and depart hence!" Then all, save those three knights, departed.

Anon they saw other knights come in with haste at the hall doors and take their harness off, who said to Sir Galahad, "Sir, we have tried sore to be with you at this table."

"Ye be welcome," said he, "but whence are ye?"

So three of them said they were from Gaul; and three from Ireland; and three from Denmark.

Then came forth the likeness of a bishop, with a cross in his hand, and four angels stood by him, and a table of silver was before them, whereon was set the vessel of the Sangreal. Then came forth other angels also—two bearing burning candles, and the third a towel, and the fourth a spear which bled marvelously, the drops wherefrom fell into a box he held in his left hand. Anon the bishop took the wafer up to consecrate it, and at the lifting up, they saw the figure of a Child, whose visage was as bright as any fire, which smote itself into the midst of the wafer and vanished, so that all saw the flesh made bread.

Thereat the bishop went to Galahad and kissed him, and bade him go and kiss his fellows; and said, "Now, servants of the Lord, prepare for food such as none ever yet were fed with since the world began."

With that he vanished, and the knights were filled with a great dread and prayed devoutly.

Then saw they come forth from the holy vessel the vision of a man bleeding all openly, whom they knew well by the tokens of His passion for the Lord Himself. At that they fell upon their faces and were dumb. Anon he brought the Holy Grail to them and spake high words of comfort, and, when they drank therefrom, the taste thereof was sweeter than any tongue could tell or heart desire. Then a voice said to Galahad, "Son, with this blood which drippeth from the spear anoint thou the maimed king and heal him. And when thou hast this done, depart hence with thy brethren in a ship that ye shall find, and go to the city of Sarras. And bear with thee the holy vessel, for it shall no more be seen in the realm of Logris."

At that Sir Galahad walked to the bleeding spear, and therefrom anointing his fingers went out straightway to the maimed King Pelles, and touched his wound. Then suddenly he uprose from his bed as whole a man as ever he was, and praised God passing thankfully with all his heart.

Then Sir Galahad, Sir Bors, and Sir Percival departed as they had been told; and when they had ridden three days they came to the sea-shore, and found the ship awaiting them. Therein they entered, and saw in the midst the silver table and the vessel of the Sangreal, covered with red samite. Then were they passing glad, and made great reverence thereto. And Sir Galahad prayed that now he might leave the world and pass to God. And presently, the while he prayed, a voice said to him, "Galahad, thy prayer is heard, and when thou asketh the death of the body thou shalt have it, and find the life of thy soul."

But while they prayed and slept the ship sailed on, and when they woke they saw the city of Sarras before them, and the other ship wherein was Sir Percival's sister. Then the three knights took up the holy table and the Sangreal and went into the city; and there, in a chapel, they buried Sir Percival's sister right solemnly.

Now at the gate of the town they saw an old cripple sitting, whom Sir Galahad called to help them bear their weight.

"Truly," said the old man, "it is ten years since I have gone a step without these crutches."

"Care ye not," said Sir Galahad, "rise now and show goodwill."

So he assayed to move, and found his limbs as strong as any man's might be, and running to the table helped to carry it.

Anon there rose a rumor in the city that a cripple had been healed by certain marvelous strange knights.

But the king, named Estouranse, who was a heathen tyrant, when he heard thereof took Sir Galahad and his fellows, and put them in prison in a deep hole. Therein they abode a great while, but ever the Sangreal was with them and fed them with marvelous sweet food, so that they fainted not, but had all joy and comfort they could wish.

At the year's end the king fell sick and felt that he should die. Then sent he for the three knights, and when they came before him prayed their mercy for his trespasses against them. So they forgave him gladly, and anon he died.

Then the chief men of the city took counsel together who should be king in his stead, and as they talked, a voice cried in their midst, "Choose ye the youngest of the three knights King Estouranse cast into prison for your king." At that they sought Sir Galahad and made him king with the assent of all the city, and else they would have slain him.

But within a twelve-month came to him, upon a certain day, as he prayed before the Sangreal, a man in likeness of a bishop, with a great company of angels round about him, who offered mass, and afterwards called to Sir Galahad, "Come forth, thou servant of the Lord, for the time hath come thou hast desired so long."

Then Sir Galahad lifted up his hands and prayed, "Now, blessed Lord! would I no longer live if it might please Thee."

Anon the bishop gave him the sacrament, and when he had received it with unspeakable gladness, he said, "Who art thou, father?"

"I am Joseph of Arimathea," answered he, "whom our Lord hath sent to bear thee fellowship."

When he heard that, Sir Galahad went to Sir Percival and Sir Bors and kissed them and commended them to God, saying, "Salute for me Sir Lancelot, my father, and bid them remember this unstable world."

Therewith he kneeled down and prayed, and suddenly his soul departed, and a multitude of angels bare it up to heaven. Then came a hand from heaven and took the vessel and the spear and bare them out of sight.

Since then was never man so hardy as to say that he had seen the Sangreal.

And after all these things, Sir Percival put off his armor and betook him to an hermitage, and within a little while passed out of this world. And Sir Bors, when he had buried him beside his sister, returned, weeping sore for the loss of his two brethren, to King Arthur, at Camelot.

THE PASSING OF ARTHUR

XIV. SIR LANCELOT AND THE FAIR ELAINE

Now after the quest of the Sangreal was fulfilled and all the knights who were left alive were come again to the Round Table, there was great joy in the court. And passing glad were King Arthur and Queen Guinevere to see Sir Lancelot and Sir Bors, for they had been long absent in that quest.

And so greatly was Sir Lancelot's fame now spread abroad that many ladies and damsels daily resorted to him and besought him for their champion; and all right quarrels did he gladly undertake for the pleasure of our Lord Christ. And always as much as he might he withdrew him from the queen.

Wherefore Queen Guinevere, who counted him for her own knight, grew wroth with him, and on a certain day she called him to her chamber, and said thus: "Sir Lancelot, I daily see thy loyalty to me doth slack, for ever thou art absent from this court, and takest other ladies' quarrels on thee more than ever thou wert wont. Now do I understand thee, false knight, and therefore shall I never trust thee more. Depart now from my sight, and come no more within this court upon pain of thy head." With that she turned from him and would hear no excuses.

So Sir Lancelot departed in heaviness of heart, and calling Sir Bors, Sir Ector, and Sir Lionel, he told them how the queen had dealt with him.

"Fair sir," replied Sir Bors, "remember what honor ye have in this country, and how ye are called the noblest knight in the world; wherefore go not, for women are hasty, and do often what they sore repent of afterwards. Be ruled by my advice. Take horse and ride to the hermitage beside Windsor, and there abide till I send ye better tidings."

To that Sir Lancelot consented, and departed with a sorrowful countenance.

Now when the queen heard of his leaving she was inwardly sorry, but made no show of grief, bearing a proud visage outwardly. And on a certain day she made a costly banquet to all the knights of the Round Table, to show she had as great joy in all others as in Sir Lancelot. And at the banquet were Sir Gawain, and his brothers Sir Agravaine, Sir Gaheris, and Sir Gareth; also Sir Modred, Sir Bors, Sir Blamor, Sir Bleoberis, Sir Ector, Sir Lionel, Sir Palomedes, Sir Mador de la Port, and his cousin Sir Patrice—a knight of Ireland, Sir Pinell le Savage, and many more.

Now Sir Pinell hated Sir Gawain because he had slain one of his kinsmen by treason; and Sir Gawain had a great love for all kinds of fruit, which, when Sir Pinell knew, he poisoned certain apples that were set upon the table, with intent to slay him. And so it chanced as they ate and made merry, Sir Patrice, who sat next to Sir Gawain, took one of the poisoned apples and eat it, and when he had eaten he suddenly swelled up and fell down dead.

At that every knight leapt from the board ashamed and enraged nigh out of their wits, for they knew not what to say, yet seeing that the queen had made the banquet they all had suspicion of her.

"My lady the queen," said Sir Gawain, "I wit well this fruit was meant for me, for all men know my love for it, and now had I been nearly slain; wherefore, I fear me, ye will be ashamed."

"This shall not end so," cried Sir Mador de la Port; "now have I lost a noble knight of my own blood, and for this despite and shame I will be revenged to the uttermost."

Then he challenged Queen Guinevere concerning the death of his cousin, but she stood still, sore abashed, and anon with her sorrow and dread, she swooned.

At the noise and sudden cry came in King Arthur, and to him appealed Sir Mador, and impeached the queen.

"Fair lords," said he, "full sorely am I troubled at this matter, for I must be rightful judge, and therein it repenteth me I may not do battle for my wife, for, as I deem, this deed was none of hers. But I suppose she will not lack a champion, and some good knight surely will put his body in jeopardy to save her."

But all who had been bidden to the banquet said they could not hold the queen excused, or be her champions, for she had made the feast, and either by herself or servants must it have come.

"Alas!" said the queen, "I made this dinner for a good intent, and no evil, so God help me in my need."

"My lord the king," said Sir Mador, "I require you heartily as you be a righteous king give me a day when I may have justice."

"Well," said the king, "I give ye this day fifteen days, when ye shall be ready and armed in the meadow beside Westminster, and if there be a knight to fight with you, God speed the right, and if not, then must my queen be burnt."

When the king and queen were alone together he asked her how this case befell.

"I wot not how or in what manner," answered she.

"Where is Sir Lancelot?" said King Arthur, "for he would not grudge to do battle for thee."

"Sir," said she, "I cannot tell you, but all his kinsmen deem he is not in this realm."

"These be sad tidings," said the king; "I counsel ye to find Sir Bors, and pray him for Sir Lancelot's sake to do this battle for you."

So the queen departed and sent for Sir Bors to her chamber, and besought his succor.

"Madam," said he, "what would you have me do? for I may not with my honor take this matter on me, for I was at that same dinner, and all the other knights would have me ever in suspicion. Now do ye miss Sir Lancelot, for he would not have failed you in right nor yet in wrong, as ye have often proved, but now ye have driven him from the country."

"Alas! fair knight," said the queen, "I put me wholly at your mercy, and all that is done amiss I will amend as ye will counsel me."

And therewith she kneeled down upon both her knees before Sir Bors, and besought him to have mercy on her.

Anon came in King Arthur also, and prayed him of his courtesy to help her, saying, "I require you for the love of Lancelot."

"My lord," said he, "ye require the greatest thing of me that any man can ask, for if I do this battle for the queen I shall anger all my fellows of the Table Round; nevertheless, for my lord Sir Lancelot's sake, and for yours, I will that day be the queen's champion, unless there chance to come a better knight than I am to do battle for her." And this he promised on his faith.

Then were the king and queen passing glad, and thanked him heartily, and so departed.

But Sir Bors rode in secret to the hermitage where Sir Lancelot was, and told him all these tidings.

"It has chanced as I would have it," said Sir Lancelot; "yet make ye ready for the battle, but tarry till ye see me come."

"Sir," said Sir Bors, "doubt not but ye shall have your will."

But many of the knights were greatly wroth with him when they heard he was to be the queen's champion, for there were few in the court but deemed her guilty.

Then said Sir Bors, "Wit ye will, fair lords, it were a shame to us all to suffer so fair and noble a lady to be burnt for lack of a champion, for ever hath she proved herself a lover of good knights; wherefore I doubt not she is guiltless of this treason."

At that were some well pleased, but others rested passing wroth.

And when the day was come, the king and queen and all the knights went to the meadow beside Westminster, where the battle should be fought. Then the queen was put in ward, and a great fire was made round the iron stake, where she must be burnt if Sir Mador won the day.

So when the heralds blew, Sir Mador rode forth, and took oath that Queen Guinevere was guilty of Sir Patrice's death, and his oath he would prove with his body against any who would say the contrary. Then came forth Sir Bors, and said, "Queen Guinevere is in the right, and that will I prove with my hands."

With that they both departed to their tents to make ready for the battle. But Sir Bors tarried long, hoping Sir Lancelot would come, till Sir Mador cried out to King Arthur, "Bid thy champion come forth, unless he dare not." Then was Sir Bors ashamed, and took his horse and rode to the end of the lists.

But ere he could meet Sir Mador he was aware of a knight upon a white horse, armed at all points, and with a strange shield, who rode to him and said, "I pray you withdraw from this quarrel, for it is mine, and I have ridden far to fight in it."

Thereat Sir Bors rode to King Arthur, and told him that another knight was come who would do battle for the queen.

"Who is he?" said King Arthur.

"I may not tell you," said Sir Bors; "but he made a covenant with me to be here to-day, wherefore I am discharged."

Then the king called that knight, and asked him if he would fight for the queen.

"Therefore came I hither, Sir king," answered he; "but let us tarry no longer, for anon I have other matters to do. But wit ye well," said he to the Knights of the Round Table, "it is shame to ye for such a courteous queen to suffer this dishonor."

And all men marveled who this knight might be, for none knew him save Sir Bors.

Then Sir Mador and the knight rode to either end of the lists, and couching their spears, ran one against the other with all their might; and Sir Mador's spear broke short, but the strange knight bore both him and his horse down to the ground. Then lightly they leaped from their saddles and drew their swords, and so came eagerly to the battle, and either gave the other many sad strokes and sore and deep wounds.

Thus they fought nigh an hour, for Sir Mador was a full strong and valiant knight. But at last the strange knight smote him to the earth, and gave him such a buffet on the helm as wellnigh killed him. Then did Sir Mador yield, and prayed his life.

"I will but grant it thee," said the strange knight, "if thou wilt release the queen from this quarrel forever, and promise that no mention shall be made upon Sir Patrice's tomb that ever she consented to that treason."

"All this shall be done," said Sir Mador.

Then the knights parters took up Sir Mador and led him to his tent, and the other knight went straight to the stair foot of King Arthur's throne; and by that time was the queen come to the king again, and kissed him lovingly.

Then both the king and she stooped down, and thanked the

knight, and prayed him to put off his helm and rest him, and to take a cup of wine. And when he put his helmet off to drink, all people saw it was Sir Lancelot. But when the queen beheld him she sank almost to the ground weeping for sorrow and for joy, that he had done her such great goodness when she had showed him such unkindness.

Then the knights of his blood gathered round him, and there was great joy and mirth in the court. And Sir Mador and Sir Lancelot were soon healed of their wounds; and not long after came the Lady of the Lake to the court, and told all there by her enchantments how Sir Pinell, and not the queen, was guilty of Sir Patrice's death. Whereat the queen was held excused of all men, and Sir Pinell fled the country.

So Sir Patrice was buried in the church of Winchester, and it was written on his tomb that Sir Pinell slew him with a poisoned apple, in error for Sir Gawain. Then, through Sir Lancelot's favor, the queen was reconciled to Sir Mador, and all was forgiven.

Now fifteen days before the Feast of the Assumption of our Lady, the king proclaimed a tourney to be held that feast-day at Camelot, whereat himself and the King of Scotland would joust with all who should come against them. So thither went the King of North Wales, and King Anguish of Ireland, and Sir Galahaut the noble prince, and many other nobles of divers countries.

And King Arthur made ready to go, and would have had the queen go with him, but she said that she was sick. Sir Lancelot, also, made excuses, saying he was not yet whole of his wounds.

At that the king was passing heavy and grieved, and so departed alone towards Camelot. And by the way he lodged in a town called Astolat, and lay that night in the castle.

As soon as he had gone, Sir Lancelot said to the queen, "This night I will rest, and to-morrow betimes will I take my way to Camelot; for at these jousts I will be against the king and his fellowship."

"Ye may do as ye list," said Queen Guinevere; "but by my counsel ye will not be against the king, for in his company are many hardy knights, as ye well know."

242

"Madam," said Sir Lancelot, "I pray ye be not displeased with me, for I will take the adventure that God may send me."

And on the morrow he went to the church and heard mass, and took his leave of the queen, and so departed.

Then he rode long till he came to Astolat, and there lodged at the castle of an old baron called Sir Bernard of Astolat, which was near the castle where King Arthur lodged. And as Sir Lancelot entered the king espied him, and knew him. Then said he to the knights, "I have just seen a knight who will fight full well at the joust toward which we go."

"Who is it?" asked they.

"As yet ye shall not know," he answered smiling.

When Sir Lancelot was in his chamber unarming the old baron came to him, saluting him, though as yet he knew not who he was.

Now Sir Bernard had a daughter passing beautiful, called the Fair Maid of Astolat, and when she saw Sir Lancelot she loved him from that instant with her whole heart, and could not stay from gazing on him.

On the morrow, Sir Lancelot asked the old baron to lend him a strange shield. "For," said he, "I would be unknown."

"Sir," said his host, "ye shall have your desire, for here is the shield of my eldest son, Sir Torre, who was hurt the day he was made knight, so that he cannot ride; and his shield, therefore, is not known. And, if it please you, my youngest son, Sir Lavaine, shall ride with you to the jousts, for he is of his age full strong and mighty; and I deem ye be a noble knight, wherefore I pray ye tell me your name."

"As to that," said Sir Lancelot, "ye must hold me excused at this time, but if I speed well at the jousts, I will come again and tell you; but in anywise let me have your son, Sir Lavaine, with me, and lend me his brother's shield."

Then, ere they departed, came Elaine, the baron's daughter, and said to Sir Lancelot, "I pray thee, gentle knight, to wear my token at to-morrow's tourney."

"If I should grant you that, fair damsel," said he, "ye might say that I did more for you than ever I have done for lady or damsel."

Then he bethought him that if he granted her request he would be the more disguised, for never before had he worn any lady's token. So anon he said, "Fair damsel, I will wear thy token on my helmet if thou wilt show it me."

Thereat was she passing glad, and brought him a scarlet sleeve broidered with pearls, which Sir Lancelot took, and put upon his helm. Then he prayed her to keep his shield for him until he came again, and taking Sir Torre's shield instead, rode forth with Sir Lavaine towards Camelot.

On the morrow the trumpets blew for the tourney, and there was a great press of dukes and earls and barons and many noble knights; and King Arthur sat in a gallery to behold who did the best. So the King of Scotland and his knights, and King Anguish of Ireland rode forth on King Arthur's side; and against them came the King of North Wales, the King of a Hundred Knights, the King of Northumberland, and the noble prince Sir Galahaut.

But Sir Lancelot and Sir Lavaine rode into a little wood behind the party which was against King Arthur, to watch which side should prove the weakest.

Then was there a strong fight between the two parties, for the King of a Hundred Knights smote down the King of Scotland; and Sir Palomedes, who was on King Arthur's side, overthrew Sir Galahaut. Then came fifteen Knights of the Round Table and beat back the Kings of Northumberland and North Wales with their knights.

"Now," said Sir Lancelot to Sir Lavaine, "if ye will help me, ye shall see yonder fellowship go back as fast as they came."

"Sir," said Sir Lavaine, "I will do what I can."

Then they rode together into the thickest of the press, and there, with one spear, Sir Lancelot smote down five Knights of the Round Table, one after other, and Sir Lavaine overthrew two. And taking another spear, for his own was broken, Sir Lancelot smote down four more knights, and Sir Lavaine a fifth. Then, drawing his sword, Sir Lancelot fought fiercely on the right hand and the left, and unhorsed Sir Safire, Sir Epinogris, and Sir Galleron. At that the Knights of the Round Table withdrew themselves as well as they were able.

"Now, mercy," said Sir Gawain, who sat by King Arthur; "what knight is that who doth such marvelous deeds of arms? I should deem him by his force to be Sir Lancelot, but that he wears a lady's token on his helm as never Lancelot doth."

"Let him be," said King Arthur; "he will be better known, and do more ere he depart."

Thus the party against King Arthur prospered at this time, and his knights were sore ashamed. Then Sir Bors, Sir Ector, and Sir Lionel called together the knights of their blood, nine in number, and agreed to join together in one band against the two strange knights. So they encountered Sir Lancelot all at once, and by main force smote his horse to the ground; and by misfortune Sir Bors struck Sir Lancelot through the shield into the side, and the spear broke off and left the head in the wound.

When Sir Lavaine saw that, he ran to the King of Scotland and struck him off his horse, and brought it to Sir Lancelot, and helped him to mount. Then Sir Lancelot bore Sir Bors and his horse to the ground, and in like manner served Sir Ector and Sir Lionel; and turning upon three other knights he smote them down also; while Sir Lavaine did many gallant deeds.

But feeling himself now sorely wounded Sir Lancelot drew his sword, and proffered to fight with Sir Bors, who, by this time, was mounted anew. And as they met, Sir Ector and Sir Lionel came also, and the swords of all three drave fiercely against him. When he felt their buffets, and his wound that was so grievous, he determined to do all his best while he could yet endure, and smote Sir Bors a blow that bent his head down nearly to the ground and razed his helmet off and pulled him from his horse.

Then rushing at Sir Ector and Sir Lionel, he smote them down, and might have slain all three, but when he saw their faces his heart forbade him. Leaving them, therefore, on the field, he hurled into the thickest of the press, and did such feats of arms as never were beheld before.

And Sir Lavaine was with him through it all, and overthrew ten knights; but Sir Lancelot smote down more than thirty, and most of them Knights of the Round Table.

Then the king ordered the trumpets to blow for the end of the tourney, and the prize to be given by the heralds to the knight with the white shield who bore the red sleeve.

But ere Sir Lancelot was found by the heralds, came the King of the Hundred Knights, the King of North Wales, the King of Northumberland, and Sir Galahaut, and said to him, "Fair knight, God bless thee, for much have ye done this day for us; wherefore we pray ye come with us and receive the honor and the prize as ye have worshipfully deserved it."

"My fair lords," said Sir Lancelot, "wit ye well if I have deserved thanks, I have sore bought them, for I am like never to escape with my life; therefore pray ye let me depart, for I am sore hurt. I take no thought of honor, for I had rather rest me than be lord of all the world." And therewith he groaned piteously, and rode a great gallop away from them.

And Sir Lavaine rode after him, sad at heart, for the broken spear still stuck fast in Sir Lancelot's side, and the blood streamed sorely from the wound. Anon they came near a wood more than a mile from the lists, where he knew he could be hidden.

Then said he to Sir Lavaine, "O gentle knight, help me to pull out this spear-head from my side, for the pain thereof nigh killeth me."

"Dear lord," said he, "I fain would help ye; but I dread to draw it forth, lest ye should die for loss of blood."

"I charge you as you love me," said Sir Lancelot, "draw it out."

So they dismounted, and with a mighty wrench Sir Lavaine drew the spear forth from Sir Lancelot's side; whereat he gave a marvelous great shriek and ghastly groan, and all his blood leaped forth in a full stream. Then he sank swooning to the earth, with a visage pale as death.

"Alas!" cried Sir Lavaine, "what shall I do now?"

And then he turned his master's face towards the wind, and sat by him nigh half an hour while he lay quiet as one dead. But at the last he lifted up his eyes, and said, "I pray ye bear me on my horse again, and lead me to a hermit who dwelleth within two miles hence, for he was formerly a knight of Arthur's court, and now hath mighty skill in medicine and herbs."

So with great pain Sir Lavaine got him to his horse, and led him to the hermitage within the wood, beside a stream. Then knocked he with his spear upon the door, and prayed to enter. At that a child came out, to whom he said, "Fair child, pray the good man thy master to come hither and let in a knight who is sore wounded."

Anon came out the knight-hermit, whose name was Sir Baldwin, and asked, "Who is this wounded knight?"

"I know not," said Sir Lavaine, "save that he is the noblest knight I ever met with, and hath done this day such marvelous deeds of arms against King Arthur that he hath won the prize of the tourney."

Then the hermit gazed long on Sir Lancelot, and hardly knew him, so pale he was with bleeding, yet said he at the last, "Who art thou, lord?"

Sir Lancelot answered feebly, "I am a stranger knight adventurous, who laboreth through many realms to win worship."

"Why hidest thou thy name, dear lord, from me?" cried Sir Baldwin; "for in sooth I know thee now to be the noblest knight in all the world—my lord Sir Lancelot du Lake, with whom I long had fellowship at the Round Table."

"Since ye know me, fair sir," said he, "I pray ye, for Christ's sake, to help me if ye may."

"Doubt not," replied he, "that ye shall live and fare right well."

Then he staunched his wound, and gave him strong medicines and cordials till he was refreshed from his faintness and came to himself again.

Now after the jousting was done King Arthur held a feast, and asked to see the knight with the red sleeve that he might take the prize. So they told him how that knight had ridden from the field wounded nigh to death. "These be the worst tidings I have heard for many years," cried out the king; "I would not for my kingdom he were slain."

Then all men asked, "Know ye him, lord?"

"I may not tell ye at this time," said he; "but would to God we had good tidings of him."

Then Sir Gawain prayed leave to go and seek that knight, which the king gladly gave him. So forthwith he mounted and rode many leagues round Camelot, but could hear no tidings.

Within two days thereafter King Arthur and his knights returned from Camelot, and Sir Gawain chanced to lodge at Astolat, in the house of Sir Bernard. And there came in the fair Elaine to him, and prayed him news of the tournament, and who won the prize. "A knight with a white shield," said he, "who bare a red sleeve in his helm, smote down all comers and won the day."

At that the visage of Elaine changed suddenly from white to red, and heartily she thanked our Lady.

Then said Sir Gawain, "Know ye that knight?" and urged her till she told him that it was her sleeve he wore. So Sir Gawain knew it was for love that she had given it; and when he heard she kept his proper shield he prayed to see it.

As soon as it was brought he saw Sir Lancelot's arms thereon, and cried, "Alas! now am I heavier of heart than ever yet."

"Wherefore?" said fair Elaine.

"Fair damsel," answered he, "know ye not that the knight ye love is of all knights the noblest in the world, Sir Lancelot du Lake? With all my heart I pray ye may have joy of each other, but hardly dare I think that ye shall see him in this world again, for he is so sore wounded he may scarcely live, and is gone out of sight where none can find him."

Then was Elaine nigh mad with grief and sorrow, and with piteous words she prayed her father that she might go seek Sir Lancelot and her brother. So in the end her father gave her leave, and she departed.

And on the morrow came Sir Gawain to the court, and told how he had found Sir Lancelot's shield in Elaine's keeping, and how it was her sleeve which he had worn; whereat all marveled, for Sir Lancelot had done for her more than he had ever done for any woman.

But when Queen Guinevere heard it she was beside herself with wrath, and sending privily for Sir Bors, who sorrowed sorely that through him Sir Lancelot had been hurt—"Have ye now heard," said she, "how falsely Sir Lancelot hath betrayed me?"

"I beseech thee, madam," said he, "speak not so, for else I may not hear thee."

"Shall I not call him traitor," cried she, "who hath worn another lady's token at the jousting?"

"Be sure he did it, madam, for no ill intent," replied Sir Bors, "but that he might be better hidden, for never did he in that wise before."

"Now shame on him, and thee who wouldest help him," cried the queen.

"Madam, say what ye will," said he; "but I must haste to seek him, and God send me soon good tidings of him."

So with that he departed to find Sir Lancelot.

Now Elaine had ridden with full haste from Astolat, and come to Camelot, and there she sought throughout the country for any news of Lancelot. And so it chanced that Sir Lavaine was riding near the hermitage to exercise his horse, and when she saw him she ran up and cried aloud, "How doth my lord Sir Lancelot fare?"

Then said Sir Lavaine, marveling greatly, "How know ye my lord's name, fair sister?"

So she told him how Sir Gawain had lodged with Sir Bernard, and knew Sir Lancelot's shield.

Then prayed she to see his lord forthwith, and when she came to the hermitage and found him lying there sore sick and bleeding, she swooned for sorrow. Anon, as she revived, Sir Lancelot kissed her, and said, "Fair maid, I pray ye take comfort, for, by God's grace, I shall be shortly whole of this wound, and if ye be come to tend me, I am heartily bounden to your great kindness." Yet was he sore vexed to hear Sir Gawain had discovered him, for he knew Queen Guinevere would be full wroth because of the red sleeve.

So Elaine rested in the hermitage, and ever night and day she watched and waited on Sir Lancelot, and would let none other tend him. And as she saw him more, the more she set her love upon him, and could by no means withdraw it. Then said Sir Lancelot to Sir Lavaine, "I pray thee set some to watch for the good knight Sir Bors, for as he hurt me, so will he surely seek for me."

Now Sir Bors by this time had come to Camelot, and was seeking for Sir Lancelot everywhere, so Sir Lavaine soon found him, and brought him to the hermitage.

And when he saw Sir Lancelot pale and feeble, he wept for pity and sorrow that he had given him that grievous wound. "God send thee a right speedy cure, dear lord," said he; "for I am of all men most unhappy to have wounded thee, who art our leader, and the noblest knight in all the world."

"Fair cousin," said Sir Lancelot, "be comforted, for I have but gained what I sought, and it was through pride that I was hurt, for had I warned ye of my coming it had not been; wherefore let us speak of other things."

So they talked long together, and Sir Bors told him of the queen's anger. Then he asked Sir Lancelot, "Was it from this maid who tendeth you so lovingly ye had the token?"

"Yea," said Sir Lancelot; "and would I could persuade her to withdraw her love from me."

"Why should ye do so?" said Sir Bors; "for she is passing fair and loving. I would to heaven ye could love her."

"That may not be," replied he; "but it repenteth me in sooth to grieve her."

Then they talked of other matters, and of the great jousting at Allhallowtide next coming, between King Arthur and the King of North Wales.

"Abide with me till then," said Sir Lancelot, "for by that time I trust to be all whole again, and we will go together."

So Elaine daily and nightly tending him, within a month he felt so strong he deemed himself full cured. Then on a day, when Sir Bors and Sir Lavaine were from the hermitage, and the knight-hermit also was gone forth, Sir Lancelot prayed Elaine to bring him some herbs from the forest.

When she was gone he rose and made haste to arm himself, and try if he were whole enough to joust, and mounted on his horse, which was fresh with lack of labor for so long a time. But when he set his spear in the rest and tried his armor, the horse bounded and leapt beneath him, so that Sir Lancelot strained to keep him back. And therewith his wound, which was not wholly healed, burst forth again, and with a mighty groan he sank down swooning on the ground.

At that came fair Elaine and wept and piteously moaned to see him lying so. And when Sir Bors and Sir Lavaine came back, she called them traitors to let him rise, or to know any rumor of the tournament. Anon the hermit returned and was wroth to see Sir Lancelot risen, but within a while he recovered him from his swoon and staunched the wound. Then Sir Lancelot told him how he had risen of his own will to assay his strength for the tournament. But the hermit bade him rest and let Sir Bors go alone, for else would he sorely peril his life. And Elaine, with tears, prayed him in the same wise, so that Sir Lancelot in the end consented.

So Sir Bors departed to the tournament, and there he did such feats of arms that the prize was given between him and Sir Gawain, who did like valiantly.

And when all was over he came back and told Sir Lancelot, and found him so nigh well that he could rise and walk. And within a while thereafter he departed from the hermitage and went with Sir Bors, Sir Lavaine, and fair Elaine to Astolat, where Sir Bernard joyfully received them.

But after they had lodged there a few days Sir Lancelot and Sir Bors must needs depart and return to King Arthur's court.

So when Elaine knew Sir Lancelot must go, she came to him and said, "Have mercy on me, fair knight, and let me not die for your love."

Then said Sir Lancelot, very sad at heart, "Fair maid, what would ye that I should do for you?"

"If I may not be your wife, dear lord," she answered, "I must die."

"Alas!" said he, "I pray heaven that may not be; for in sooth I may not be your husband. But fain would I show ye what thankfulness I can for all your love and kindness to me. And ever

251

will I be your knight, fair maiden; and if it chance that ye shall ever wed some noble knight, right heartily will I give ye such a dower as half my lands will bring."

"Alas! what shall that aid me?" answered she; "for I must die," and therewith she fell to the earth in a deep swoon.

Then was Sir Lancelot passing heavy of heart, and said to Sir Bernard and Sir Lavaine, "What shall I do for her?"

"Alas!" said Sir Bernard, "I know well that she will die for your sake."

And Sir Lavaine said, "I marvel not that she so sorely mourneth your departure, for truly I do as she doth, and since I once have seen you, lord, I cannot leave you."

So anon, with a full sorrowful heart, Sir Lancelot took his leave, and Sir Lavaine rode with him to the court. And King Arthur and the Knights of the Round Table joyed greatly to see him whole of his wound, but Queen Guinevere was sorely wroth, and neither spake with him nor greeted him.

Now when Sir Lancelot had departed, the Maid of Astolat could neither eat, nor drink, nor sleep for sorrow; and having thus endured ten days, she felt within herself that she must die.

Then sent she for a holy man, and was shriven and received the sacrament. But when he told her she must leave her earthly thoughts, she answered, "Am I not an earthly woman? What sin is it to love the noblest knight of all the world? And, by my truth, I am not able to withstand the love whereof I die; wherefore, I pray the High Father of Heaven to have mercy on my soul."

Then she besought Sir Bernard to indite a letter as she should devise, and said, "When I am dead put this within my hand, and dress me in my fairest clothes, and lay me in a barge all covered with black samite, and steer it down the river till it reach the court. Thus, father, I beseech thee let it be."

Then, full of grief, he promised her it should be so. And anon she died, and all the household made a bitter lamentation over her.

Then did they as she had desired, and laid her body, richly dressed, upon a bed within the barge, and a trusty servant steered it down the river towards the court.

Now King Arthur and Queen Guinevere sat at a window of the palace, and saw the barge come floating with the tide, and marveled what was laid therein, and sent a messenger to see, who, soon returning, prayed them to come forth.

When they came to the shore they marveled greatly, and the king asked of the serving-man who steered the barge what this might mean. But he made signs that he was dumb, and pointed to the letter in the damsel's hands. So King Arthur took the letter from the hand of the corpse, and found thereon written, "To the noble knight, Sir Lancelot du Lake."

Then was Sir Lancelot sent for, and the letter read aloud by a clerk, and thus it was written:—

"Most noble knight, my lord Sir Lancelot, now hath death forever parted us. I, whom men call the Maid of Astolat, set my love upon you, and have died for your sake. This is my last request, that ye pray for my soul and give me burial. Grant me this, Sir Lancelot, as thou art a peerless knight."

At these words the queen and all the knights wept sore for pity.

Then said Sir Lancelot, "My lord, I am right heavy for the death of this fair damsel; and God knoweth that right unwillingly I caused it, for she was good as she was fair, and much was I beholden to her; but she loved me beyond measure, and asked me that I could not give her."

"Ye might have shown her gentleness enough to save her life," answered the queen.

"Madam," said he, "she would but be repaid by my taking her to wife, and that I could not grant her, for love cometh of the heart and not by constraint."

"That is true," said the king; "for love is free."

"I pray you," said Sir Lancelot, "let me now grant her last asking, to be buried by me."

So on the morrow, he caused her body to be buried richly and solemnly, and ordained masses for her soul, and made great sorrow over her.

Then the queen sent for Sir Lancelot, and prayed his pardon for her wrath against him without cause. "This is not the first time it hath been so," answered he; "yet must I ever bear with ye, and so do I now forgive you."

So Queen Guinevere and Sir Lancelot were made friends again; but anon such favor did she show him, as in the end brought many evils on them both and all the realm.

XV. THE WAR BETWEEN ARTHUR AND
LANCELOT AND THE PASSING OF ARTHUR

Within a while thereafter was a jousting at the court, wherein Sir Lancelot won the prize. And two of those he smote down were Sir Agravaine, the brother of Sir Gawain, and Sir Modred, his false brother—King Arthur's son by Belisent. And because of his victory they hated Sir Lancelot, and sought how they might injure him.

So on a night, when King Arthur was hunting in the forest, and the queen sent for Sir Lancelot to her chamber, they two espied him; and thinking now to make a scandal and a quarrel between Lancelot and the king, they found twelve others, and said Sir Lancelot was ever now in the queen's chamber, and King Arthur was dishonored.

Then, all armed, they came suddenly round the queen's door, and cried, "Traitor! now art thou taken."

"Madam, we be betrayed," said Sir Lancelot; "yet shall my life cost these men dear."

Then did the queen weep sore, and dismally she cried, "Alas! there is no armor here whereby ye might withstand so many; wherefore ye will be slain, and I be burnt for the dread crime they will charge on me."

But while she spake the shouting of the knights was heard without, "Traitor, come forth, for now thou art snared!"

"Better were twenty deaths at once than this vile outcry," said Sir Lancelot.

Then he kissed her and said, "Most noble lady, I beseech ye, as I have ever been your own true knight, take courage; pray for my soul if I be now slain, and trust my faithful friends, Sir Bors and Sir Lavaine, to save you from the fire."

But ever bitterly she wept and moaned, and cried, "Would God that they would take and slay me, and that thou couldest escape."

"That shall never be," said he. And wrapping his mantle round his arm he unbarred the door a little space, so that but one could enter.

Then first rushed in Sir Chalaunce, a full strong knight, and lifted up his sword to smite Sir Lancelot; but lightly he avoided him, and struck Sir Chalaunce, with his hand, such a sore buffet on the head as felled him dead upon the floor.

Then Sir Lancelot pulled in his body and barred the door again, and dressed himself in his armor, and took his drawn sword in his hand.

But still the knights cried mightily without the door, "Traitor, come forth!"

"Be silent and depart," replied Sir Lancelot; "for be ye sure ye will not take me, and to-morrow will I meet ye face to face before the king."

"Ye shall have no such grace," they cried; "but we will slay thee, or take thee as we list."

"Then save yourselves who may," he thundered, and therewith suddenly unbarred the door and rushed forth at them. And at the first blow he slew Sir Agravaine, and after him twelve other knights, with twelve more mighty buffets. And none of all escaped him save Sir Modred, who, sorely wounded, flew away for life.

Then returned he to the queen, and said, "Now, madam, will I depart, and if ye be in any danger I pray ye come to me."

"Surely will I stay here, for I am queen," she answered; "yet if to-morrow any harm come to me I trust to thee for rescue."

"Have ye no doubt of me," said he, "for ever while I live am I your own true knight."

Therewith he took his leave, and went and told Sir Bors and all his kindred of this adventure. "We will be with thee in this quarrel," said they all; "and if the queen be sentenced to the fire, we certainly will save her."

Meanwhile Sir Modred, in great fear and pain, fled from the court, and rode until he found King Arthur, and told him all that had befallen. But the king would scarce believe him till he came and saw the bodies of Sir Agravaine and all the other knights.

Then felt he in himself that all was true, and with his passing grief his heart nigh broke. "Alas!" cried he, "now is the fellowship of the Round Table forever broken: yea, woe is me! I may not with my honor spare my queen."

Anon it was ordained that Queen Guinevere should be burned to death, because she had dishonored King Arthur.

But when Sir Gawain heard thereof, he came before the king, and said, "My lord, I counsel thee be not too hasty in this matter, but stay the judgment of the queen a season, for it may well be that Sir Lancelot was in her chamber for no evil, seeing she is greatly beholden to him for so many deeds done for her sake, and peradventure she had sent to him to thank him, and did it secretly that she might avoid slander."

But King Arthur answered, full of grief, "Alas! I may not help her; she is judged as any other woman."

Then he required Sir Gawain and his brethren, Sir Gaheris and Sir Gareth, to be ready to bear the queen to-morrow to the place of execution.

"Nay, noble lord," replied Sir Gawain, "that can I never do; for neither will my heart suffer me to see the queen die, nor shall men ever say I was of your counsel in this matter."

Then said his brother, "Ye may command us to be there, but since it is against our will, we will be without arms, that we may do no battle against her."

So on the morrow was Queen Guinevere led forth to die by fire, and a mighty crowd was there, of knights and nobles, armed and unarmed. And all the lords and ladies wept sore at that piteous sight. Then was she shriven by a priest, and the men came nigh to bind her to the stake and light the fire.

At that Sir Lancelot's spies rode hastily and told him and his kindred, who lay hidden in a wood hard by; and suddenly, with twenty knights, he rushed into the midst of all the throng to rescue her.

But certain of King Arthur's knights rose up and fought with them, and there was a full great battle and confusion. And Sir Lancelot drave fiercely here and there among the press, and smote on every side, and at every blow struck down a knight, so that many were slain by him and his fellows.

Then was the queen set free, and caught up on Sir Lancelot's saddle and fled away with him and all his company to the Castle of La Joyous Garde.

Now so it chanced that, in the turmoil of the fighting, Sir Lancelot had unawares struck down and slain the two good knights Sir Gareth and Sir Gaheris, knowing it not, for he fought wildly, and saw not that they were unarmed.

When King Arthur heard thereof, and of all that battle, and the rescue of the queen, he sorrowed heavily for those good knights, and was passing wroth with Lancelot and the queen.

But when Sir Gawain heard of his brethren's death he swooned for sorrow and wrath, for he wist that Sir Lancelot had killed them in malice. And as soon as he recovered he ran in to the king, and said, "Lord king and uncle, hear this oath which now I swear, that from this day I will not fail Sir Lancelot till one of us hath slain the other. And now, unless ye haste to war with him, that we may be avenged, will I myself alone go after him."

Then the king, full of wrath and grief, agreed thereto, and sent letters throughout the realm to summon all his knights, and went with a vast army to besiege the Castle of La Joyous Garde. And Sir Lancelot, with his knights, mightily defended it; but never would he suffer any to go forth and attack one of the king's army, for he was right loth to fight against him.

So when fifteen weeks were passed, and King Arthur's army wasted itself in vain against the castle, for it was passing strong, it chanced upon a day Sir Lancelot was looking from the walls and espied King Arthur and Sir Gawain close beside.

"Come forth, Sir Lancelot," said King Arthur right fiercely, "and let us two meet in the midst of the field."

"God forbid that I should encounter with thee, lord, for thou didst make me a knight," replied Sir Lancelot.

Then cried Sir Gawain, "Shame on thee, traitor and false knight, yet be ye well assured we will regain the queen and slay thee and thy company; yea, double shame on ye to slay my brother Gaheris

258

unarmed, Sir Gareth also, who loved ye so well. For that treachery, be sure I am thine enemy till death."

"Alas!" cried Sir Lancelot, "that I hear such tidings, for I knew not I had slain those noble knights, and right sorely now do I repent it with a heavy heart. Yet abate thy wrath, Sir Gawain, for ye know full well I did it by mischance, for I loved them ever as my own brothers."

"Thou liest, false recreant," cried Sir Gawain, fiercely.

At that Sir Lancelot was wroth, and said, "I well see thou art now mine enemy, and that there can be no more peace with thee, or with my lord the king, else would I gladly give back the queen."

Then the king would fain have listened to Sir Lancelot, for more than all his own wrong did he grieve at the sore waste and damage of the realm, but Sir Gawain persuaded him against it, and ever cried out foully on Sir Lancelot.

When Sir Bors and the other knights of Lancelot's party heard the fierce words of Sir Gawain, they were passing wroth, and prayed to ride forth and be avenged on him, for they were weary of so long waiting to no good. And in the end Sir Lancelot, with a heavy heart, consented.

So on the morrow the hosts on either side met in the field, and there was a great battle. And Sir Gawain prayed his knights chiefly to set upon Sir Lancelot; but Sir Lancelot commanded his company to forbear King Arthur and Sir Gawain.

So the two armies jousted together right fiercely, and Sir Gawain proffered to encounter with Sir Lionel, and overthrew him. But Sir Bors and Sir Blamor, and Sir Palomedes, who were on Sir Lancelot's side, did great feats of arms, and overthrew many of King Arthur's knights.

Then the king came forth against Sir Lancelot, but Sir Lancelot forbore him and would not strike again.

At that Sir Bors rode up against the king and smote him down. But Sir Lancelot cried, "Touch him not on pain of thy head," and going to King Arthur he alighted and gave him his own horse, saying, "My lord, I pray thee forbear this strife, for it can bring to neither of us any honor."

And when King Arthur looked on him the tears came to his eyes as he thought of his noble courtesy, and he said within himself, "Alas! that ever this war began."

But on the morrow Sir Gawain led forth the army again, and Sir Bors commanded on Sir Lancelot's side. And they two struck together so fiercely that both fell to the ground sorely wounded; and all the day they fought till night fell, and many were slain on both sides, yet in the end neither gained the victory.

But by now the fame of this fierce war spread through all Christendom, and when the Pope heard thereof he sent a Bull, and charged King Arthur to make peace with Lancelot, and receive back Queen Guinevere; and for the offense imputed to her absolution should be given by the Pope.

Thereto would King Arthur straightway have obeyed, but Sir Gawain ever urged him to refuse.

When Sir Lancelot heard thereof, he wrote thus to the king: "It was never in my thought, lord, to withhold thy queen from thee; but since she was condemned for my sake to death, I deemed it but a just and knightly part to rescue her therefrom; wherefore I recommend me to your grace, and within eight days will I come to thee and bring the queen in safety."

Then, within eight days, as he had said, Sir Lancelot rode from out the castle with Queen Guinevere, and a hundred knights for company, each carrying an olive branch, in sign of peace. And so they came to the court, and found King Arthur sitting on his throne, with Sir Gawain and many other knights around him. And when Sir Lancelot entered with the queen, they both kneeled down before the king.

Anon Sir Lancelot rose and said, "My lord, I have brought hither my lady the queen again, as right requireth, and by commandment of the Pope and you. I pray ye take her to your heart again and forget the past. For myself I may ask nothing, and for my sin I shall have sorrow and sore punishment; yet I would to heaven I might have your grace."

But ere the king could answer, for he was moved with pity at his words, Sir Gawain cried aloud, "Let the king do as he will, but be sure, Sir Lancelot, thou and I shall never be accorded while we live, for thou has slain my brethren traitorously and unarmed."

"As heaven is my help," replied Sir Lancelot, "I did it ignorantly, for I loved them well, and while I live I shall bewail their death; but to make war with me were no avail, for I must needs fight with thee if thou assailest, and peradventure I might kill thee also, which I were right loth to do."

"I will forgive thee never," cried Sir Gawain, "and if the king accordeth with thee he shall lose my service."

Then the knights who stood near tried to reconcile Sir Gawain to Sir Lancelot, but he would not hear them. So, at the last, Sir Lancelot said, "Since peace is vain, I will depart, lest I bring more evil on my fellowship."

And as he turned to go, the tears fell from him, and he said, "Alas, most noble Christian realm, which I have loved above all others, now shall I see thee never more!" Then said he to the queen, "Madam, now must I leave ye and this noble fellowship forever. And, I beseech ye, pray for me, and if ye ever be defamed of any, let me hear thereof, and as I have been ever thy true knight in right and wrong, so will I be again."

With that he kneeled and kissed King Arthur's hands, and departed on his way. And there was none in all that court, save Sir Gawain alone, but wept to see him go.

So he returned with all his knights to the Castle of La Joyous Garde, and, for his sorrow's sake, he named it Dolorous Garde thenceforth.

Anon he left the realm, and went with many of his fellowship beyond the sea to France, and there divided all his lands among them equally, he sharing but as the rest.

And from that time forward peace had been between him and King Arthur, but for Sir Gawain, who left the king no rest, but constantly persuaded him that Lancelot was raising mighty hosts against him.

So in the end his malice overcame the king, who left the government in charge of Modred, and made him guardian of the queen, and went with a great army to invade Sir Lancelot's lands.

Yet Sir Lancelot would make no war upon the king, and sent a message to gain peace on any terms King Arthur chose. But Sir Gawain met the herald ere he reached the king, and sent him back with taunting and bitter words. Whereat Sir Lancelot sorrowfully called his knights together and fortified the Castle of Benwicke, and there was shortly besieged by the army of King Arthur.

And every day Sir Gawain rode up to the walls, and cried out foully on Sir Lancelot, till, upon a time, Sir Lancelot answered him that he would meet him in the field and put his boasting to the proof. So it was agreed on both sides that there should none come nigh them or separate them till one had fallen or yielded; and they two rode forth.

Then did they wheel their horses apart, and turning, came together as it had been thunder, so that both horses fell, and both their lances broke. At that they drew their swords and set upon each other fiercely, with passing grievous strokes.

Now Sir Gawain had through magic a marvelous great gift. For every day, from morning till noon, his strength waxed to the might of seven men, but after that waned to his natural force. Therefore till noon he gave Sir Lancelot many mighty buffets, which scarcely he endured. Yet greatly he forbore Sir Gawain, for he was aware of his enchantment, and smote him slightly till his own knights marveled. But after noon Sir Gawain's strength sank fast, and then, with one full blow, Sir Lancelot laid him on the earth. Then Sir Gawain cried out, "Turn not away, thou traitor knight, but slay me if thou wilt, or else I will arise and fight with thee again some other time."

"Sir knight," replied Sir Lancelot, "I never yet smote a fallen man."

At that they bore Sir Gawain sorely wounded to his tent, and King Arthur withdrew his men, for he was loth to shed the blood of so many knights of his own fellowship.

But now came tidings to King Arthur from across the sea, which caused him to return in haste. For thus the news ran, that no sooner was Sir Modred set up in his regency, than he had forged false tidings from abroad that the king had fallen in a battle with Sir

Lancelot. Whereat he had proclaimed himself the king, and had been crowned at Canterbury, where he had held a coronation feast for fifteen days. Then he had gone to Winchester, where Queen Guinevere abode, and had commanded her to be his wife; whereto, for fear and sore perplexity, she had feigned consent, but, under pretext of preparing for the marriage, had fled in haste to London and taken shelter in the Tower, fortifying it and providing it with all manner of victuals, and defending it against Sir Modred, and answering to all his threats that she would rather slay herself than be his queen.

Thus was it written to King Arthur. Then, in passing great wrath and haste, he came with all his army swiftly back from France and sailed to England. But when Sir Modred heard thereof, he left the Tower and marched with all his host to meet the king at Dover.

Then fled Queen Guinevere to Amesbury to a nunnery, and there she clothed herself in sackcloth, and spent her time in praying for the king and in good deeds and fasting. And in that nunnery evermore she lived, sorely repenting and mourning for her sin, and for the ruin she had brought on all the realm. And there anon she died.

And when Sir Lancelot heard thereof, he put his knightly armor off, and bade farewell to all his kin, and went a mighty pilgrimage for many years, and after lived a hermit till his death.

When Sir Modred came to Dover, he found King Arthur and his army but just landed; and there they fought a fierce and bloody battle, and many great and noble knights fell on both sides.

But the king's side had the victory, for he was beyond himself with might and passion, and all his knights so fiercely followed him, that, in spite of all their multitude, they drove Sir Modred's army back with fearful wounds and slaughter, and slept that night upon the battle-field.

But Sir Gawain was smitten by an arrow in the wound Sir Lancelot gave him, and wounded to the death. Then was he borne to the king's tent, and King Arthur sorrowed over him as it had been his own son. "Alas!" said he; "in Sir Lancelot and in you I had my greatest earthly joy, and now is all gone from me."

And Sir Gawain answered, with a feeble voice, "My lord and king, I know well my death is come, and through my own wilfulness, for I am smitten in the wound Sir Lancelot gave me. Alas! that I have been the cause of all this war, for but for me thou hadst been now at peace with Lancelot, and then had Modred never done this treason. I pray ye, therefore, my dear lord, be now agreed with Lancelot, and tell him, that although he gave me my death-wound, it was through my own seeking; wherefore I beseech him to come back to England, and here to visit my tomb, and pray for my soul."

When he had thus spoken, Sir Gawain gave up his ghost, and the king grievously mourned for him.

Then they told him that the enemy had camped on Barham Downs, whereat, with all his hosts, he straightway marched there, and fought again a bloody battle, and overthrew Sir Modred utterly. Howbeit, he raised yet another army, and retreating ever from before the king, increased his numbers as he went, till at the farthest west in Lyonesse, he once more made a stand.

Now, on the night of Trinity Sunday, being the eve of the battle, King Arthur had a vision, and saw Sir Gawain in a dream, who warned him not to fight with Modred on the morrow, else he would be surely slain; and prayed him to delay till Lancelot and his knights should come to aid him.

So when King Arthur woke he told his lords and knights that vision, and all agreed to wait the coming of Sir Lancelot. Then a herald was sent with a message of truce to Sir Modred, and a treaty was made that neither army should assail the other.

But when the treaty was agreed upon, and the heralds returned, King Arthur said to his knights, "Beware, lest Sir Modred deceive us, for I in no wise trust him, and if swords be drawn be ready to encounter!" And Sir Modred likewise gave an order, that if any man of the king's army drew his sword, they should begin to fight.

And as it chanced, a knight of the king's side was bitten by an adder in the foot, and hastily drew forth his sword to slay it. That saw Sir Modred, and forthwith commanded all his army to assail the king's.

So both sides rushed to battle, and fought passing fiercely. And when the king saw there was no hope to stay them, he did right mightily and nobly as a king should do, and ever, like a lion, raged in the thickest of the press, and slew on the right hand and on the left, till his horse went fetlock deep in blood. So all day long they fought, and stinted not till many a noble knight was slain.

But the king was passing sorrowful to see his trusty knights lie dead on every side. And at the last but two remained beside him, Sir Lucan, and his brother, Sir Bedivere, and both were sorely wounded.

"Now am I come to mine end," said King Arthur; "but, lo! that traitor Modred liveth yet, and I may not die till I have slain him. Now, give me my spear, Sir Lucan."

"Lord, let him be," replied Sir Lucan; "for if ye pass through this unhappy day, ye shall be right well revenged upon him. My good lord, remember well your dream, and what the spirit of Sir Gawain did fore-warn ye."

"Betide me life, betide me death," said the king; "now I see him yonder alone, he shall never escape my hands, for at a better vantage shall I never have him."

"God speed you well," said Sir Bedivere.

Then King Arthur got his spear in both his hands, and ran towards Sir Modred, crying, "Traitor, now is thy death-day come!" And when Sir Modred heard his words, and saw him come, he drew his sword and stood to meet him. Then King Arthur smote Sir Modred through the body more than a fathom. And when Sir Modred felt he had his death wound, he thrust himself with all his might up to the end of King Arthur's spear, and smote his father, Arthur, with his sword upon the head, so that it pierced both helm and brain-pan.

And therewith Sir Modred fell down stark dead to the earth, and King Arthur fell down also in a swoon, and swooned many times.

Then Sir Lucan and Sir Bedivere came and bare him away to a little chapel by the sea-shore. And there Sir Lucan sank down with the bleeding of his own wounds, and fell dead.

And King Arthur lay long in a swoon, and when he came

to himself, he found Sir Lucan lying dead beside him, and Sir Bedivere weeping over the body of his brother.

Then said the king to Sir Bedivere, "Weeping will avail no longer, else would I grieve forevermore. Alas! now is the fellowship of the Round Table dissolved forever, and all my realm I have so loved is wasted with war. But my time hieth fast, wherefore take thou Excalibur, my good sword, and go therewith to yonder water-side and throw it in, and bring me word what thing thou seest."

So Sir Bedivere departed; but as he went he looked upon the sword, the hilt whereof was all inlaid with precious stones exceeding rich. And presently he said within himself, "If I now throw this sword into the water, what good should come of it?" So he hid the sword among the reeds, and came again to the king.

"What sawest thou?" said he to Sir Bedivere.

"Lord," said he, "I saw nothing else but wind and waves."

"Thou hast untruly spoken," said the king; "wherefore go lightly back and throw it in, and spare not."

Then Sir Bedivere returned again, and took the sword up in his hand; but when he looked on it, he thought it sin and shame to throw away a thing so noble. Wherefore he hid it yet again, and went back to the king.

"What saw ye?" said King Arthur.

"Lord," answered he, "I saw nothing but the water ebbing and flowing."

"Oh, traitor and untrue!" cried out the king; "twice hast thou now betrayed me. Art thou called of men a noble knight, and wouldest betray me for a jewelled sword? Now, therefore, go again for the last time, for thy tarrying hath put me in sore peril of my life, and I fear my wound hath taken cold; and if thou do it not this time, by my faith I will arise and slay thee with my hands."

Then Sir Bedivere ran quickly and took up the sword, and went down to the water's edge, and bound the girdle round the hilt and threw it far into the water. And lo! an arm and hand came forth above the water, and caught the sword, and brandished it three times, and vanished.

So Sir Bedivere came again to the king and told him what he had seen.

"Help me from hence," said King Arthur; "for I dread me I have tarried over long."

Then Sir Bedivere took the king up in his arms, and bore him to the water's edge. And by the shore they saw a barge with three fair queens therein, all dressed in black, and when they saw King Arthur they wept and wailed.

"Now put me in the barge," said he to Sir Bedivere, and tenderly he did so.

Then the three queens received him, and he laid his head upon the lap of one of them, who cried, "Alas! dear brother, why have ye tarried so long, for your wound hath taken cold?"

With that the barge put from the land, and when Sir Bedivere saw it departing, he cried with a bitter cry, "Alas! my lord King Arthur, what shall become of me now ye have gone from me?"

"Comfort ye," said King Arthur, "and be strong, for I may no more help ye. I go to the Vale of Avilion to heal me of my grievous wound, and if ye see me no more, pray for my soul."

Then the three queens kneeled down around the king and sorely wept and wailed, and the barge went forth to sea, and departed slowly out of Sir Bedivere's sight.

THE END

Printed in France by Amazon
Brétigny-sur-Orge, FR

15042597R00157